T0259646

Pro Microsoft Power Platform

Solution Building for the Citizen Developer

Mitchell Pearson
Brian Knight
Devin Knight
Manuel Quintana

Apress®

Pro Microsoft Power Platform: Solution Building for the Citizen Developer

Mitchell Pearson
Fleming Island, FL, USA

Brian Knight
Green Cove Springs, FL, USA

Devin Knight
Green Cove Springs, FL, USA

Manuel Quintana
Jacksonville, FL, USA

ISBN-13 (pbk): 978-1-4842-6007-4
https://doi.org/10.1007/978-1-4842-6008-1

ISBN-13 (electronic): 978-1-4842-6008-1

Copyright © 2020 by Mitchell Pearson, Brian Knight, Devin Knight, Manuel Quintana

This work is subject to copyright. All rights are reserved by the Publisher, whether the whole or part of the material is concerned, specifically the rights of translation, reprinting, reuse of illustrations, recitation, broadcasting, reproduction on microfilms or in any other physical way, and transmission or information storage and retrieval, electronic adaptation, computer software, or by similar or dissimilar methodology now known or hereafter developed.

Trademarked names, logos, and images may appear in this book. Rather than use a trademark symbol with every occurrence of a trademarked name, logo, or image we use the names, logos, and images only in an editorial fashion and to the benefit of the trademark owner, with no intention of infringement of the trademark.

The use in this publication of trade names, trademarks, service marks, and similar terms, even if they are not identified as such, is not to be taken as an expression of opinion as to whether or not they are subject to proprietary rights.

While the advice and information in this book are believed to be true and accurate at the date of publication, neither the authors nor the editors nor the publisher can accept any legal responsibility for any errors or omissions that may be made. The publisher makes no warranty, express or implied, with respect to the material contained herein.

Managing Director, Apress Media LLC: Welmoed Spahr
Acquisitions Editor: Jonathan Gennick
Development Editor: Laura Berendson
Coordinating Editor: Jill Balzano

Cover image designed by Freepik (www.freepik.com)

Distributed to the book trade worldwide by Springer Science+Business Media New York, 233 Spring Street, 6th Floor, New York, NY 10013. Phone 1-800-SPRINGER, fax (201) 348-4505, e-mail orders-ny@springer-sbm.com, or visit www.springeronline.com. Apress Media, LLC is a California LLC and the sole member (owner) is Springer Science + Business Media Finance Inc (SSBM Finance Inc). SSBM Finance Inc is a **Delaware** corporation.

For information on translations, please e-mail booktranslations@springernature.com; for reprint, paperback, or audio rights, please e-mail bookpermissions@springernature.com.

Apress titles may be purchased in bulk for academic, corporate, or promotional use. eBook versions and licenses are also available for most titles. For more information, reference our Print and eBook Bulk Sales web page at http://www.apress.com/bulk-sales.

Any source code or other supplementary material referenced by the author in this book is available to readers on GitHub via the book's product page, located at www.apress.com/9781484260074. For more detailed information, please visit http://www.apress.com/source-code.

Printed on acid-free paper

Table of Contents

About the Authors

Mitchell Pearson is a business intelligence consultant and the training content manager for Pragmatic Works. He has authored books on SQL Server and Power BI and spends his time at Pragmatic Works developing new courses on business intelligence and Microsoft Azure. Mitchell has experience developing enterprise-level BI solutions using the full suite of products offered by Microsoft (SSRS, SSIS, SSAS, Power BI, and Azure). He is active in the community, running the local Power BI user group, presenting at SQL Saturday events and at PASS virtual chapters, and giving free webinars for Pragmatic Works.

Brian Knight is a Power Apps MVP and the founder of Pragmatic Works and cofounder of SQLServerCentral.com and JumpstartTV.com. He has won the CEO of the year award given by the *Jacksonville Business Journal,* and Pragmatic Works has ranked up on the top growing companies in the country for many years in a row. Brian runs the local SQL Server user group in Jacksonville (JSSUG), is a contributing columnist for SQL Server Standard, maintains a regular column for the database website SQLServerCentral.com, and does regular webcasts at Jumpstart TV. He has authored and coauthored more than nine SQL Server books. Brian has spoken at conferences such as PASS, SQL Connections, and TechEd and many Code Camps.

Devin Knight is a Microsoft Data Platform MVP and the President of Pragmatic Works Training. He is an author of nine SQL Server, Power Platform, and Business Intelligence books. You can find him speaking at conferences like the Microsoft Business Applications Summit, PASS Summit, SQL Saturdays, and Code Camps. He is also a contributing member to several Virtual User Group Chapters. Making his home in Jacksonville, FL, Devin contributes locally at the Jacksonville Power BI User Group.

Manuel Quintana is a training content manager at Pragmatic Works. Previously, he was a senior manager working in the hotel industry. He joined the Pragmatic Works team in 2014 with no knowledge in the business intelligence space, but now speaks at SQL Saturdays and SQL Server user groups locally and virtually. He also teaches various BI technologies to many Fortune 500 companies on behalf of Pragmatic Works. Since 2014, he has called Jacksonville, Florida, home and now lives in Orlando with his beautiful wife, but he was born on the island of Puerto Rico and loves to go back and visit his family. When he is not working on creating new content for Pragmatic Works, you can probably find him playing board games or watching competitive soccer matches.

About the Technical Reviewer

Treb Gatte is a business intelligence analyst with many years of industry experience. He is an entrepreneur and a teacher with a passion for helping people to get the value they deserve from the software they have purchased. He is a technical expert and early adopter, with 24 combined years of software experience spanning the banking, government, and transaction processing industries.

Acknowledgments

Mitchell Pearson

I would like to thank God for the gifts and opportunities afforded me and most of all for sending his son Jesus Christ. I would like to thank my beautiful wife Jen for her incredible support and patience. I also thank my children, Brookelynne, Braxton, and Bella, for their unconditional love and great personalities! I thank Brian Knight for changing my life and giving me an incredible opportunity with no previous experience in the field of business intelligence. I would also like to thank the many mentors that have provided guidance and encouragement along the way. Thank you Anthony Martin, Dustin Ryan, Bradley Schacht, Devin Knight, Jorge Segarra, Bradley Ball, and many others!

Brian Knight

Thanks to everyone who made this book possible. As always, I owe a huge debt to my wife, Jenn, for putting up with my late nights. I wouldn't be here if it weren't for your tireless dedication to lifting me up. Also to my children, Colton, Liam, Camille, and John, for being so patient with their tired dad who has always overextended himself.

Finally, I would like to thank Shawn Trautman, my line dancing instructor. This will be the year that we complete the United Country Western Dance Council's goal of making line dancing a competitive sport worldwide.

Devin Knight

I must give thanks to God; without God in my life, I would not be as blessed as I am daily. Thanks for the amazing team of authors: Brian, Mitchell, and Manuel have put in time after hours away from their families to bring this great book together. To my wife, Erin, and three children, Collin, Justin, and Lana, who were all patient during nights that daddy had to spend writing. Finally, I would like to thank Alan "Nasty" Nash, my personal Toe Wrestling coach, for training a rising star like myself in the fine techniques of professional Toe Wrestling. I know this will be the year that we earn the world championship title.

ACKNOWLEDGMENTS

Manuel Quintana

Thank you to all my family and friends who support me in all of my endeavors. Special praise must be given to my wife for supporting me during late hours working and some weekends being dedicated to writing this book; without her I wouldn't be the person I am proud of being today. Also, I must say thank you to all my coworkers at Pragmatic Works; each one of them has mentored me in one way or another, and all my success can be traced back to them. I hope to make everyone mentioned here proud of what I have done and what I will achieve.

Introduction

Pro Microsoft Power Platform dives into the world of the citizen developer and explores the suite of powerful no-code/low-code tools made available by Microsoft. This book is divided into four parts; the first three parts cover the technologies of Power Apps, Power Automate, and Power BI individually and in depth. The fourth and last part focuses on how each of these tools integrates with one another to extend their capability. With the suite of Power Platform tools, self-sufficient citizen developers can drive change in their organization, multiply their productivity, and save the company significant money. Tasks that were once reserved for consultants or the IT Department can now be easily and quickly accomplished by an empowered workforce with little to no IT background!

Who Is This Book For?

This book has been designed specifically with the "citizen developer" in mind. The citizen developer is a problem solver, generally with little to no background in code, but usually has experience in Microsoft Excel or other self-service analytical tools. *Pro Microsoft Power Platform* is for Power users, analysts, and problem solvers that need access to a comprehensive set of tools to accomplish complex challenges and bring their visions to life. The reader may sometimes be considered part of a "Rogue IT" department that takes on tough projects that need to be done quickly, but if put in IT's hands could take months or even years to complete. The reader of *Pro Microsoft Power Platform* is likely familiar with one of the three Power Platform tools but has yet to be exposed to the other two in a way that fully explains how they all integrate. Every department in an organization has a "problem solver," the person everyone looks to when others have tried but failed. This book gives every "problem solver" the support they need to become efficient citizen developers.

What This Book Covers

Part 1: Building Line of Business Applications with Power Apps

Often, the first step when developing Power Platform solutions is to build a data collection application. Part 1 of this book covers how citizen developers can build their own applications. Building an application sounds like an impossible task, even to some of us that work in IT. However, building applications in Power Apps is surprisingly easy! Power Apps offers a low-code and easy-to-understand development interface for application development.

In Part 1, the reader will learn how to create apps, how to customize those apps to make them more dynamic and responsive, how to leverage the formula language, and finally how to manage sharing and administration.

Part 2: Task automation with Power Automate

Part 2 is about creating automated workflows with Power Automate to reduce redundant tasks and improve consistency across processes within an organization. With Power Automate, the reader will learn how to design workflows from existing templates and from a blank canvas leveraging a low-code development environment with an intuitive and clear graphical user interface. The reader will also learn how to build dynamic approval flows and how to extend that capability further with conditional logic, dynamic content, and automation. Finally, the reader will learn how to share workflows and perform necessary administrative tasks.

Part 3: Dashboards, Reporting, and Analytics with Power BI

Part 3 explores the building of interactive reports and dashboards with Power BI. Power BI provides unmatched analytical performance with its in-memory technology. The reader will learn how to connect to data sources, cleanse the data, build a data model, and provide additional value through Data Analysis Expressions, also known as DAX. DAX is an easy-to-learn expression language for creating calculated columns and measures to further extend the analytical capabilities of Power BI. The reader will learn about the rich analysis that can be performed through the building of interactive reports and responsive dashboards. Finally, the reader will learn about the Power BI service and how to share reports and dashboards with others.

Part 4: Integrating the Power Platform Tools Together

In Part 4, the reader will learn how each of these technologies can be integrated together expanding their capabilities. Independently, each of the Power Platform tools can be leveraged to add great value to any organization. However, Microsoft's suite of self-service tools can unlock endless possibilities when used together. Common scenarios for how these tools can easily integrate with one another will be highlighted in this section.

PART I

Building Line of Business Applications with Power Apps

CHAPTER 1

Introduction to Power Apps

Over the past few years, Power Apps' popularity has gone from a little-known edge product to one that's being used by millions of people monthly. Power Apps allows you to build applications fast. So fast, you can deliver value to your business in just a few minutes. In this chapter, you'll learn about the types of Power Apps you can build and the tools of the trade. This chapter sets the stage for getting your hands dirty in subsequent chapters.

What Is Power Apps

Power Apps is a low-code/no-code solution platform for building applications quickly. It enables almost anyone to build applications quickly with minimal IT intervention. The ideal Power Apps solution built replaces a manual process or paperwork and is accessed generally with employees in the Active Directory. Power Apps can also be accessed with guest accounts for outside partners or vendors and can also be accessed anonymously for portal applications.

Types of Apps

The first decision you must make when you're looking to create a Power App is what type of Power App you want to create. There are three types of applications – canvas, model-driven, and portal applications – and each has its pros and cons. One of the main drivers in the past was a licensing decision, but that's now changed as Power Apps has unified most of its pricing. Now, the decision is more about functionality and what you want the app to do.

© Mitchell Pearson, Brian Knight, Devin Knight, Manuel Quintana 2020
M. Pearson et al., *Pro Microsoft Power Platform*, https://doi.org/10.1007/978-1-4842-6008-1_1

Canvas Applications

Canvas applications (shown in Figure 1-1) allow you to create pixel-perfect applications for your users but require a bit more work to implement in many cases. Canvas applications can connect to hundreds of data sources (called connectors) and can even use some connectors for initiating an action, like texting a customer or displaying a map. Because it is pixel-perfect, the use cases for canvas applications are endless, and there is very little that can't be done with this type of application.

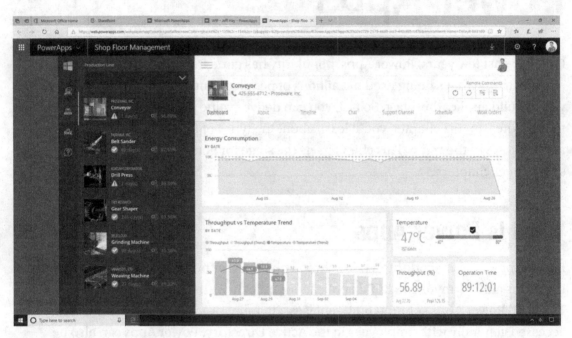

Figure 1-1. *Canvas application with Power BI reporting*

Model-Driven Applications

Model-driven applications focus on creating simple data entry style applications that can have a defined workflow. A perfect use case for this type of application is an employee onboarding application where there is a defined business process where data flows from onboarding the tax records, then payroll, and finally security access. This type of business process can be seen in Figure 1-2 with the dots on top of the screen. One key requirement of model-driven applications is they use Common Data Services, which will be discussed later in this chapter.

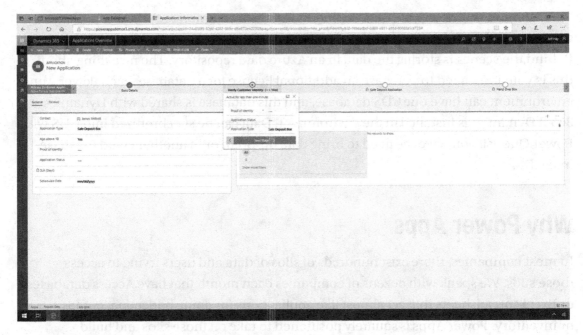

Figure 1-2. *Model-driven applications*

Portal Applications

Portal applications create intranet or extranet sites for you and your customers or
partners. They allow for anonymous access to the application, or you can force users
to authenticate with numerous providers like Active Directory, Facebook, or LinkedIn.
These applications also require Common Data Services as the data repository. A perfect
use case for a portal application is a county's website where they might have dozens of
forms they want to expose to their citizens.

Common Data Services

When you're looking to create any type of application, you typically first create a
database schema to store your data and then build the application to interface with that
schema. This can take time to build the perfect schema to store employees, products,
and other common objects. Common Data Services provides the application builder a
set of common objects called entities that can store that data.

Common Data Services (CDS) includes dozens of common entities you're likely going to need, and this list can be extended or existing ones modified by the developer. Behind the scenes is storing the data in an Azure data repository. The nice thing about this is you don't need to purchase an additional license for a database. Each Power Apps environment can have one CDS database, and this database is shared with Dynamics 365 if Dynamics is installed in the environment. Data can be synchronized into CDS with Power Query if you have the need to bring data on-prem or in another cloud database into CDS.

Why Power Apps

In most companies, there exist hundreds of silos of data and users trying to access those silos. We speak with dozens of companies each month that have Access databases or Excel spreadsheets that act almost like applications for doing budgeting, quotas, or inventory. Power Apps is squarely positioned to take on those silos and build applications quickly to enable users to access that data quickly and from any device.

You can build a Power App in two ways: by starting with data or from scratch. If you start with data, you can build the application by pointing to a data store (Excel, a table, or a cloud resource, to name just a few), and Power Apps will create the core screens for you in under a minute. For many people who want just an application to read and write to a data store, this application is all they'll ever need. For others, this may just be the starting point, or they'll choose to build the application from scratch to have full control of the experience.

Each time you build an application, it's accessible through a web link, a phone device, or other support Microsoft tools like SharePoint, Dynamics 365, or Teams. For phone access, there is a native Power Apps application that presents the user an internal company store of applications that they have access to, so you don't have to worry about submitting your applications to Apple or Google. As you share your Power Apps, those applications are centrally managed, and you can see who has used your application and some of the telemetry around their usage.

Creating Power Apps

Power Apps are created through a browser at `https://make.powerapps.com`. There is no classic application builder outside the browser because the design interface changes online at least monthly with new improvements and features. Once you log in with your credentials, you can create an application from scratch, by starting with data or by using templates of beautiful prebuilt applications.

This book is a hands-on book after this introductory chapter. To roll your sleeves up and get your hands dirty with the authors, you'll want to have at least a trial account to do the examples and get the most out of this book. If your company does not have Power Apps deployed, you can use the Community Plan to try all the concepts of this book out for free. To sign up for the Community Plan, simply go to `https://powerapps.microsoft.com/en-us/communityplan/`. The apps you build with this plan are meant for individual use only.

Environments

Environments are used to segment applications and data in the Power Platform. Each environment can have its own CDS database. Most companies use environments to segment development from production. A minority of other companies use them to segment various major departments like HR and Sales. You can navigate between environments on the top bar of `https://make.powerapps.com`.

If you do decide to create an environment for development, QA, and production, mechanisms exist to export applications, data, and connections out of one environment and import into another environment.

Admin Interface

To administer Power Apps, click the gearbox on the top right and select Admin Center (`https://admin.powerapps.com/`). This is where you can create and modify environments, modify the security, and set up data retention policies to prevent data from leaving your company. If you don't have a CDS database already created, you can create a new one by clicking Create Database while viewing the properties of an environment.

Each application also has an administration interface to set security, deploy, and roll back versions. You can access this interface by clicking the ellipsis button next to your application name and selecting Details. From there, you'll also be able to export the application for use by a customer or another environment.

Try It Out

For our first "Try It Out" section, you're going to confirm that your environment is set up and ready for the rest of the chapters around Power Apps and that the CDS database is created.

Lesson Requirements

To perform the examples in this book, you'll want to have access to an environment or create a new one with a CDS database. If your company does not have one, you can sign up for a personal Community Plan account and configure it.

Hints

Navigate to the Admin Center at https://make.powerapps.com and select the environment that you want to use throughout this book. Alternatively, you can create a new environment and CDS database.

Step by Step

Don't forget, if you're not an administrator of your environment, you can sign up for the Community Plan individually (https://powerapps.microsoft.com/en-us/communityplan/) to make sure you can do the full extent of the book.

---

1. Open https://make.powerapps.com and click the gearbox on the top right. Select Admin Center.

2. If you want to create a new fresh environment, select New
    Environment. Give the new environment a name (your choice)
    and specify the type. You might not have any more production
    environments remaining, so Trial will work fine if you think you
    can finish this book in under two weeks. We think you're going
    to love this book so much you'll finish in the next few days. Click
    Create Environment to create the environment. This might take up
    to five minutes.

3. You might also just want to use an existing environment and
    that's fine. If so, make sure you have a CDS database by clicking
    the environment. Then, select Create Database on the right side.
    Select your Currency for your country and language and select
    Create My Database. If you already have the database, this Create
    Database option won't exist, and you're ready to go.

Summary

Power Apps gives you the ability to create applications rapidly that work on a browser,
mobile device, and across the Microsoft tool stack. There are three types of applications
you can build: model-driven, canvas, and portal applications. Model-driven and portal
applications require Common Data Services (CDS), which gives you prebuilt data
models that can be extended. In the next chapter, you're going to see how to build your
first application in Power Apps.

CHAPTER 2

Building Your First Power App

In this chapter, you'll learn how to build your first application with the Start with Data option. This one-screen wizard builds a quick application with the core screens and is a great start for most organizations that just need an application to add, insert, and delete data.

Starting with Data

The easiest way to build an application is to start with an existing connection. Simply go to https://make.powerapps.com and select your data source from the Start with Data section. If you don't see your data source, you can click "Other data sources" to choose a less commonly used data source.

These connections can be used to connect ot nearly any database, SharePoint or Excel, to name just a few. Once you select a connection, you will be asked which table you want to build an application from, and then the basic application will be built to read, update, delete, and insert new records. These functions are broken into three screens: one screen to browse and search the records, one to view the details of a record, and a final one to add or update the record.

That's all there is to building your first application! After you build the core application, you can then modify it. The wizard only creates applications that are optimized for phones at first, but you can then change them to be a different orientation also. A common thing that you may need to fix, for example, is adding drop-down boxes to make the application more usable. For example, you might have a department name in a list that better fits a drop-down box.

© Mitchell Pearson, Brian Knight, Devin Knight, Manuel Quintana 2020
M. Pearson et al., *Pro Microsoft Power Platform*, https://doi.org/10.1007/978-1-4842-6008-1_2

The Development Environment

Once your application is created, you're taken to the Power Apps designer as shown in Figure 2-1. This designer is constantly being improved by Microsoft to make it easier to build and debug an application. Let's break down the core parts of the designer from Figure 2-1:

1. **Left Navigation Bar** – Here, you'll find the screens and controls you're using in your application.

2. **Middle Pane (Current Screen)** – A design preview of your application.

3. **Right-Hand Pane** – Used to configure the various controls in your application.

4. **Property Drop-Down List** – Similar to the right-hand pane, you can use this area to choose which property to configure for a control.

5. **Formula Bar** – Used to add your code to Power Apps for a given property or action.

6. **Ribbon** – Like Office, use the top ribbon to flip between major areas of the designer.

7. **Breadcrumb Navigation** – Shows what part of the application you have selected.

8. **Preview Button (F5)** – Click here to run the application in preview mode.

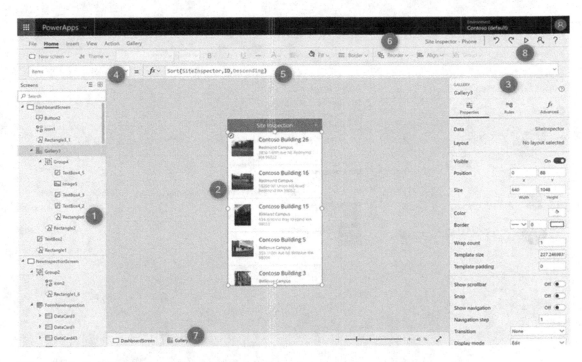

Figure 2-1. *The Power Apps designer environment*

Saving and Version Control

Each time you save in Power Apps, it creates a new version of the application. To save, click File ➤ Save. Before you save, you can also go to File ➤ Settings to change the application's name, icon, and color. This is the same icon that will show up prior to launching the application.

After you save, you can then share the application with others by clicking Share. Simply type the name or email of each person you wish to share the application with, and they can optionally receive an email telling them they have access. By default, they will be a user of the application (shown in Figure 2-2), but you can also make them a co-owner by clicking the Co-owner check box.

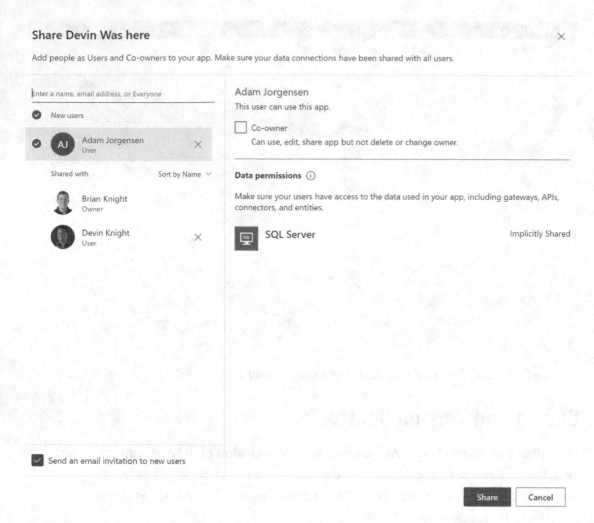

Figure 2-2. Sharing your application with others

Previewing the Application

There are two ways to interact with the application that you're building. You can
click the Preview Play button on the top right in Figure 2-1. This opens a preview of
the application like what your users will experience. For many interactions, you can
alternatively hold the ALT key down on your keyboard and click selectable items in your
application. You can do most actions but type inside a form or text input.

Try It Out

In this "Try It Out" section, you'll build your first Power App using the Start with Data option. You'll save the application and test run it. For the purpose of this section, please download the source files from the book's asset files: chapter2.zip. Unzip that file and place it in a folder on your Microsoft OneDrive. In this section, you're going to create an application against that workbook.

Lesson Requirements

In this excercise, the goal is to build a simple application using the Start with Data option to read, add, delete, and update lead records from the Chapter2LeadList.xlsx file. Once you have the application built, add some flair to it by changing the title of the app to Lead Management App.

Hints

Open `https://make.powerapps.com` and click Excel Online. This will take you to the area to create your connection. Select either OneDrive or OneDrive for Business based on what plan you have and then the LeadList.xlsx spreadsheet to create the application.

Step by Step

1. Unzip Chapter2.zip into a folder on OneDrive or OneDrive for Business.

2. Open `https://make.powerapps.com` to open the Power Apps environment.

3. Click Excel Online from the Start from Data section.

4. You'll then be taken to the beginning of the designer experience.

5. From the connection pane on the left, select either OneDrive or OneDrive for Business based on where you uploaded you unzipped the Chapter2LeadList.xlsx file and click Create.

6. Select Table1 and click Connect.

7. The core application will then automatically build in a few
    moments and look like Figure 2-3. We can do better than that
    though!

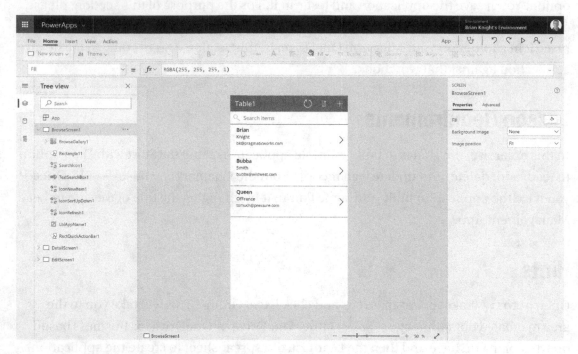

Figure 2-3. *Application created from the wizard*

8. Double-click Table1, and in the formula bar, change "Table1"
    to "Lead Management System." Click each of the other screens
    on the left, and you can repeat this for each of the other screens
    named DetailScreen1 and EditScreen1.

9. Click the Play button on the top right to test drive the application.

10. Save the application by clicking File ➤ Save.

Summary

The easiest way to build a simple application in Power Apps is to start with data. This can
build a quick application optimized for the phone form factor. The application will be
able to create, read, update, and delete data in almost any data connection.

CHAPTER 3

Exploring Power Apps Screens and Controls

In this chapter, you will learn how to build an application from scratch. As part of that, you will see how to use some of the many common controls and connectors for building those apps and how to change some of the common settings.

Building an App from Scratch

As you saw in the last chapter, you can build an application by starting from data which can build an application fast but is less flexible than building one from scratch. This chapter will focus on how most professionals build applications from scratch. By building an application from scratch, you start by choosing whether you want to build a tablet-focused application or a phone-based application. This decision does not mean that a tablet application can't be used on a phone or a phone application can't be used on a tablet. A tablet application will simply open horizontally on a phone.

To start building an application, go to `https://make.powerapps.com` and click Canvas App from Blank. You can then select if you would prefer that the app be optimized for tablet or phone format. This can always be changed at a later time in the App Settings section, and just because you select tablet, for example, doesn't mean the app won't work on a phone. Power Apps will simply orient the application horizontally for tablets. After you choose between tablet and phone, give it a name and click OK to create the base application.

Using and Reusing Connections

Once you create a connection, it is available to any other app in the environment if the user has access to it. You can create the connection prior to creating the application

© Mitchell Pearson, Brian Knight, Devin Knight, Manuel Quintana 2020
M. Pearson et al., *Pro Microsoft Power Platform*, https://doi.org/10.1007/978-1-4842-6008-1_3

or while you create the application. To access the connectors during the app building process, go to the left bar and click the database icon as shown in Figure 3-1.

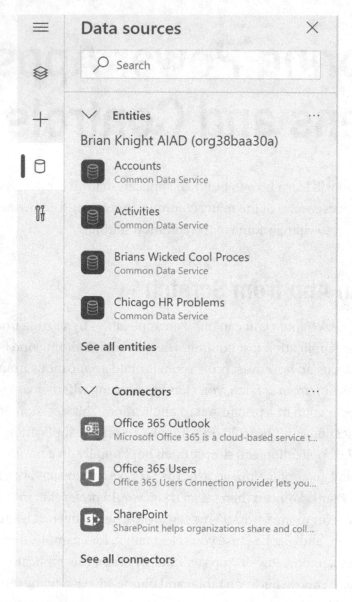

Figure 3-1. *Connector tab in Power Apps*

The Entities group of the Data Source section shows you the Common Data Services entities (tables) for that environment. The Connectors group shows you existing connections you have already created. Connectors can be traditional database connections or nontraditional connections like one to send emails or text a user.

To create a new connection, click See All Connectors and click where you want to connect to. As you can imagine, with more than 300 connectors, the search bar on top becomes handy to find your connector faster.

Common Controls You'll Need and Love

Your application is going to consist of numerous controls like galleries to show data and forms to enter and update data. You can access some of these controls under the Insert ribbon or the + ribbon (Insert) on the left of your screen. Once the control is inserted, you can control it in the Properties drop-down box or the window on the right that was discussed in the last chapter.

Displaying Data

To display data, you'll likely want to use a gallery or data table in Power Apps. The gallery gives you a lot more fine-tooth control of how to display your data. For example, you can add icons to delete a record or take you to another screen. Data tables are excellent for showing lots of rows in a clean table. You can still interact with the table by clicking a row or column to do something like navigate to a new screen or filter another gallery, but icons cannot be added, and limited tweaking can be done.

You can add a gallery by going to the Insert ribbon and selecting Gallery. Then, select what type of gallery you wish to insert. The most common example is a vertical gallery that shows you rows in a clean vertical format. If you want even more refined control, select one of the blank ones. Once added, you will be asked what connection has your data and how you want it formatted. The last step is to go to the right window and select what type of layout you want to use. Once you select the layout, click the Edit button in the Fields area above the layout to select what fields you want to display in the gallery. Don't worry, you can add more later.

For data tables, it's even easier since you don't have as much control. Add your data table under the Insert ribbon. Then select what fields you want to show in the table by clicking Edit Fields. Some fields will be added automatically, and you might want to refine them further.

Adding and Editing Data

The most common way to edit or add rows to a data connection is by using forms from the Insert ribbon. The configuration of a form is like a data table after you select the Data Source (connection). Simply click Edit Fields to select the fields that you want to show up on the form and add a button later to send the data. There's also an important property called Default Mode, which by default is set to Edit. This mode specifies whether you want to Edit data or Insert data (New mode).

Once you add a button from the Insert ribbon, you will need to add some code to the button to have it submit data to the data source. Whether you want to add data (New mode) or edit data (Edit mode), the code will be the same for the OnSelect property:

```
SubmitForm(FormName)
```

To select which row you want to edit, you'll need to configure the Item property for the form. This property is ignored when the form is in New mode, but in Edit mode the property is used to select a single row for modification. For example, if you want to edit a row from a gallery, you can configure the Items property to be the following, which will pass whatever row was selected from the gallery into the form to edit.

```
GalleryName.Selected
```

Try It Out

Now that you know about forms and galleries, it's time to try to spend the next few chapters building an end-to-end application for filing expenses. For this chapter, we're going to build a gallery and form for entering and viewing expense reports. To start building the application, you'll need to configure the data source we'll be using for the next few sections (over all the Power Apps and Power Automate chapters).

Setup

During much of this book, we will be using an expense report example. To store this data, you'll need to use a SharePoint Online list (SharePoint is included in Office 365). Under normal circumstances, it would likely make sense to store this type of data in a database like SQL Server, but the author team wanted to find a place where most readers could easily set up.

To start, create two lists in SharePoint – Customers and Expenses – by following these steps:

1. Sign in to SharePoint Online. If you don't know where this might be, go to `https://portal.office.com`, click the Sign In button, and then click SharePoint once in.

2. Pick any site where you can create a SharePoint list. If you don't
    know where that might be, you can always click Create Site and
    create a Team Site for the purpose of the book.

3. Once the site is open, click + New and select List. Name your first
    list Customers.

4. Select the Title column and click Column Settings ➤ Rename.
    Rename the column to Customer Name.

5. Click + Add Column and select Person. Name this column
    Expense Approver.

6. Add a final Date column called Expenses End Date. No time is
    needed for this column. (Figure 3-2 shows the complete list.)

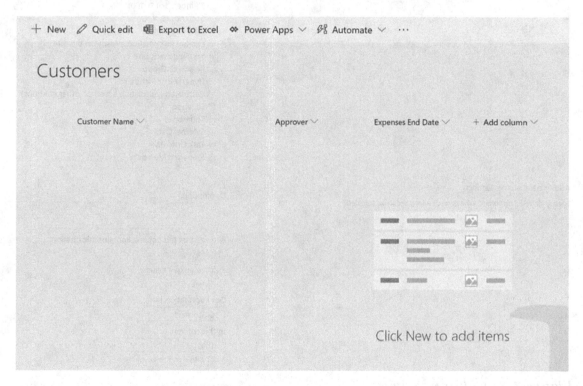

Figure 3-2. *Final Customer list*

7. Go back to the home page for the site. With the first list now
    created, create another list called Expenses.

8. Rename Title this time to Report Name just as you did before for Customer Name.

9. Create a new Column that's a lookup to Customer. To do this, click Add Column, and when it asks the data type, select Other. Then name the column Customer and choose Lookup as the data type. Finally, click Customers for the Get information from drop-down box and click OK. The complete screen looks like Figure 3-3.

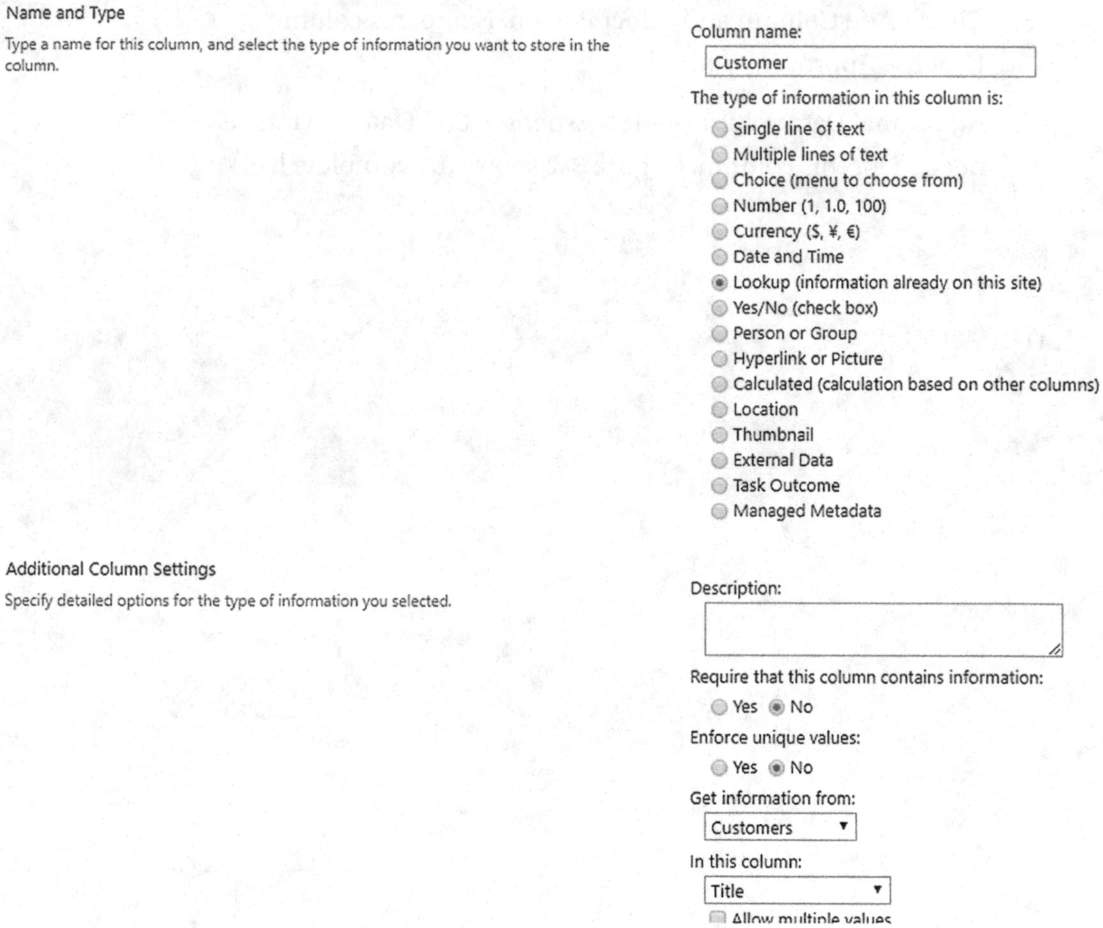

Name and Type

Type a name for this column, and select the type of information you want to store in the column.

Column name:

Customer

The type of information in this column is:

○ Single line of text
○ Multiple lines of text
○ Choice (menu to choose from)
○ Number (1, 1.0, 100)
○ Currency ($, ¥, €)
○ Date and Time
◉ Lookup (information already on this site)
○ Yes/No (check box)
○ Person or Group
○ Hyperlink or Picture
○ Calculated (calculation based on other columns)
○ Location
○ Thumbnail
○ External Data
○ Task Outcome
○ Managed Metadata

Additional Column Settings

Specify detailed options for the type of information you selected.

Description:

Require that this column contains information:

○ Yes ◉ No

Enforce unique values:

○ Yes ◉ No

Get information from:

Customers ▼

In this column:

Title ▼

☐ Allow multiple values

Figure 3-3. Column settings

10. Add the following other columns with the data type of Single Line of Text:

   a. Merchant

   b. Category

   c. From Email

   d. Approver Email

   e. Status

11. Add a Total column with the Currency data type.

12. Add a Comment column that is a Multiple Lines of Text data type.

13. Add an Is Approved column that's a Yes/No column which defaults to No.

14. Add a column called DateSubmitted that is a date.

15. Lastly, add a few customers and expense reports for those customers for the two lists.

Lesson Requirements

In this lesson, you'll use the SharePoint lists you just created to make an expense report application. You will need to show a list of all customers on the left and a list of past expense reports on the lower right. On the upper-right zone of the application, allow an employee to enter a new expense report. The final product should look like Figure 3-4.

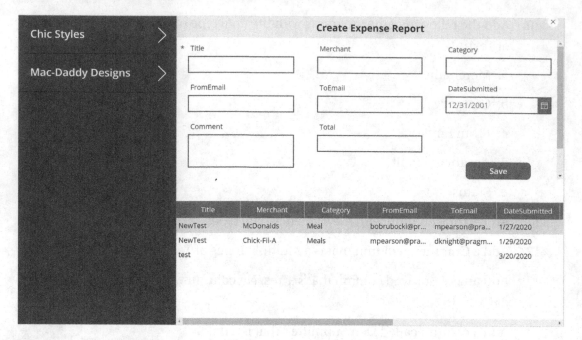

Figure 3-4. *View of the expense report app*

Hints

To accomplish the goals, you'll need a gallery to display old expense reports and another gallery or a data table to display customers (projects). Lastly, you'll need a form to submit an expense report. Watch out for the form modes. By default, the form mode will be looking to edit a record vs. adding a new expense report.

Step by Step

1. Before you begin, make sure you've done the setup steps to create the SharePoint lists. Make sure you've also created a few records in each list to experiment.

2. Let's begin by going to `http://make.powerapps.com` and clicking Create Canvas App from Blank. Choose a tablet form factor and name it something like Expense Report App.

3. Create your connection first to the two SharePoint lists by clicking the database icon on the left of the screen and selecting Connectors ➤ SharePoint (you might have to click See all Connectors to discover this connector). Once you put your credentials in, select the site you created from the setup step earlier and select the Customers and Expense Reports lists and click Connect.

4. Add a gallery by going to the Insert ribbon and selecting Gallery ➤ Vertical Gallery. When the Select Data Source dialog opens, select Customers. Alternatively, you can select Customers from the Data Source option on the right side after selecting the gallery. In the right pane, change the layout to Title. Adjust the gallery to where it fits nicely on the left side. Change the Color property of the gallery (on the right pane) to a dark color. Lastly, change the text color (by selecting the first row and the arrow next to that row) to white. The final gallery should look something like Figure 3-5.

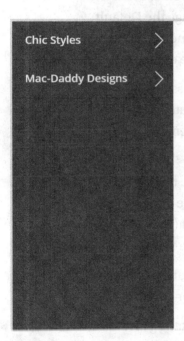

Figure 3-5. *First gallery now created*

5. Go to the Insert ribbon and select Data Table to add a data table to the pane. Alternatively, you could have used a gallery, but since there are so many columns to show, a data table will give the rows an Excel look. Point this table to the Expense Reports list by selecting it from the Data Source property in the right pane. Position the data table to occupy about half the right area of our app.

6. Now, you need somewhere to add new expense reports. From the Insert ribbon, select Form ➤ Edit. Point this form to the Expense Report list from the Data Source property as you did before. In the right properties pane, click Fields to open the field pane. Change Comments to Edit Multi-line Text. Click the ellipsis button next to Attachments and select Remove to delete that field from the form. Do the same thing for the Is Approved column. Lastly, change the DefaultMode property in the right pane to New.

7. Select the Status field in the form (not the card) and click Unlock to Change Property in the Advanced right tab. Change the Default property from the Properties drop-down box to "Pending." In the right properties pane, change Visible to False for the entire card.

8. Above the form, go to Insert ➤ Label. Stretch it across the app above the form and change the text property to Create Expense Report. Make the font as large as you think makes sense and change the fill color to light gray.

9. Insert a button from the Insert ribbon and name the button Save by double-clicking the text in the button. Change the OnSelect property from False to `SubmitForm(Form1);NewForm(Form1)` on the button. This will save the data and then reset the form.

10. Other optional things you could do are change the labels for the field names to add spaces and make them more user-friendly.

11. You're ready to now play with the application by entering an expense report. The only field required is the Title field.

Summary

In this chapter, you learned about the most common Power Apps components used to build an application. The two major components you'll need to interact with data are forms (for modifying data) and galleries (for showing data). We didn't do a lot of coding though, and that's the point. In our next chapter, we'll start to build a deeper understanding of coding in Power Apps.

CHAPTER 4

Working with Power Apps Expressions

Now that you've seen some of the power in building apps with Power Apps, it's time to unlock the full potential of the application we've built with the expression language. Power Apps expressions are meant to resemble Excel expressions to simplify adoption, and, in this chapter, we'll cover some of the most common functions you'll use in Power Apps.

Functions You Need to Memorize

While there are hundreds of functions in Power Apps that are useful, there are a few that you should commit to memory because they'll be used daily as a Power Apps developer. Pay special attention that the entire Power Apps expression language is case sensitive.

Filter Function

The Filter function limits the rows by some sort of criteria. Filter is used by passing in the data source or collection and then how you wish it to be filtered:

```
Filter(source, logical test)
```

For example, if you wanted to filter the Customers SharePoint list or table to only active records, you might do something like the following if the Status column had character data inside of it:

```
Filter(Customers, Status="Active")
```

© Mitchell Pearson, Brian Knight, Devin Knight, Manuel Quintana 2020
M. Pearson et al., *Pro Microsoft Power Platform*, https://doi.org/10.1007/978-1-4842-6008-1_4

Please note that if your computer has a regional settings set to use the comma for its decimal space like in much of Europe, your formula will need to use a semicolon instead of a comma throughout this chapter and in the Power Apps product. For example, the previous command would look like this:

```
Filter(Customers; Status="Active")
```

Filter also allows multiple conditions to be searched by adding a comma after each condition. Alternatively, you can use a && for a logical AND or || for a logical OR condition. In the following example, we're looking for Active customers, where the name of the customer is pulled from a text input box called txtCustomerInput.

```
Filter(Customers, Status="Active", Name=txtCustomerInput.Text)
```

Each of the preceding examples provided assumes the input is an exact match. You could specify a query where the input starts with a certain word using the StartsWith condition, or you can use the "in" condition to specify that a piece of text can be anywhere in that field. The following are two different ways of seeing very similar results:

```
Filter(Customers, StartsWith(Name=txtCustomerInput.Text))
```

Or you could specify that a user could type in any part of the company's name by using something like this:

```
Filter(Customers, txtCustomerInput.Text in Name)
```

Search Function

The Search function is like the Filter command where it will reduce the number of rows you see in a connection or data source. Again, you'll see these generally in galleries, data tables, or drop-down boxes typically. The best thing about the Search function is it's always considered a contains search like the "in" example we saw moments ago in the Filter section, and it can also search multiple columns in one command. Imagine you want to search the Customers table for anywhere a customer's first, last, or company name contains the words in a search bar called txtSearchInput; you would use code like

```
Search(Customers, txtSearchInput.Text, "First Name", "Last Name", "Company")
```

User Function

The User function allows you to retrieve the information for a user that's signed in and using your application. Typically, you'll use the function in forms to save who is updating or saving data into your data source. There are three properties you can access about the user: Email, FullName, and Image. All the information is pulled from the information that the user or administrator inputted into the Azure Active Directory. To access the function, simply use it as shown in the following and append what information you want:

```
User().Email
```

Lookup Function

The Lookup function is used typically to return a single value from a different sheet, table, collection, or list in Power Apps. It's similar to a SQL Server join if you come from the SQL Server world or a vLookup if you come from the Excel world. To use, you'll show the data source and how you want to join to that connection and lastly what value you want to return.

```
Lookup(DataSource, Condition, ReturnValue)
```

For example, when an order is selected, you could return the customer information by using the Lookup function as shown here:

```
Lookup(Customers, CustomerID=galOrder.Selected.CustomerID, CustomerName)
```

We should spend a moment talking about performance and consequences. If you were to add a Lookup function, for example, into a gallery item, every row will need to perform that lookup, and it could cause performance problems and overload your data source with connections. Instead, you might want to flatten the data in these instances with a database view or a collection ahead of time.

If Function

Every programming language has a variant of an If function, and Power Apps is no different. Its expression language uses an If function similar to how it's used in Excel. You'll find yourself using If statements all over your application to set a default text value, hide objects, or potentially conditionally color text labels. To use, the syntax will resemble this:

```
If(Condition, ThenResult, ElseCondition)
```

Let's imagine you want to highlight the value that was selected in a gallery to a light blue color; you could use code like the following on the TemplateFill property in the gallery:

```
If(ThisItem.IsSelected,LightBlue)
```

You might also want to show an error message if the value of a text box was left blank by using something like this:

```
If(IsBlank(txtSearch.Text), "Need to specify a value to search for", "Ready to search")
```

If statements can be nested by using a series of ElseConditions. If you have more than a few nested If statements, a Switch function might make more sense as it's cleaner to write.

SubmitForm

We reviewed SubmitForm in our last chapter and how it can insert or update data in a data collection or connection from a form by passing in the form name like `SubmitForm(FormName)`. A form can start in multiple modes – view, edit, and insert – and these modes impact what action will be done by SubmitForm. For example, if you want to force the form to be in New mode, you can use the following command:

```
NewForm(FormName)
```

If you want to force the form to be in edit mode where SubmitForm would update the row, simply use `EditForm(FormName)`. After specifying the form is in edit mode, you'll need to set the Item property in the form to select the row that you want to edit. You can do that with the Filter, Search, or more likely a gallery selection. You can also reset the values back to the default values by using `ResetForm(FormName)`. This might be used on a cancel button in many cases.

Common Date Functions

There is a litany of functions to help you handle dates in Power Apps. The most common one to use is `Now()`, which returns the current date and time for the user's time zone, or `Today()`, which just returns the current date. There are also many other important functions for handling various date operations that you're going to want to keep note of.

Parsing Dates

Often, you'll want to retrieve a piece of the date. For example, if you want to return only the year from the current date, you could use something like `Year(Now())`. Likewise, other functions to retrieve a piece of a date are

- `Month(Now())` – Returns the month number.
- `Text(Month(Today()), "mmmm")` – Returns the month name fully spelled out. Use "mmm" if you want the month's abbreviation.
- `Day(Now())` – Returns the day number of the month.
- `Hour(Now())` – Returns the hour of the day.
- `Weekday(Now())` – Returns the day number of the week.
- `Text(Weekday(Today()), "dddd")` – Returns the day name. You can use "ddd" to return the day abbreviation.

DateAdd and DateDiff

The DateAdd function adds the provided number of days, months, or years to a given date. You can use this to find when an invoice might be due, for example. The DateDiff function is used to determine the difference between two provided dates. This could be used to determine how many days an invoice is past due by passing the DueDate column as shown in the following:

`DateDiff(DateValue("1/1/2020"), Now(),Days)`

In the preceding expression, when you pass in a date within double quotes, you must wrap that date in a `DateValue` function to convert the text into a date. The following function uses DateAdd to add four days to today's date. You can try these functions in this section by dropping a label into your application and typing in this code:

```
DateAdd( Now(), 4, Days)
```

Remove

The Remove function can delete a row from a data source or collection. To use the function, specify the data source or collection you want to remove the record from and then the record as in the following example:

```
Remove(Customers, ThisItem)
```

By using ThisItem as in the preceding example, you'll remove the current row in a gallery or data table. It passes the entire row into the Remove function. Alternatively, you could specify the item in the gallery that was selected by using `Remove(Customers, Gallery1.Selected)`. You could also use the Filter command to specify the row or rows you want filtered. Lastly, you can use the RemoveIf function to eliminate rows based on a condition as shown here:

```
RemoveIf(Customers, AccountBalance=0)
```

Delegation in Power Apps

One of the biggest gotchas in Power Apps is the notion of delegation. When everything is operating normal, a Filter function, for example, will pass the command to your data source and only return the rows you care about. In other words, all the work is being done on the data source's server in its native server language.

The exception to that is when you get a delegation warning. A delegation warning happens when the data source doesn't know how to interpret your function, and it must return all the rows to Power Apps and let Power Apps do the operation on the application side. This makes the application run much slower and has a larger issue. By default, only 500 rows will be returned to Power Apps, which could potentially give you the wrong answer if you have more rows than that in your data source. You can optionally change the 500-row evaluation option to 2000 rows at a maximum by going to File ➤ Settings ➤ Advanced Settings as shown in Figure 4-1.

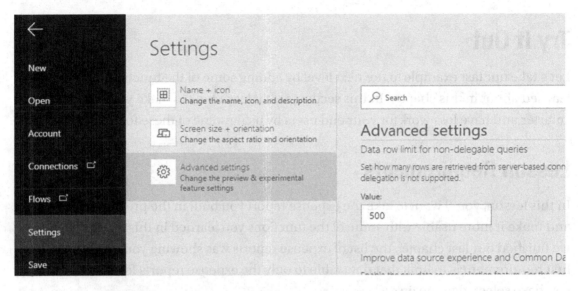

Figure 4-1. Delegation setting

If you have more than 2000 rows in your data source and you run a count function, you would get the wrong answer if more than 2000 are valid to be counted if there is a delegation problem. You would always get the answer of 2000 rows in this scenario. This is what makes delegation warnings so important to pay attention to and work around.

To determine if this is a problem in your application, look for the following warning message that would appear on your expression.

Delegation warning. The "Filter" part of this formula might not work correctly on large data sets.

Some of the techniques we'll use in our next chapter with collections and variables will help you get around this warning message. Delegation can happen more in some data sources than others. For example, SharePoint will give you many more delegation warnings than SQL Server as a source. Although this is changing frequently, delegation will occur often in SharePoint when using the Search function but not the Filter function.

It will also give you issues if you use the Filter function with an In clause. Delegation warnings should rarely be ignored, but an example where it might be permissible to ignore is with small datasets that you never expect to exceed a few hundred rows.

Try It Out

Let's take our last example to the next level by adding some of the functions you've learned about in this chapter. In this section, you'll learn how to make your application smarter and have less work for your end users by using some of these formulas.

Lesson Requirements

In this lesson, you'll want to take the expense report you built in the previous chapter and make it more usable with some of the functions you learned in this chapter. When we finished our last chapter, the list of expense reports was showing you all reports. Your first requirement is to limit that data table to only the expense reports for the customer you have selected in the first.

You will also want to make it where you can edit an existing report by selecting it in the data table. Finally, set the DateSubmitted column to the current date and FromEmail to the email address of the user. For bonus points, set the ToEmail as the ExpenseApprover's email address from the Customer SharePoint list for the customer you have selected.

Hints

For reducing the rows in the data table, use the Filter function and pass in the value from the gallery by using the expression `GalleryName.Selected.Name`. To make the form editable, add the `EditForm(FormName)` function on the OnSelect event in the data table. You'll also need to specify the Item property to pass the entire row into the form.

To set the DateSubmitted property to today's date, set the DefaultDate property of the date picker to `Today()`. Use the User() function to set the email address for who submitted the expense report.

Step by Step

1. Open the expense report app we built in the previous chapter to edit at `https://make.powerapps.com`. Click the ellipsis button next to the application's name and select Edit.

2. Select the entire data table that shows the expense reports. You may have to select the data table from the Tree View from the left to ensure you have the entire table selected. To filter the data to only show expense reports for the customer selected in the gallery, change the Items property to this:

   ```
   Filter('Expense Reports', Customer.Value=Gallery1.Selected.
   Name)
   ```

Your gallery name might be different than Gallery1, which was the default gallery name from the previous chapter. Because Customer was a SharePoint lookup column, you can see numerous columns under the Customer list after you type period. In most data sources, you would match based on the ID of the column and not the name. If we used the ID in this instance, it would cause a delegation warning.

---

3. Choose a column that you want your users to select to edit the record. In reality, you'd want to repeat this step for all the columns to make it obvious, but one is enough for here. Change the OnSelect property of this column to the following code (note that your form might not be called Form1):

   ```
   EditForm(Form1)
   ```

4. Select the entire form and change the Item property to the row that was selected by using the following code:

   ```
   DataTable1.Selected
   ```

5. Now, when you select the row from the data table (for the column that you added the EditForm code to), you'll see your row in the form to edit. Click the Play button to preview to play with the functionality by changing a row.

6. Select the DateSubmitted date picker (make sure the entire card is not selected but only the date picker). Notice that when you got to the Advanced right properties pane, the field is presently locked. Unlock it in the Advanced properties pane by selecting Unlock to Change Properties. Then set the DefaultDate property to Today().

7. Repeat the same unlock step for FromEmail and set its default value to User().Email to lock the user submitting the expense report. The issue with this is that when you're in edit mode of the form, it will overwrite any existing value with this new default value. To fix that, you can use code like the following for FromEmail, which detects if the form is in edit or new mode. If it's in edit mode, it pulls the existing value to update. If it's in new mode, it will set the input box to the user's email address that's signed in.

    ```
    If(Form1.Mode=FormMode.Edit, ThisItem.FromEmail, User().
    Email)
    ```

8. Likewise, the same problem exists for the SubmitDate column.

    ```
    If(Form1.Mode=FormMode.Edit, ThisItem.DateSubmitted,
    Today())
    ```

9. Next, you want to set the default value for the ToEmail (who will receive the expense report) to the customer's approver. To do this, we need to enlist the help of the Lookup function as shown in the following to compare the customer's name to what was selected in the gallery and retrieve the email address of the approver.

    ```
    LookUp(Customers, Title = Gallery1.Selected.Name,'Expense
    Approver'.Email)
    ```

10. We also want to default the customer selection in the form to what was selected in the gallery on the left. To do this, you're going to use the Lookup function to match against the gallery. The Choices function you see in the following code populates the drop-down box from a SharePoint lookup column.

```
LookUp(
    Choices('Expense Reports'.Customer),
    Id = Gallery1.Selected.ID)
```

11. Add a button next to the Save button to cancel your edits. Change the text of the button to Cancel and change the fill color to something a little different than the Save button. Add the following code to the OnSelect property, which resets the form and then switches the mode back to NewForm mode.

```
ResetForm(Form1);NewForm(Form1)
```

12. Add a button next to the Save button to delete an expense report. Add the following code to remove the record that's selected from the data table.

```
Remove('Expense Reports', DataTable1.Selected)
```

13. You will want to make sure that the Delete Report button is only showing when the form is in Edit mode. Change the visibility property to the following to ensure the button is only available when you're viewing a record.

```
If(Form1.Mode=FormMode.Edit, true, false)
```

14. Congrats! You've really added a lot of functionality to this application and learned more about the Power Apps expression language. The final product will resemble Figure 4-2.

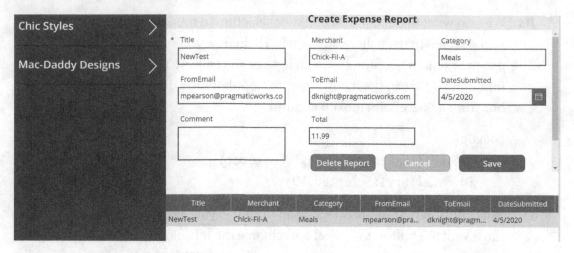

Figure 4-2. *Final created form*

Summary

While there are hundreds of functions in Power Apps, many of the core ones you will want to memorize were covered in this chapter. Many of them like Filter, Search, and Lookup limit the rows you see in a Power Apps object like a gallery. Others are focused on data manipulation like SubmitForm or Remove. In our next chapter, we'll cover the key functions that were left out of this chapter: the functions to create variables and collections.

CHAPTER 5

Leveraging Variables and Collections

To finish the basics of learning Power Apps, you must also know how to deal with variables and collections. Variables allow you to store a value or set of values in the application memory. Collections allow you to store tables of rows and columns in memory to be worked on locally. Both of these help you get around delegation warnings in many cases.

Variables

Variables are used in Power Apps to store values in memory and can be created on any actionable area like OnSelect events or when an application starts in the OnStart event, to name a few. Variables can be created at a global level where they can be seen across multiple screens, where contextual variables can be seen in a single screen.

Global

Global variables are used to store values globally in memory and can be accessed by any screen in your application. There's the most common way to create variables because typically you're going to use variables throughout the application. To set a global variable, use the Set command as shown here:

```
Set(variable, value)
```

When using the Set command, it will create the variable if it doesn't exist, or if it does exist, it will update the variable value. A common variable that you might create for every application you build is the signed-in user details. Sometimes, using the User() function

41

© Mitchell Pearson, Brian Knight, Devin Knight, Manuel Quintana 2020
M. Pearson et al., *Pro Microsoft Power Platform*, https://doi.org/10.1007/978-1-4842-6008-1_5

will cause delegation when used in a Filter command. By pushing the user's info into a variable as shown here, you can save that delegation warning:

```
Set(varUserEmail, User().Email)
```

To then retrieve the value of the variable, just call out to its name like in this filter command:

```
Filter('Expense Reports', FromEmail=varUserEmail)
```

You can see what variables have been created at any time by going to the View ribbon and selecting Variables (shown in Figure 5-1). If you see the variable here with no value, chances are the event has not executed yet, like no one has clicked the button you tied the variable to. If you want the variable to be created when the application first starts, select App from the Tree View left pane and put your code into the OnStart event of the app. After setting it there, you can either close and reopen the application or simply click the ellipsis button on the App in the Tree View and select Run OnStart.

Figure 5-1. *Variable list*

You may have noticed in Figure 5-1 that the varUser variable's value looked quite different, showing a table icon instead of a value. This is because the variable is storing every column in the User() function like this:

```
Set(varUser, User())
```

To reference these variables, it will require that you specify which column in that variable you want to call. For example, to reference the email address in varUser, add that column name to the variable name as shown here:

```
varUser.Email
```

Contextual Variables

Contextual variables are used to store values in memory that are only accessible in the screen where they were created. You'll use these less than global variables and should only be created when you truly know you're not going to use it outside the single screen. These variables are typically created on buttons with the OnSelect event or when a screen opens in the OnVisible event. To create these types of variables, use the UpdateContext function like this:

```
UpdateContext({varShowButton:true})
```

You can also set multiple values at one time by separating the values with a comma as shown in the following:

```
UpdateContext({varShowButton:true, varCustomer:"Cammie Cakes"})
```

Additionally, you can set a variable in a new screen while you navigate to the screen by including the variable update in the Navigate function as shown here:

```
Navigate(TargetScreenName, ScreenTransition.Fade, ({varShowButton:false})
```

Collections

Collections are like variables but can store entire tables in memory reference, manipulation, or staging of data. You might use a variable to store data offline when your user is on an unreliable data connection or try to store a local shopping cart. These collections can be created in a few different ways, but in this chapter, let's focus on the most common: Collect and ClearCollect.

In both functions, the collection will be created and loaded within the same command. Both functions are similar, but the decision on which one you use is based on one question. Do you want to wipe and load the collection or just add new data to the collection? The syntax for both is the same and will look like this:

```
Collect (CollectionName, Item)
```

The item is represented as an array with {} representing each row. Imagine you want to store a collection of superheroes.

```
ClearCollect (
    colSuperHeroes,
    {
        Hero: "Hulk",
        Power: "Strength"
    },
    {
        Hero: "Ironman",
        Power: "Rich"
    },
     {
        Hero: "Thor",
        Power: "Lightning"
    }
)
```

After you create the collection, you can reference it like any other data source in Power Apps. It even shows up in the list of data sources for you to create galleries, forms, or data tables from. If you want to see a list of collections that are available to you, select Collections from the View ribbon (shown in Figure 5-2).

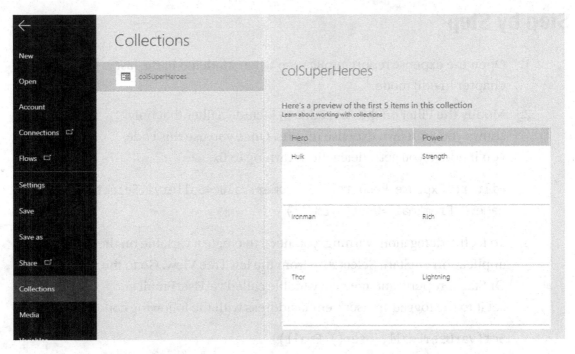

Figure 5-2. *Collection listing*

Try It Out

You can use collections to avoid delegation warnings we spoke about in our last chapter. It can also be used to store user preferences or show dialog boxes to confirm values.

Lesson Requirements

In this chapter, try to make the data table also filter the FromEmail column based on the email address for who is signed in. That way, a user can only alter his or her own expense reports.

Hints

Create the variable on the application OnStart event by using the Set command. Then, modify the filter to include the newly created variable.

Step by Step

1. Open the expense report application when modified in the last chapter in edit mode.

2. Modify the Filter on the data table to include a filter that only shows you your own expense reports. Once you use this code, you'll notice you get a delegation warning to fix.

    ```
    Filter('Expense Reports', Customer.Value=Gallery1.Selected.
    Name,  FromEmail=User().Email)
    ```

3. To fix the delegation warning, you need to create a variable on the application OnStart. Select App from the left Tree View. Go to the OnStart property and create a variable called varUserEmail and set it to the logged-in user's email address with the following code:

    ```
    Set(varUserEmail, User().Email)
    ```

4. Select the ellipsis button next to App in the Tree View and select Run OnStart.

5. Now you'll need to modify the filter on the data table to use the newly created variable. After you do this, you'll notice the delegation goes away and the filter runs much faster.

    ```
    Filter('Expense Reports', Customer.Value=Gallery1.
    Selected.Name,  varUserEmail)
    ```

6. Great job. You've now created a variable to help you get around delegation problems.

Summary

Variables are used to store data in the application's memory, while collections can store tables consisting of rows and columns. Variables can help you get around delegation warnings in some cases or control the visibility of an object, like a dialog box. You can retrieve data from a collection by using the same mechanisms you use to retrieve data from any other data source like galleries or data tables, to name just a few.

CHAPTER 6

Securing and Sharing Apps

Sharing applications in Power Apps is as easy as sharing a document in Word or an email. In this chapter, you'll learn how to share your applications with others and how to invite others to collaborate on those canvas applications. You can share applications with internal or external users, but they must have a license.

Sharing an Application

When you have a Power App open in design mode, you can save the application while designing it by going to File ➤ Save. Once you save the application, it's only available for you to use. You can share with others by clicking File ➤ Share while you have the application in design mode or by clicking the ellipsis button next to the app at `https://make.powerapps.com` and selecting Share (shown in Figure 6-1).

© Mitchell Pearson, Brian Knight, Devin Knight, Manuel Quintana 2020
M. Pearson et al., *Pro Microsoft Power Platform*, https://doi.org/10.1007/978-1-4842-6008-1_6

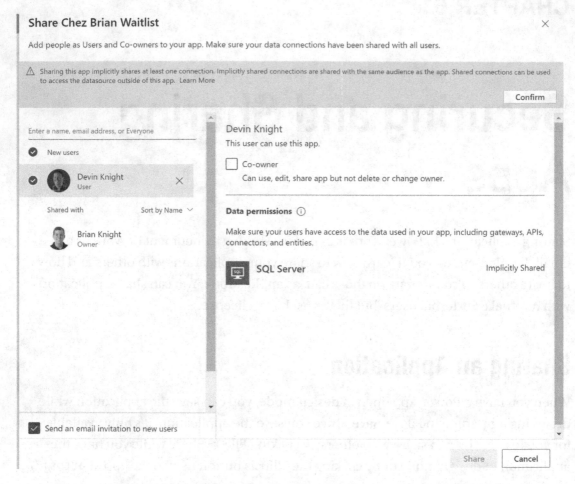

Figure 6-1. Sharing an application

On this screen, you can add individuals, groups, or the entire company to have access to the application by the user's name or email address. To add the entire company, type Everyone for the name. You can also check "Send an email invitation to new users" to send them a notification of the new application and a link to it.

By default, the user will have access to run the published application on their phone, link, or through a partner application like Microsoft Teams. Once you add people to your application, you can click Co-owner to grant the users authorization to edit the application.

If you have a SQL Server connection and use SQL Server authentication, when you share the application, you also implicitly give the user rights to use that connection to create their own application. The user would have to have rights to create apps in the environment for this implicit right to have any effect.

Running Apps in Microsoft Teams

A great way to increase adoption in your application internally is to add it to your collaboration environment for your company, Microsoft Teams. It makes the Power App easier to find and lands the application where they spend much of their time. There are two ways to create a Power App in Teams based on your needs.

The first way to create an application is to make it discoverable in the Apps section of Teams. The first step is to go to https://make.powerapps.com and click the ellipsis button next to the application and select Add to Teams. This downloads the application as a .zip file that can then in turn be uploaded into Teams. To upload it, go to Teams and click Apps in the lower left of Teams.

In this area, you can add new packaged applications into the collaboration tool. You can also upload the custom application you've built by clicking "Upload a Custom App" from the lower left. You can then select whether you want the Power App to be available for you or the entire organization. Then, select the downloaded zip file and click Add. This application is now available for anyone to search for and add to their Teams channel.

You might have to have your administrator upload the application into Teams if you do not have permissions.

The other way to add an application is by adding it directly to a Teams channel. When you add an app this way, it will not be available to be discovered in the App section but is perfect if you only see yourself adding it to one channel. To add the Power App, go to your Teams channel and click + to add a new tab. Click the Power Apps icon and click Add. Finally, search for your application (shown in Figure 6-2) and select the application to add. You can also notify members in the team by checking "Post to the channel about this tab."

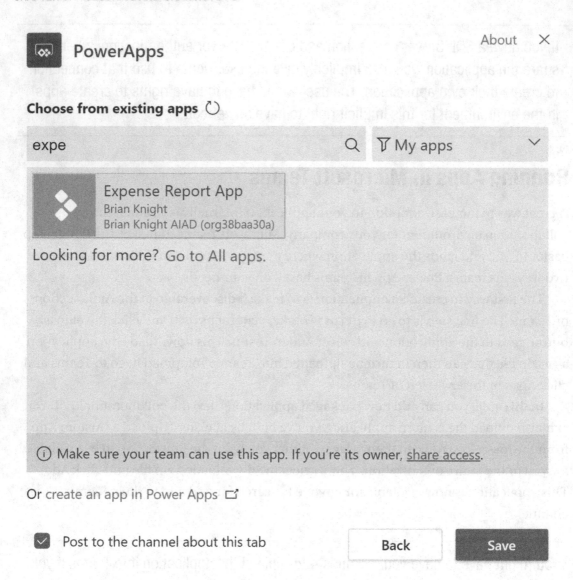

Figure 6-2. Adding an app to teams

As you update the application by publishing new versions for your users, the Teams app will also replicate the change.

Running Apps on Mobile

As you build applications in Power Apps, the applications are automatically cross-platform. They can be opened in a browser, inside of other Microsoft tools like SharePoint or Teams, or with the native application on the Apple or Android. Simply download the Power Apps application in the Apple store or Android store. Once you sign in to the Power Apps app, you'll see all the apps you have access to in your tenant. You can tap the app you wish to open and swipe right to go back to the app listing.

Try It Out

In this simple "Try It Out" section, you'll want to share the application with another user in your organization.

Lesson Requirements

To complete this section, share your application with another user of your choice.

Step by Step

1.   Open the application in design mode you have been building for the past two chapters.

2.   Save the application by clicking File ➤ Save.

3.   Share the application by going to File ➤ Share.

4.   Type a user that you wish to share the application with and click Share.

Summary

In this chapter, you saw how to share an application with other users or groups. You also saw how you can increase the adoption of your applications by deploying your applications to Teams or the mobile app. In the next chapter, you'll see how to manage the applications.

CHAPTER 7

Managing Power Apps

Power Apps gathers like resources into environments. In this chapter, you'll learn how to manage Power Apps environments. You'll see how to create environments for your development, test, and production migration processes and how to promote applications between those environments.

Power Apps Environments

Power Apps and Power Automate group resources into Environments. The environment brings together all the apps, flows, components, and connections, to name just a few. At a minimum, you'll want a Dev, Test, and QA environment to help with your application life cycle. You can always switch environments at `https://make.powerapps.com` in the top right.

To create an environment, you will need to go to the Admin Center at `https://admin.powerplatform.com`, click Environments, and click New (Figure 7-1). You can then name the environment and state the purpose. A Sandbox environment is a development environment for testing applications and concepts. If you need a temporary space for your environment, choose Trial. Lastly, if you're ready to start using the applications in production, select Production. To complete the first screen, give a good description of the environment and a region that represents where most of your users are at.

If you toggle the "Create a database for this environment" option to true, a Common Data Services (CDS) database will be created after you're asked a few questions. This is covered completely in the next chapter, and this can always be created later if you're unsure. In short, the CDS database provides you a location to store your data instead of having to provision a new database, and this is included in your Power Apps plan. It is a premium connector so you will only be allowed to read and write to the database if you're on a premium plan.

53

© Mitchell Pearson, Brian Knight, Devin Knight, Manuel Quintana 2020
M. Pearson et al., *Pro Microsoft Power Platform*, https://doi.org/10.1007/978-1-4842-6008-1_7

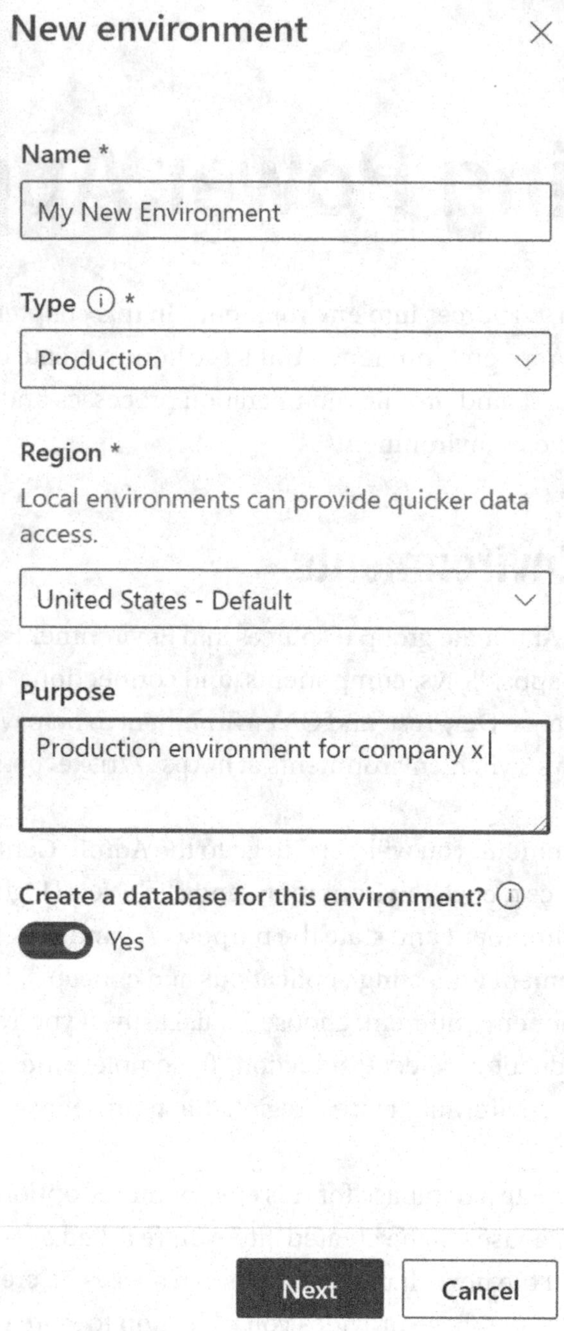

New environment   ✕

Name *

My New Environment

Type ⓘ *

Production   ⌄

Region *

Local environments can provide quicker data
access.

United States - Default   ⌄

Purpose

Production environment for company x

Create a database for this environment? ⓘ

◉ Yes

Next   Cancel

Figure 7-1. *Creating a new environment*

After clicking Save, the environment is provisioned. If you want the CDS database created, you'll be asked what language you want the database to use and your currency. You'll also be asked about security groups on the next screen, and those roles will be covered in the next section.

Once you create the environment, you can select the environment in the earlier screen to review some of the core settings as shown in Figure 7-2. You can, for example, in this screen click the Edit button in the Details section to rename your environment or change the URL for your environment. You might find in this screen that you aren't running the latest release of Power Apps, and you can turn on the latest release here.

Figure 7-2. Settings pane

Backing Up and Restoring

Backing up an environment happens automatically, but you can at any point manually create a backup or restore to a point in time. To create a manual backup, click Backup ➤ Create. Simply name the backup and provide an optional description and click Create. Manual backups come in handy before you do a big deployment or upgrade the environment to a new release.

To restore the environment, click Backup ➤ Restore or Manage from the environment details screen. On the Manage Backups screen (Figure 7-3), choose a date and time to restore from and click Continue. Alternatively, you can click the Manual tab to select a manual backup to recover. Once you choose the backup or time to restore from, select an environment to restore the backup to. The downside is that the environment must be a Sandbox environment.

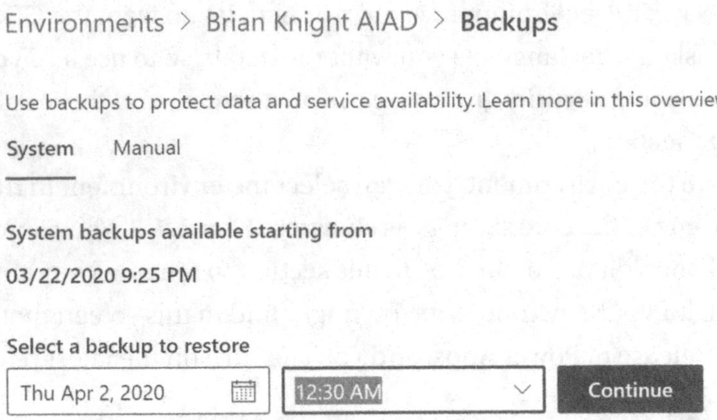

Environments > Brian Knight AIAD > **Backups**

Use backups to protect data and service availability. Learn more in this overview .

System   Manual

System backups available starting from

03/22/2020 9:25 PM

Select a backup to restore

| Thu Apr 2, 2020 | 🗓 | 12:30 AM | ⌄ | | Continue |

Figure 7-3. *Restoring an environment*

Securing Environments

By default, users may not have access to a newly created environment (depending on their role in the organization). Typically, there are three levels that you may want your users to have: admin, maker rights, or rights to see applications in the environment. There are also additional roles for the Common Data Services, which will be discussed more in the next chapter.

To grant someone rights to your environment, go to `https://admin.powerapps.com` (yes, this is a different URL but can also be accessed through the main admin center for the Power Platform). Select the Environment you wish to secure and click the Security tab. The first step is to type the email address for someone you wish to grant rights to and click Add User. This might take a few moments for the user to be provisioned, and after it's ready, the user will have basic rights to the environment. If your user doesn't even see your environment in the listing, it's because this step hasn't been done typically.

After the user has been added, click Assign Security Roles. This opens the Enabled User view to manage the roles. Click the user you just added and click Manage Roles from the top ribbon. The Environment Maker role grants the user rights to create their own apps in your environment if they're licensed. You can also make the user an administrator of the environment by clicking System Administrator, or if you wish to give the user rights to the CDS, click Common Data Services User. The latter right might not grant the user rights to the custom entities you create but gives basic rights to CDS. Click OK to save that and wait a minute to see if the role assignment has worked.

Application Versioning

Every time you save your application, a new version is created of the application. The versions aren't available to people you have shared the application with until you publish the version. As soon as you click the Save button when editing the application, it will turn to a Publish button. If you click Publish, the version is now live seconds later for anyone you have shared the app.

Versions can also be rolled back in case you mess something up in development. Before rolling the application back, make sure everyone is out of designing the application. Then go to `https://make.powerapps.com` and select the ellipsis button next to the application you want to restore and select Details. Then, click Versions. This takes you to the Versions page (Figure 7-4) where you can see what version has been published to your users and recover.

Figure 7-4. *Restoring a version of an app*

In this list, you'll see 6 months of old versions of your application, and you're able to recover any of those. Simply select the version you want to restore and select Restore from the top menu bar. Your old version will then become a new version number of the application, and you can publish it to make it available for users.

Migrating Apps Between Environments

As mentioned earlier, it is recommended that each company have at least three environments: development, test, and production. To build in the development environment and deploy to test and finally to production reduces the risk of bugs in your final application. There are two ways to create this migration process between environments: solutions and exporting of the application.

Solutions are the more formal and complex of the two processes but support more rigorous application lifecycle management (ALM) processes. It has a formal source control system with integration into Azure DevOps and build cycles. To work with solutions, go to `https://make.powerapps.com` and go to Solutions from the left menu. You then add the applications, connections, flows, and other components into the solution, and it will provide a .zip file to import into the other environment.

The largest advantage of solutions is it allows you to package up a multi-app Power Apps solution unlike the second option which focuses on a single application. It also can provide a way to bring over all your data schema changes for CDS entities and fields. Lastly, it has things like environment variables to make your solution more dynamic.

The simpler technique for some is to simply export a copy of the application out of one environment and then import it into another environment or email it to a customer. To do this, click the ellipsis button next to the application at `https://make.powerapps.com` and select Export Package to go to the Export Package screen shown in Figure 7-5. You will then see a listing of all the applications, flows, and connections that are required for the application.

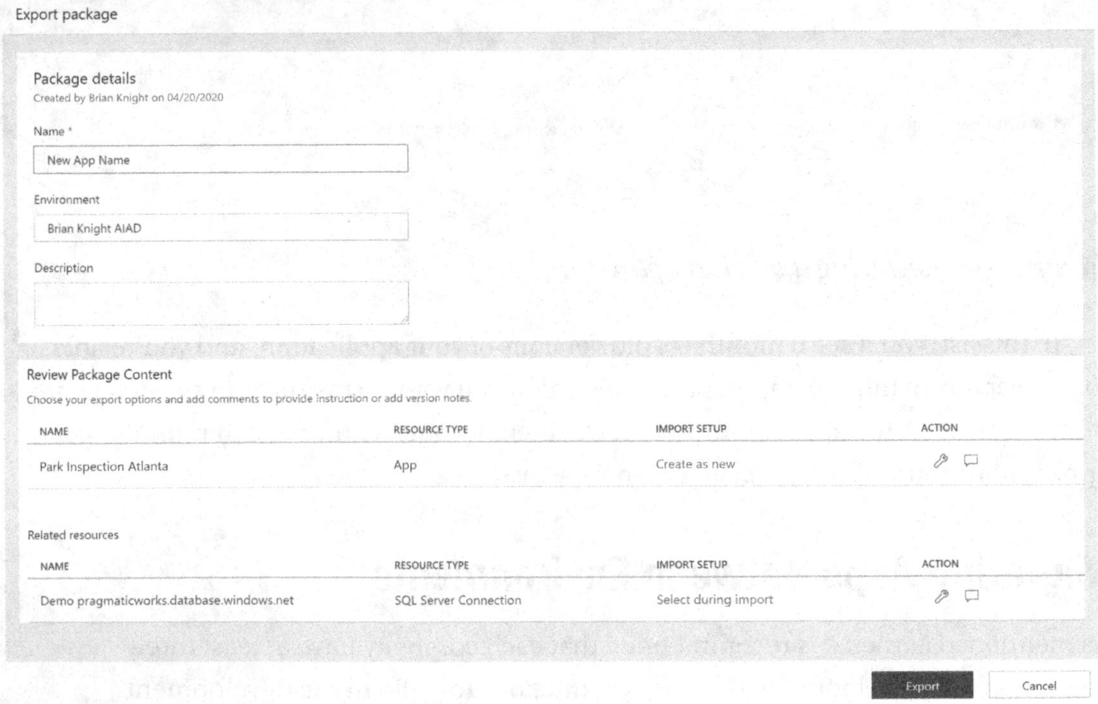

Export package

Package details
Created by Brian Knight on 04/20/2020

Name *

New App Name

Environment

Brian Knight AIAD

Description

Review Package Content
Choose your export options and add comments to provide instruction or add version notes.

NAME	RESOURCE TYPE	IMPORT SETUP	ACTION
Park Inspection Atlanta	App	Create as new	

Related resources

NAME	RESOURCE TYPE	IMPORT SETUP	ACTION
Demo pragmaticworks.database.windows.net	SQL Server Connection	Select during import	

Export   Cancel

Figure 7-5. Exporting an application

On the screen, type the name that you want the app to have in the new environment and select if this is the first time the app will be seen in the environment by changing Update to "Create as new" for Import Setup. The connection option "Select during import" means that the importing administrator will be prompted to select an existing connection when they import your package. This requires that the admin will have to have the connection already created prior to running the import for the deployment to be successful.

Try It Out

For this "Try It Out" section, you're going to put to work what you learned when creating environments and deploying applications.

Lesson Requirements

For this lesson, try to create a new environment for Power Apps and move an application from your old environment to a new environment. Keep in mind that you might not have permissions to create environments in your company. If that's the case for you, try migrating an app from your personal Community Plan license to another environment that you might have access.

Step by Step

1. To create the environment, go to the admin portal at `https://admin.powerplatform.microsoft.com/`.

2. Click the New button in the Environments tab.

3. Name the environment and choose Trial (you can always change it to production later).

4. Click Save to create the environment.

5. To export the application, go to an environment with a canvas application at `https://make.powerapps.com`. Click the ellipsis button next to the application and click Export Package.

6. Change the Import Setup option on the application to Create as New and name the application. Click Export and download the file.

7. Switch to a new environment to migrate the application to in the upper right at `https://make.powerapps.com`.

8. If the application you exported had any connections, ideally you would create those connections prior to importing the application under Data ➤ Connections.

9. In the Apps tab, click "Import canvas app" from the top ribbon and browse to your .Zip file you just downloaded.

10. Select the connection that you just created and click Import. A minute or so should pass and your application will be created. Additionally, if you had any Power Automate flows, those would also be created.

Summary

In this chapter, you saw how to administer Power Apps environments, which help you segment your various resources like connections, applications, and Power Automate flows. You can use these environments to segment development, testing, and production and give a clean environment for important departments. Now, let's get back into development in Power Apps with Common Data Services (CDS).

CHAPTER 8

Common Data Services and Model-Driven Apps

When you want to build an application, one of the first decisions you must make is where you are going to store data. Whether you store the data in SharePoint, Excel, or SQL Server, you then must design your lists, worksheets, or tables before getting too far into your application construction. Common Data Services (CDS) provides an easier place to store your data and contains some of the common plumbing you will need to build an intelligent application.

CDS is made up of entities, which equate to SQL Server tables or lists in SharePoint. When you first install your environment, you will be prompted to create the CDS database, and the newly created database will have many common entities out of the box like Contacts and Accounts. These common entities can be extended and added upon. If you didn't create the database at the creation of the environment, you can do it later by going to `https://make.powerapps.com` and go to Data ➤ Entities. You will then be prompted to create the database.

Designing Your Entities

You can add new entities or extend the existing entities by going to Data ➤ Entities at `https://make.powerapps.com`. Once there, you can click New entity to create a new entity (Figure 8-1). Name the entity whatever you wish in the Display Name, and spaces are allowed. The Primary Name property is the name of the field that contains a unique value for each record. In the case of the example in Figure 8-1, the Primary Name might be a text field with the license tag number.

61

© Mitchell Pearson, Brian Knight, Devin Knight, Manuel Quintana 2020
M. Pearson et al., *Pro Microsoft Power Platform*, https://doi.org/10.1007/978-1-4842-6008-1_8

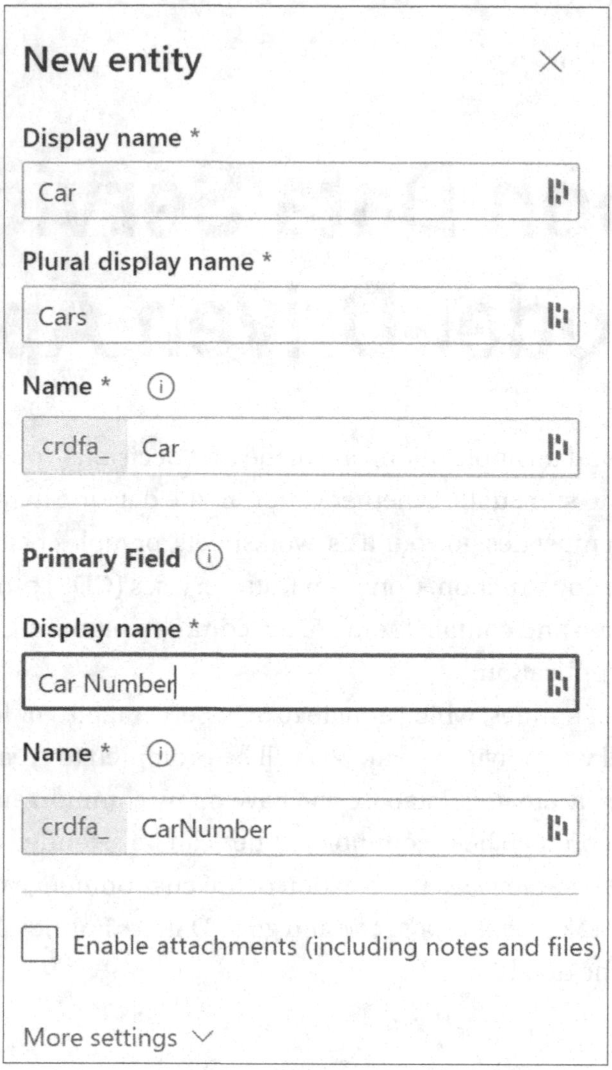

Figure 8-1. *Creating a new entity*

Once you click Create, the entity will be created. You'll notice at first only your Primary Field will be displayed. Moments later, a number of other fields will be created automatically, which contain a lot of the plumbing for CDS, like when the record was created and by whom. For this example, let us change the Primary Field, Car Number, into an autonumber field by clicking it and changing the field from Text to Autonumber. This, by default, will start each new car at 1000 and increment by one as you add new records. Click Done to accept that change.

You can then click Add Field from the top left to create new fields. For example, create a new field called Make and Model for a text field. Add one more field called Car Owner. This time, change the data type to Lookup and its Related entity to Contact. By doing this, users will receive a pop-up asking which of your contacts in the Contact entity is the owner of the car. This also helps later with record-level security where a person can only see his or her own car.

You will notice that some of the fields have bold names. When you click Save entity, it will convert them into a regular font, meaning that those fields are now saved. If you built your entities within a solution, you can also easily package those changes for other environments.

Creating Views

Views are used in model-driven applications to see the records that have been created. They also can be used to list data in a Power Apps portal application. To create a view, go to the entity you wish to create the view for and select the View tab. The default view is called Active <Entity Name> like Active Cars, and you can alter this one to fit your needs.

To create a new one, click Add View. Name the view and proceed to the View Editor. You can then drag and drop the fields from the field listing to the view or click Add Columns. You can then add any filters or sorting on the right pane. Click Save and then Publish to make it available to your users and applications. Any applications will automatically be updated as soon as you publish the view.

Creating Forms

Forms are used to create, edit, and delete records from an entity. To create an entity form, open the entity and click Forms. The default form is the Information form that is the form type of Main. You can modify an existing one or create a new one by clicking Add Form ➤ Main Form.

You are then taken to the New Form Screen (shown in Figure 8-2). Click the white background to name the form in the right pane. On the left pane, you will see a list of fields that you can drag over to the form. If you don't want people to make the mistake of typing into the autonumber field, click the field and check Read-Only. You can also rename any of the display names for the fields to make them more user-friendly.

You can also click the Components icon to create new sections and other ways of visualizing the data. Components allow you to add reusable styling to your form and ultimately your application. Once your changes are complete, click Save and then Publish to make the form available to other model-driven apps and Power Apps Portals applications.

Figure 8-2. *Creating a new form*

To test drive your views and forms, go to your entity, and click Data. You will see the list of views on the top right of the data tab. Click Add Record to see the main form and add records. You can also select a record and click Edit Record to pull the same form up in Edit mode.

The best part about forms and views in CDS is the ability to modify the entity one time and have it roll out to any application that might use that form. This includes any model-driven application or portal. If you add business rules, those are also available in all application types, including canvas apps.

Creating a Model-Driven Application

CDS works as a source for canvas applications, portals, or model-driven applications. Model-driven apps are the easiest way to interact with your entities though. Creating a model-driven application is much easier than canvas applications, but you have much less control over the look and feel.

To create the application, go to `https://make.powerapps.com` and click "Model-driven app from blank." Click Create and then name the app (Figure 8-3). You can optionally give a different icon for your application. Once you are ready, click Done to be taken to the App Designer.

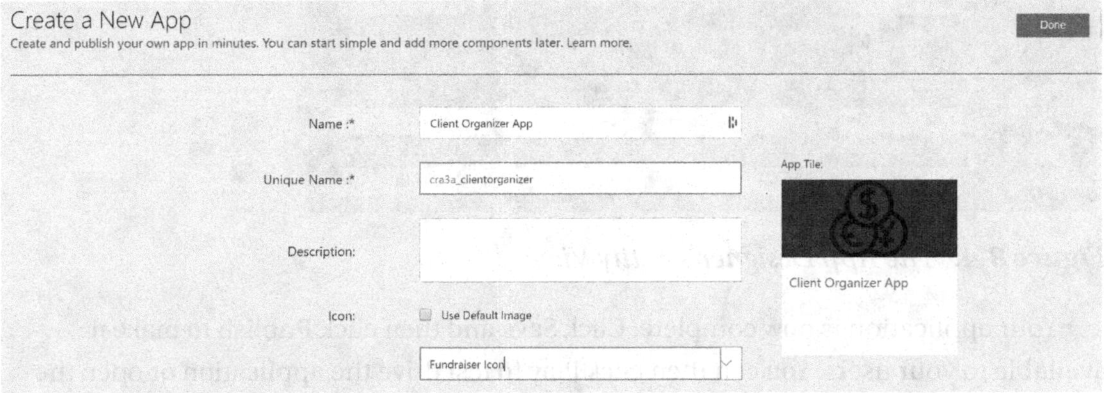

Figure 8-3. *Creating a new App*

As you will see, the App Designer screen looks much different than how you build canvas applications. Start building your application by clicking the pencil next to Site Map to configure what the application will contain. This opens the Sitemap Designer screen.

In this screen, you will need to define an Area, Group, and Subarea. An area is a major section of your company like HR. Then, a group might equate to a smaller department like Payroll. Lastly, the subareas are the entities to have in that Payroll group like Employees, Paychecks, and Timecards.

Select the area and define the name on the right and a unique ID. You can also define a better icon for it. Repeat that same step for the group. Lastly, for the subarea, select entity for the type and select the entity you want from the entity drop-down box. You can add additional entities by clicking Add and selecting Subarea.

Your application is largely complete. Click Save and Close to go back to the App Designer. This time, you will notice that the entity View is filled out (Figure 8-4). You can click the Forms option for a given entity and force the app to open with a specified form on the right. You can also do the same thing for Views.

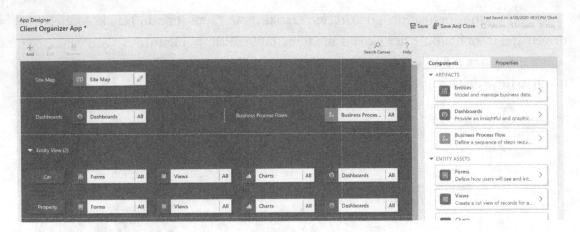

Figure 8-4. *The App Designer's entity View*

Your application is now complete. Click Save and then click Publish to make it available to your users. You can then click Play to test drive the application or open the application back on the home screen.

For deploying model-driven applications to another environment, you'll need to create a solution like what was discussed in the last chapter.

Try It Out

For this "Try It Out" section, let's create a CDS entity and build a model-driven application on top of it. Follow along with the instructions that come next.

Lesson Requirements

For this chapter, create an entity called Property to store your customer properties into. Create an entity with the following fields:

- Property Number – Autonumbered field

- Address

- City

- State

- Zip

- Country

- Value of Property – Currency

- Property Owner – Customer lookup

Create a new view on the entity and a form to enter data. After those have been created, create a model-driven application to combine the Property, Account, and Contact entities.

Hints

When you're creating a model-driven entity, start with the site map configuration first. Define your area, subarea, and entities and then publish the app. Don't forget to save and publish each view and form as you change them.

Step by Step

The following is the step-by-step process for creating the model-driven CDS application:

1. Go to `https://make.powerapps.com` and go to Data ➤ Entities.

2. Click New entity. Name the entity Property and change the Primary Field property to Property Number. Click Create to create the entity.

3. Click the Property Number field and change the Data Type property to Autonumber. Click Done to save.

4. Click Add Field to add the next field. Name this field Address and keep the rest of the default values. Click Done to save.

5. Repeat those same steps for the City, State, Country, and Zip fields.

6. Add the Property Value field with the same steps, but this time change the data type to Currency.

7. Add the Property Owner field with the same steps, but this time change the data type to Customer.

8. Click Save entity.

9.   In the Views tab, click Add View. Name the view Owner Properties.

10.   Drag the columns you created over to the view or click Add
Column alternatively as shown in Figure 8-5. Click Save and then
click Publish to make the view available to others.

Figure 8-5. *Adding columns to the view*

11.   Go back to the Property entity and go to the Forms tab. Click the
Main Form to edit the form.

12.   Drag the fields you created over to the form wherever makes sense
for you. Make the Property Number read only by selecting the field
and clicking Read-only field on the right pane. Click Save and then
Publish to make this form available. The final product will look
something like Figure 8-6.

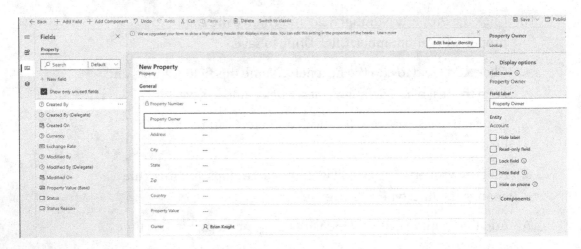

Figure 8-6. *Creating the application form*

13. You are now done with the entity and can go back to the Home tab to create the model-driven app. From the Home tab, click "Model-driven app from blank."

14. After clicking Create, name the application whatever you want and click Done.

15. In the App Designer screen, click the pencil next to the Site Map to open the Sitemap Designer. Select New Area and change the name to Client Backoffice. Change the group name to Organizer. For the subarea, select entity as the Type and Properties for your entity. Repeat the same steps for the Accounts and Contacts entity. Click Save and Close to go back to the App Designer.

16. In App Designer, you can isolate the forms, or views can be seen for each of those entities if you would like, but it's not required. Click Save and Publish. Then click Play to preview the application.

17. Great job! You have built your first entity and model-driven application! Your final product resembles Figure 8-7.

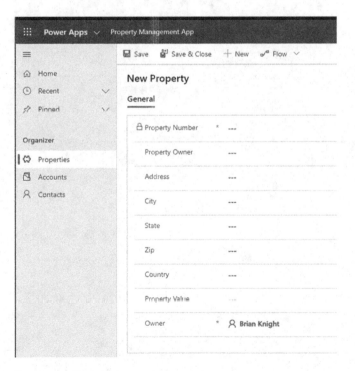

Figure 8-7. *The final application*

Summary

Common Data Services (CDS) allows you to create entities to store your data with business rules, data entry forms, and views. In this chapter, you saw how entities can be used to create reusable forms and views that can be shared across multiple applications and even a Power Apps Portal. Great job! You've now built applications using Power Apps and are ready to go to the next part of the Power Platform.

PART II

Task Automation with Power Automate

CHAPTER 9

Introduction to Power Automate

Working with Power Automate

Power Automate functions incredibly well as a stand-alone tool for workflow automation, similar to how Power Apps and Power BI are great at what they are designed to do. However, the underlying theme to the Power Platform is really the "better together" story. Each of the tools is further improved and their capabilities amplified when built within a framework that leverages each tool effectively. The integration of each of the Power Platform tools is discussed in depth later in the final chapters of this book after the reader has a firm grasp on each service.

What Is Power Automate?

Power Automate is a "low-code" development platform for building automated workflows. The development is driven by a simple and intuitive graphical user interface that comes with over 275 existing prebuilt connectors and thousands of prebuilt templates to start from. These connectors, actions, and templates allow the citizen developer to easily connect to popular apps and services during the workflow development process.

Figure 9-1 is a visual depiction of a workflow performing many automated and intelligent tasks. The workflow automatically triggers when an event occurs in SharePoint. It then automatically retrieves information from SharePoint and Office 365 for the current user. Leveraging the information from previous steps, an approval process is created and immediately followed by a conditional logic to perform specific actions

73

© Mitchell Pearson, Brian Knight, Devin Knight, Manuel Quintana 2020
M. Pearson et al., *Pro Microsoft Power Platform*, https://doi.org/10.1007/978-1-4842-6008-1_9

based on user input and responses. Note the flow also has built-in error handling that will send an email if the approval creation process fails, and all of this is accomplished with no code!

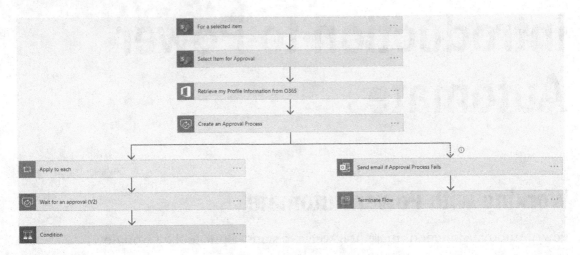

Figure 9-1. *Visual depiction of an automated workflow*

Who Is Power Automate Designed For?

Like all the tools described in this book, development in Power Automate does not require a background in .NET programming or app development. In fact, it is designed specifically for the citizen developer. The astute reader may assume from this description that Power Automate lacks flexibility and intelligent decision-making automation tools. However, automated workflows are extremely valuable for the business user and the IT professional alike.

Power Automate is derived from Azure Logic Apps, a tool known as an IT developer tool, and they share the same code base. They both leverage the Workflow Definition Language for building expressions, and there is almost perfect feature parity between the two tools being discussed with very few exceptions. Feature parity plainly means that they share the same feature functionality and capabilities. In fact, flows can be easily exported from Power Automate and deployed as an Azure Logic App; this will be discussed later in the book.

The Power of Automation

In today's nonstop, fast-paced world, who has the time to stop and spend a few hours building an automated workflow? If you did have time, would you really stop and spend that time working in Power Automate? Consider for a moment the importance of automation. Rory Vaden, *New York Times* bestselling author of *Take the Stairs*, said it best when he said:

> *Automation is to your time; exactly what compounding interest is to your money. Just like compounding interest takes money and makes it into more money, automation takes time and it makes it into more time.*

When time is invested in automating repetitive tasks, it yields more time in the future. At some point, you break even on that time invested, and then you have earned more time in each day to accomplish additional and more important tasks.

Evaluating time spent in respect to "return on time invested" results in a fundamental paradigm shift in how time is assessed. Taking time to build an automated process becomes a natural occurring process when considered within these new parameters. For example, one philosophy may be "I don't have three hours to waste building an automated workflow." However, another philosophy might be "Of course I have three hours to build an automated workflow that will replace a manual notification process that currently takes twenty minutes each day."

This shift in one's philosophy allows a realization and a thought process to occur that understands there will be a return on time invested. In this scenario, it will only take nine days before the initial time invested will reach a breakeven point, and from that point on, 25 minutes have been gained each day thereafter. Each process automated results in more available time for accomplishing and prioritizing other tasks.

Intelligent and Dynamic Workflows

What can be accomplished within Power Automate is truly limited by one's imagination. Imagine a flow that has been designed to simply insert a record into a database anytime a new tweet is posted. The tweets are in a centralized location and easily analyzed for historical analysis.

But why stop there? With intelligent workflows, so much more can be accomplished! Instead of just loading the tweet, sentiment analysis can be performed by analyzing the tweet with Azure Cognitive Services. The next step can be routing those tweets based on what information is returned. For example, generating sales leads automatically in Dynamics, routing support requests to the support team, creating follow-up requests with clients, or even automatically replying on tweets.

I remember, not too long ago, seeing a tweet where an individual was sharing with the world their terrible experience of buying an appliance. The appliance did not perform well and ultimately was returned. The first response came in seconds and was by a competitor in the appliance space. The store empathized with the customer and offered their immediate assistance in getting them set up and on their way. This is the power of automation; this is making actionable, real-time business decisions through process automation!

Automation is a big piece when it comes to why Power Automate is such a necessary tool, but Power Automate goes much deeper than just creating basic workflows. The tools are in place to create intelligent and dynamic workflows that can accomplish truly incredible things.

Power Automate Use Cases

Naturally, Power Automate is deeply integrated with Microsoft tools, making integration with SharePoint, Dynamics, and other related Microsoft technologies a seamless process. However, it doesn't stop there; with over 275 built-in connectors, the reach of Power Automate extends far beyond just Microsoft technologies.

There are many common patterns and use cases that have emerged from automated workflows, and this section will briefly cover a few of those to provide some perspective and inspiration on what can be achieved. The next chapter focuses on the available templates; templates are a great place to see what others have achieved and automated. The following is just a very small list of use cases for Power Automate; many more will be discussed in later chapters.

- Create automated approval processes

- Create an automated and intelligent notification framework

- Livestream social media data to a Power BI dashboard

- Automate sentiment analysis with Azure Cognitive Services

- Run stored procedures for Power Apps and return results back to the application

Subscribing to Power Automate

There are a couple of licensing options available for exploring and working with Power Automate. The first is a free for personal use option that is available with the Community Plan, and the second is the official paid licensing plan which will be discussed here as well.

Community Plan

The Community Plan is a free environment available for personal use so that aspiring citizen developers have a way to learn and explore the capabilities. Signing up for the Community Plan requires a work or school account. Sign up for the Community Plan with the following link:

```
https://aka.ms/communityplan/
```

Licensing Plan

In this section, the licensing options for Power Automate will be briefly discussed, and links will be provided for follow-up reading. The licensing options are pretty straightforward, but they are also changing rapidly, and therefore the best source is going to be the official Microsoft documentation.

```
https://us.flow.microsoft.com/en-us/pricing/
```

When licensing Power Automate, there are two primary licensing options available: *license by user* and *license by flow*.

License by User

The first licensing option is *license by user* and comes with two available levels:

- Per user plan ($15 per user/month)

- Per user plan with attended RPA ($40 per user/month)

Each of these plans allows individual users to create unlimited flows. The per user plan with attended RPA, which stands for robotic process automation, allows users to automate legacy applications through RPA and AI.

License by Flow

The second licensing option is license by flow. License by flow allows the implementation of flows with reserved capacity that serve unlimited users across an organization. The cost of license per flow is currently *$500 per five flows per month*. Additional flows may be purchased and added to this plan for $100 per flow/month.

Should You Choose the Per User Plan or Per Flow Plan?

A very common question is, which plan do I choose? Well, that depends on how you plan to roll out Power Automate within your organization. Today, the most common licensing model employed is the per user plan. The following is the FAQ response directly from Microsoft (`https://docs.microsoft.com/en-us/power-platform/admin/powerapps-flow-licensing-faq#power-automate`):

> *The per user plan is intended to support the broad adoption of an automation culture in an organization. Every user with this plan is entitled to use an unlimited number of flows, within service limits. The per flow plan provides an organization with the flexibility to license by the number of flows, instead of licensing each user accessing the flows individually with the per user plan.*

CHAPTER 10

Building Your First Flow

Power Automate ships with an abundance of prebuilt templates across many categories which include approvals, productivity, email, and more. Templates are an exciting and useful way to familiarize yourself with workflows. These templates are a great place to start when building a new flow, especially if you are new to Power Automate.

Templates

Templates provide many benefits to the citizen developer. Firstly, you can create new flows by leveraging design patterns already built. Secondly, exploring the available templates will undoubtedly give you creative ideas for flows that you can design on your own. Thirdly, you can customize these templates to fit your specific business needs. Finally, you can reverse engineer existing templates to learn how to leverage existing connectors, triggers, and actions within your own flows.

Available Templates

The first decision you must make when creating a new flow is whether to start from scratch or start from a template. Templates provide you with a fully functional flow that can be customized and modified to fit your organizational needs. Furthermore, templates come in many different flavors; therefore, templates are a very logical place to start when working with Power Automate. In Figure 10-1, you will learn how to find and explore templates.

First, log in to www.powerautomate.microsoft.com.

© Mitchell Pearson, Brian Knight, Devin Knight, Manuel Quintana 2020
M. Pearson et al., *Pro Microsoft Power Platform*, https://doi.org/10.1007/978-1-4842-6008-1_10

Figure 10-1. *Find and explore existing templates*

1) Click Templates from the navigation pane to explore.

2) Sort the displayed templates. Available options are popularity, name, and published time.

3) Select a category to narrow down the list of options provided.

4) Select the template you would like to work with.

Categories

Surprisingly, there are currently 14 available categories for templates. The list seen in Figure 10-1 is not a comprehensive list; click the ellipsis (…) to see additional categories. The full list of categories is viewable in Figure 10-2.

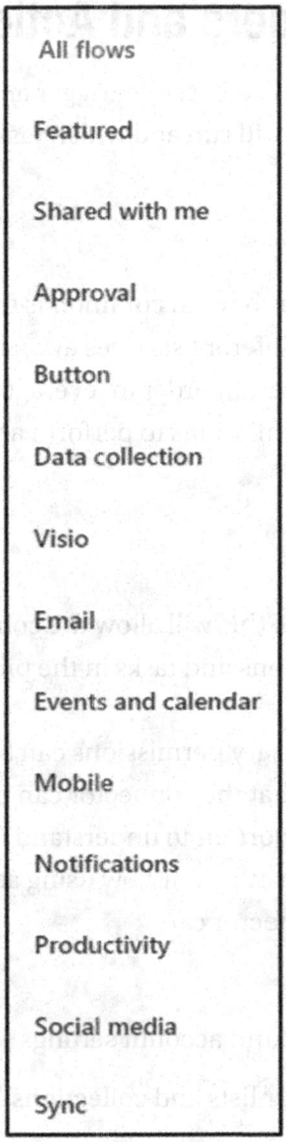

All flows

Featured

Shared with me

Approval

Button

Data collection

Visio

Email

Events and calendar

Mobile

Notifications

Productivity

Social media

Sync

Figure 10-2. *Available template categories*

Introduction to Triggers and Actions

A fully functional flow will contain at least one trigger and one action. These triggers and actions determine when the flow will run and which tasks will be performed.

Connectors

One thing that triggers and actions have in common is that they both leverage connectors to gain access to the different services available. Power Automate currently provides access to over 275 services. In order to leverage these services, you can provide the necessary credentials and permissions to perform a wide array of activities within the selected service.

Permissions

Providing permissions is required; this will allow the connector to act as a proxy on your behalf, performing necessary actions and tasks in the provided service to support your automated workflow.

However, providing the necessary permissions can be quite intimidating, especially if you read the full list of actions that the connector can perform on your behalf with your provided credentials. It's important to understand that these actions will only be performed if you design that logic into your flow using actions.

For example, the Twitter connector can

- Post and delete tweets

- See your Twitter profile and account settings

- See your tweets and your lists and collections

- Modify or delete your lists and collections

- And more!

Take a look at the full list of permissions provided to the Twitter connector in Figure 10-3.

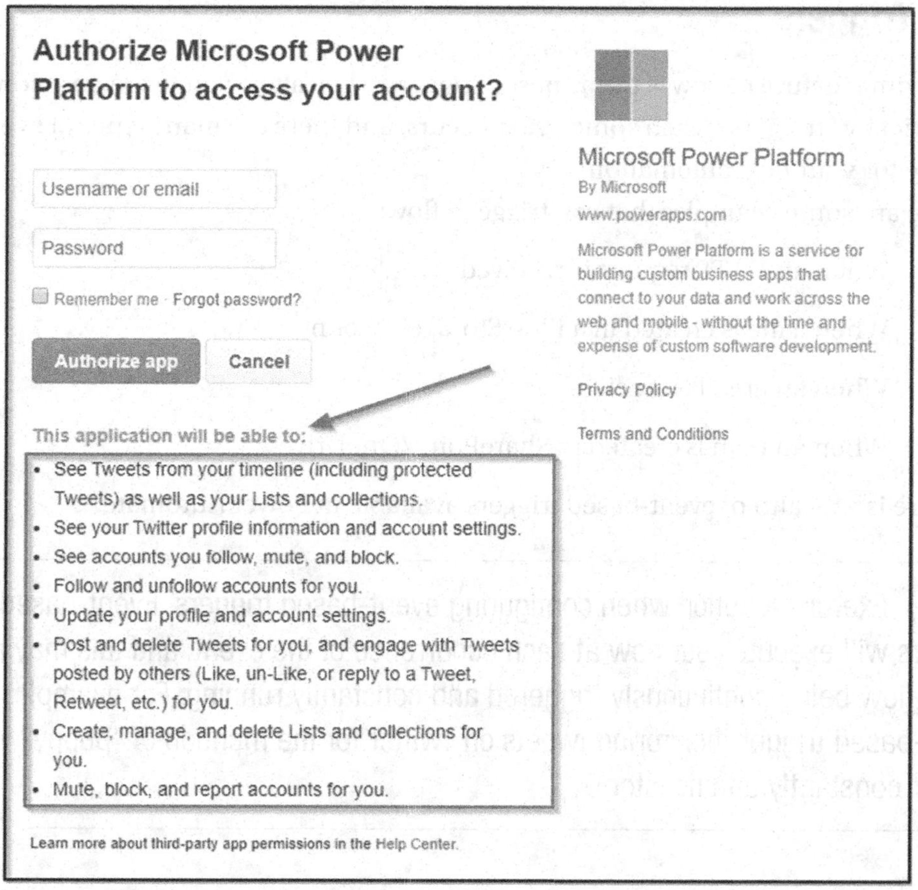

Authorize Microsoft Power Platform to access your account?

Username or email

Password

☐ Remember me · Forgot password?

[Authorize app] Cancel

Microsoft Power Platform
By Microsoft
www.powerapps.com

Microsoft Power Platform is a service for building custom business apps that connect to your data and work across the web and mobile - without the time and expense of custom software development.

Privacy Policy

Terms and Conditions

This application will be able to:

- See Tweets from your timeline (including protected Tweets) as well as your Lists and collections.
- See your Twitter profile information and account settings.
- See accounts you follow, mute, and block.
- Follow and unfollow accounts for you.
- Update your profile and account settings.
- Post and delete Tweets for you, and engage with Tweets posted by others (Like, un-Like, or reply to a Tweet, Retweet, etc.) for you.
- Create, manage, and delete Lists and collections for you.
- Mute, block, and report accounts for you.

Learn more about third-party app permissions in the Help Center.

Figure 10-3. Find and explore existing templates

Trigger Types

Automated workflows are designed to do just that, run automatically and without any manual intervention; this is accomplished through the use of triggers. There are three main trigger types to be aware of in Power Automate:

- Event triggers
- Scheduled triggers
- Push button triggers

Event Triggers

An awesome feature of flow is event-based triggers. They allow you to create a flow that automatically "triggers" when some event occurs, and there are many types of events available for your flow automation.

Here are some examples that can trigger a flow:

- When an HTTP request is received

- When a file is created in a Blob Storage account

- When an email is received

- When an item is created in SharePoint/OneDrive

There is a wealth of event-based triggers available in Power Automate.

Note   Exercise caution when configuring event-based triggers. Event-based triggers will execute your flow at each occurrence of the event, and this may result in the flow being continuously triggered and constantly running. For example, an event-based trigger monitoring tweets on Twitter for the mention of "puppy" would trigger constantly and nonstop!

Scheduled Triggers

Scheduled triggers allow flows to run on a regular schedule. Generally, scheduled triggers are used to perform work that occurs on a periodic basis. For example, perform some operation every night at a specified time.

Push Button Triggers

Push button triggers allow the execution of flow runs with the push of a button. Push button triggers grant the ability to execute flows from any place at any time. This includes executing automated workflows from a mobile device. The ability to execute a flow from a push button trigger opens a broad array of design possibilities not available with the two other triggers discussed in this section.

Actions

Power Automate has an extensive list of operations that can be performed in the 200+ available services. In flow, all operations are facilitated through actions. With actions, you can send emails, post tweets, livestream data to a Power BI dashboard, approve expense reports, and many other operations. This book will dive much deeper into actions in later chapters.

Customizing Templates

The prebuilt templates available are fully functional automated flows. These templates come in many different variations. Some of them are very simple, and others are very complex. The one thing they all have in common is that they can be customized.

Customizing existing templates is not limited to changing or modifying properties on existing triggers and actions. Within a template, you can remove existing triggers and actions; you can also add new actions. The ability to customize templates means that you can make your automated workflow even more intelligent and dynamic.

Creating Templates

Wouldn't it be awesome if you could create templates yourself? Well you can!

One requirement is that the flow must have run successfully at least once since the last save; if this requirement is not met, then a template cannot be created. See Figure 10-4.

Figure 10-4. Template error

To submit a flow as a template, you will first select that flow from the My Flows section of your navigation pane. Next, select "Submit as template" from the menu bar across the top. See Figure 10-5.

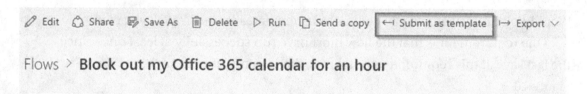

Figure 10-5. Submit flow as template

If the flow has met the minimum requirement of running successfully at least once since the last save, then the form in Figure 10-6 will appear.

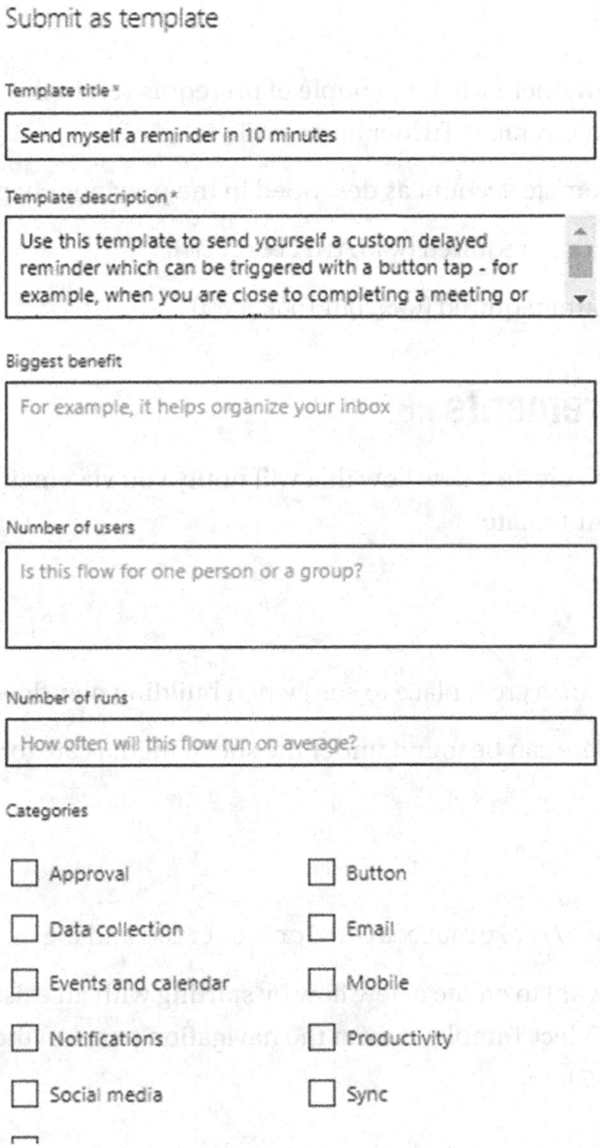

Submit as template

Template title *

Send myself a reminder in 10 minutes

Template description *

Use this template to send yourself a custom delayed
reminder which can be triggered with a button tap - for
example, when you are close to completing a meeting or

Biggest benefit

For example, it helps organize your inbox

Number of users

Is this flow for one person or a group?

Number of runs

How often will this flow run on average?

Categories

☐ Approval   ☐ Button

☐ Data collection   ☐ Email

☐ Events and calendar   ☐ Mobile

☐ Notifications   ☐ Productivity

☐ Social media   ☐ Sync

☐

Figure 10-6. Template submission form

Try It Out

To build your first flow, there will be a couple of prerequisites. In this section, you will create a template that leverages Twitter and email.

- Power Automate account as described in the previous chapter

- Twitter account required (`www.twitter.com`)

- Email account required (`www.outlook.com`)

Lesson Requirements

In this lesson, you will create a new flow that will notify you via email whenever someone tweets about Power Automate!

Hints

- Templates are a great place to start when building new flows.

- This template can be found under the social media category.

Step by Step

1. Open `https://powerautomate.microsoft.com` and log in.

2. Next, you want to create a new flow by starting with an existing template. Select Templates from the navigation pane on the left (Figure 10-7).

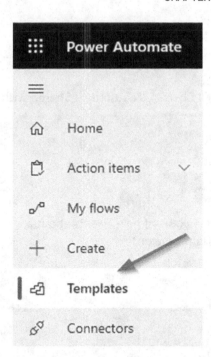

Figure 10-7. *Templates from the navigation pane*

3. Now you want to select an existing template that is triggered by monitoring tweets and contains a single action to send an email. There are a couple of methods for exploring templates. Across the top of the screen, you will see a search box with the hint text "Search templates...." Type email tweets into the search box. See Figure 10-8.

4. Select the template "Email yourself new Tweets about a certain keyword."

Figure 10-8. *Search templates*

5. On the next screen, you will be required to provide credentials
    for each of the connectors used in the template selected. This
    template contains two connectors. The first is to Twitter and the
    second is to Outlook. Click Sign in for each of the connectors
    (Figure 10-9).

Figure 10-9. *Sign in to the service*

6. Once you have authenticated and granted permissions to each of
    the connectors, click Continue.

7. The next screen is the actual design interface for Power Automate.
    There are a couple of required fields that must be completed
    before this flow can be saved and run successfully.

8. The first required element is the search text. The search text
    provided is what will trigger this automated workflow. This
    trigger will monitor Twitter for the text provided, and when a new
    tweet appears with that text, the workflow will run. Type "Power
    Automate" into the search box; refer to Figure 10-10.

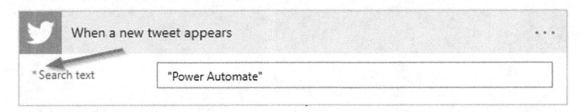

Figure 10-10. *Providing search text*

Note   Required fields are denoted with a red asterisk next to the field name. See
Figure 10-10.

---

9. The next required field can be found in the send email action. Fill in
    the email address of the person who should be notified when this
    flow is run. The final completed flow can be seen in Figure 10-11.

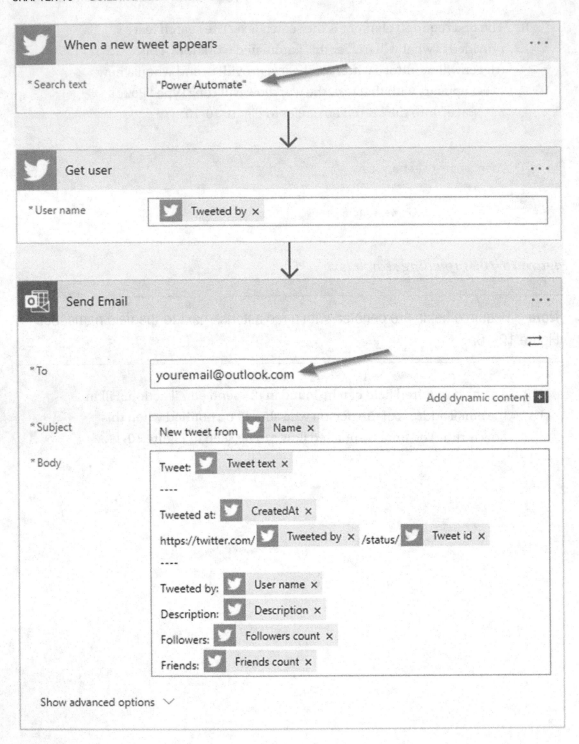

Figure 10-11. Completed flow example

10.   The current name of your flow is displayed in the top left of the
      design window. This name can be modified. To change the name of
      your flow, simply click the text of the existing name and change it.

11.   Now it's time to save the work you have done. In the top-right
      corner of the design window, there is a Save option; click Save. See
      Figure 10-12.

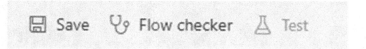

Figure 10-12. *Save the flow*

12.   Once the flow has been saved, navigate back to the previous
      screen by selecting the left arrow (←) icon located next to the
      flow's name in the top left of the design window.

13.   This screen is an administrative view of your flow. Here, you have
      many options which will be discussed in detail in later chapters. For
      now, the most important thing on this screen is the ability to *turn off*
      the flow. It is important to remember that the flow will continue to
      trigger so long as it is enabled. Click "Turn off" from the menu bar
      located across the top of the screen. See Figure 10-13.

Figure 10-13. *Disable a flow*

14.   Congratulations, you have created your first flow!

CHAPTER 11

Exploring Different Trigger Types

Power Automate has three primary methods for triggering an automated workflow. These three methods were briefly mentioned in the previous chapter. In this chapter, we will dive deeper and explore all three trigger types available in Power Automate.

Triggers

A trigger in Power Automate simply determines when an automated workflow will run. Triggers can be event based, schedule based, or on-demand. On-demand and scheduled triggers are self-explanatory, for the most part. The event-based triggers are very dynamic and contain many exciting and cool options for determining when to run a workflow. This capability can be further expanded by using trigger conditions, which will be explained shortly.

Furthermore, in this section, we will explore the settings that can be set up and configured for the various trigger options.

Scheduled Triggers

Many times, a flow will be required to run on a set schedule, for example, a flow needs to run every night at 9 o'clock or every Saturday morning at 6 o'clock. This is the simplest kind of trigger to set up and configure.

© Mitchell Pearson, Brian Knight, Devin Knight, Manuel Quintana 2020
M. Pearson et al., *Pro Microsoft Power Platform*, https://doi.org/10.1007/978-1-4842-6008-1_11

Recurrence triggers are used to schedule a flow to run on a set schedule. To create a scheduled flow, follow the steps outlined in the following and seen in Figure 11-1:

1) Select My Flows from the navigation window.

2) Click + New.

3) Select + Scheduled—from blank.

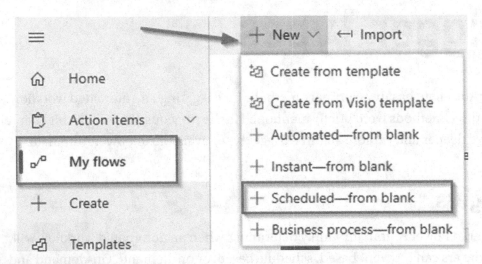

Figure 11-1. *Creating a new scheduled flow from blank*

After choosing to create a new scheduled flow, a pop-up window will appear. This window provides a wizard-based experience for configuring your recurrence trigger. This window is optional and can be skipped by selecting Skip located in the bottom-right corner. See Figure 11-2.

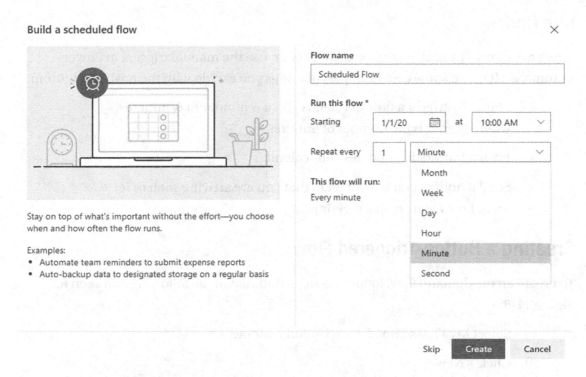

Figure 11-2. *Configuration options for scheduled flows*

Once configuration is complete, click Create. Now a new flow has been created with a recurrence trigger. The settings can be modified and adjusted as necessary by simply clicking the recurrence trigger to expand the available options.

On-Demand Triggers

Manually triggering a flow is accomplished by using a button trigger that is manually executed from a mobile device. This is an awesome and cool concept that, interestingly enough, is only available in Power Automate and can't be found in Azure Logic Apps. As we discussed in the introduction, Power Automate shares a code base with Azure Logic Apps but has been designed with the citizen developer in mind. It is rare to find a feature that exists in Power Automate and not in Azure Logic Apps, but this is one such situation.

The following steps are necessary to leverage the capabilities of button triggers in flow:

1) Create a new flow using the option *Instant—from blank*.

2) Download Power Automate from the app store on your mobile device.

Use Cases

There are many applicable examples for when to use the manual triggers in Power Automate. Here are some cool examples of things you can do with the push of a button:

- Manually trigger a flow that sends you a reminder in N minutes, where N equals the number of minutes.

- Push a button that updates your calendar.

- Send a notification to your team that you are arriving soon or let them know you are in a meeting.

Creating a Button-Triggered Flow

To create an on-demand flow, follow the steps outlined in the following and seen in Figure 11-3:

1) Select My Flows from the navigation window.

2) Click + New.

3) Select + Instant—from blank.

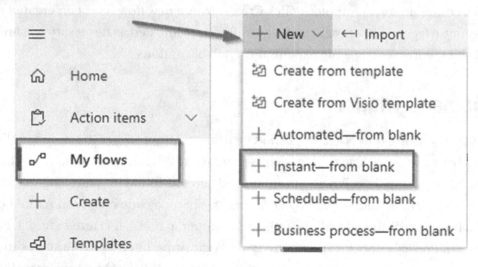

Figure 11-3. *Creating a new on-demand flow*

From the pop-up window that appears, select *Manually trigger a flow* and then click Create. See Figure 11-4.

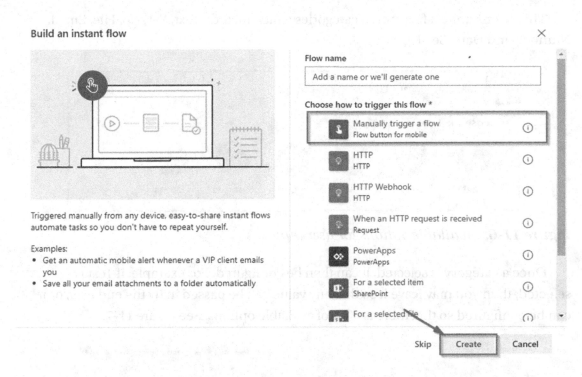

Figure 11-4. Choosing the correct text-wrapping option

Configuring Parameters

Configuring a button flow also comes with some additional functionality, specifically the ability to pass in input parameters. Previously, you learned you could send yourself, or someone else, a notification in *N* minutes; the number of minutes can be determined by parameters. Parameters configured on push button flows allow the end user to select parameters which will impact the actions defined within that automated workflow. To add parameters to a push button flow, simply click + *Add an Input*. See Figure 11-5.

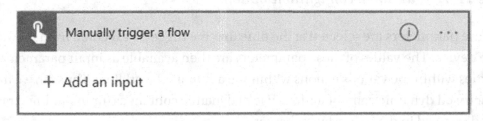

Figure 11-5. Adding an input parameter

This opens quite a few option categories which include Text, Yes/No, File, Email, Number, and Date. See Figure 11-6.

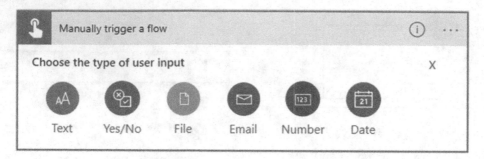

Figure 11-6. *Available options for user inputs*

Once a category is selected, it can then be configured. For example, if Text is selected, then you may leave it so that any value can be passed in by the end user, or it can be configured so that there is a list of available options. See Figure 11-7.

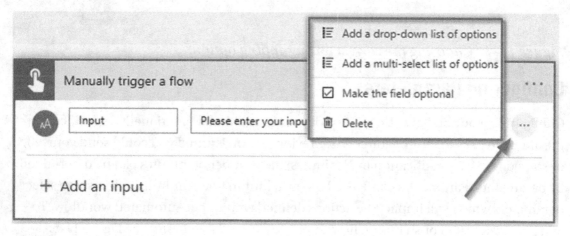

Figure 11-7. *Additional configurable options*

These parameters are selected at the time that the trigger is executed from the mobile device. The values of these parameters are then available as input parameters to properties within the various actions within the automated workflow. Thus far, we have not discussed dynamic content and the use of dynamic content as input parameters; this will be discussed in depth in a later chapter.

Event-Based Triggers

With event-based triggers, you can be very creative and have fun with deciding how to trigger your automated workflows. An event-based trigger will begin a flow execution upon the occurrence of an event in another service. This can be as simple as when a new file is created in one drive, when a new item is added to a SharePoint list, or when a new record is inserted into a database.

However, a flow is not limited to these basic everyday events; you can trigger a flow by sending an HTTP request from another application, or a flow can be triggered based on when someone enters a defined location. Yes, locations can be defined, and once a user enters that location, the flow will trigger and perform the actions defined within that flow. You can have a flow that clocks you in and out, sends an email to the team letting them know you're close, and any number of other creative actions you can think of.

Trigger Settings

There is a settings section on triggers that allows further configuration. This menu is somewhat hidden, but Microsoft often uses the ellipsis (...) icon to denote additional options are available. The available options do not require an explanation; the following is a list of the options available. See Figure 11-8 for a visual depiction of where these additional options are located.

1) Rename

2) Add a comment

3) Settings

4) Configure run after (not available for triggers, only actions)

5) Peek code

6) Delete

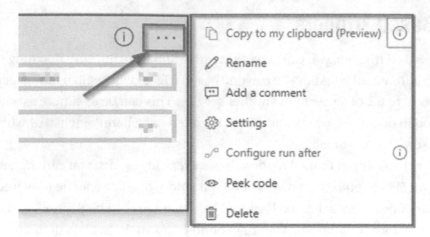

Figure 11-8. *Additional configuration options*

Selecting *Settings* opens up an editor window for configuration.

Split On

Custom Tracking ID

Retry Policy

Concurrency Control – *Important if you are doing a for loop and need items to execute in a particular order.*

Trigger Conditions

Trigger Conditions

An event-based trigger can further be defined by configuring trigger conditions. An existing flow may be set up and configured to execute anytime a new item is added to a list in SharePoint, but what if the flow should only execute if the item added was created by a specific individual or the product was *xyz*?

Adding trigger conditions can add significant value to your flows. Firstly, trigger conditions increase flexibility and reusability. Secondly, adding conditions can greatly reduce the number of times that an automated flow executes. Furthermore, the logic within the app can be simplified because you have filtered out unnecessary items and therefore are not required to build additional logic into the flow to handle those records.

Defining trigger conditions requires the use of expressions, and they are somewhat tricky to configure. Unfortunately, at the time of this writing, there is not an easy and intuitive way to define these trigger conditions.

> **Tip**   Event-based triggers, if not properly tested and left unchecked, can execute an excessive number of times unexpectedly. It's very important to take time and consider the various scenarios and possibilities that may cause an event to trigger. For example, a flow monitoring a social media platform may unexpectedly see a high number of executions based on a news event, new product release, or better-than-expected earnings.

Try It Out

Build a new flow using an event-based trigger, specifically when a new item is added to a SharePoint list. For this "Try It Out" section, there are a couple of prerequisites including the SharePoint list created in Chapter 3. This SharePoint list will be utilized in the remaining Power Automate chapters.

Lesson Requirements

In this lesson, you will build a new Power Automate workflow that is triggered whenever a new item is added to a SharePoint list. This example will leverage the SharePoint list created in Chapter 3.

- Power Automate account

- SharePoint (https://<your company>.sharepoint.com)

Hints

- Choose + *Automated—from blank* when creating a new event-based flow.

Creating an Event-Based Flow

1. Navigate to `https://flow.microsoft.com`.

2. Select My Flows from the navigation pane on the left.

3. Select + New and then choose + Automated—from blank. See
    Figure 11-9.

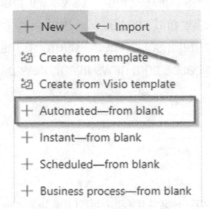

Figure 11-9. *Creating a new event-based flow*

4. Name the flow Chapter 11 – Event Based Flow.

5. Search for SharePoint in the provided search box. See Figure 11-10.

6. Select When an item is created.

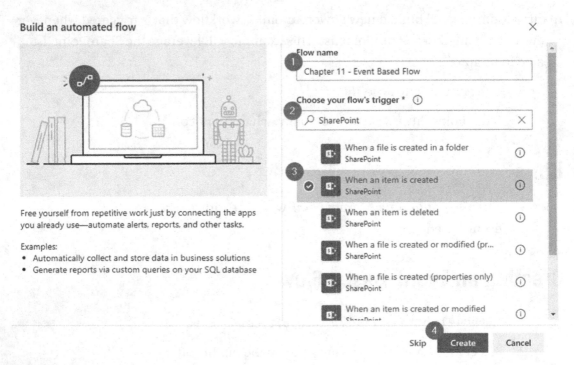

Figure 11-10. *SharePoint as an event-based trigger*

7. The next step is to configure the trigger. Select your SharePoint site from the drop-down menu.

8. For the List Name, choose the list Expenses. See Figure 11-11.

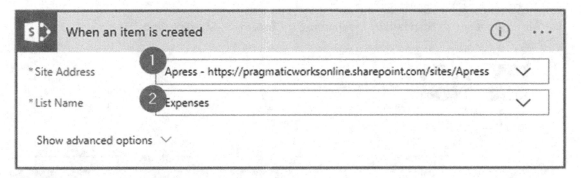

Figure 11-11. *Choosing the SharePoint list*

Testing the Trigger

Now it is time to validate the trigger is working. The next step is to add an action to complete the flow, and then testing can begin. In this section, the compose action is added to the workflow; the flow is saved and then a test will be performed.

Tip   The compose action can require very little setup, and as you will see, it is a very quick and easy way to validate event-based triggers, conditional actions, and expressions within Power Automate.

---

1. Click the button titled + New Step.

2. Once a new step is selected, you will see a list of available actions; type Compose into the search box and then select Compose from the list of Actions available. See Figure 11-12.

Figure 11-12.   Choosing the compose action

3.   For the inputs, just type in some plain text. For example, "This is a
     test." See Figure 11-13.

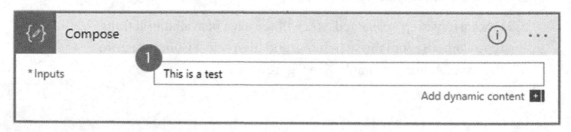

Figure 11-13.   This is a test

4. Click the Save button found below the compose action to save your flow.

5. Now navigate back.

6. Enter some sample data into the Expense list located in SharePoint; you can perform this task manually or by using the Power App created previously. See Figures 11-14 and 11-15 for manually entering a new item.

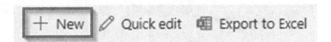

Expense Reports

Figure 11-14. *Create a new item in SharePoint*

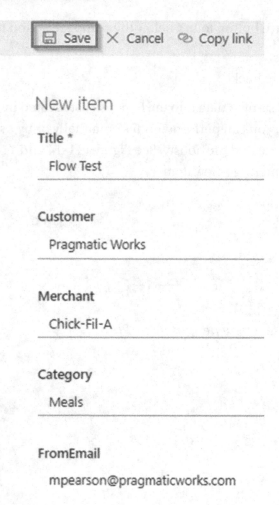

Figure 11-15. *Enter data and click Save*

7. A new item has now been added to the SharePoint list, and the flow created and saved earlier will now trigger and execute.

8. Navigate back to your flow, which should still be open in another web browser tab, and click the back arrow to navigate back to the previous screen. See Figure 11-16.

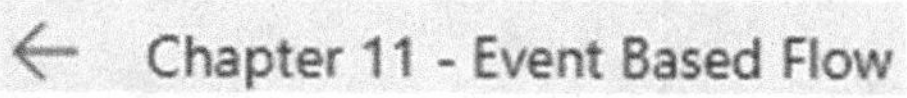

←   Chapter 11 - Event Based Flow

Figure 11-16. *Navigate back to the previous screen*

9. From this screen, you can perform some management and administration tasks which include viewing a history of flow executions.

10. Find the section titled Runs and click the most recent execution in that list; note that there should only be one unless you added multiple items to your SharePoint list.

11. This will provide a UI-based representation of the flow and provide very granular details about each step in the flow which includes input and output values. Click the Compose activity to expand the window. See Figure 11-17.

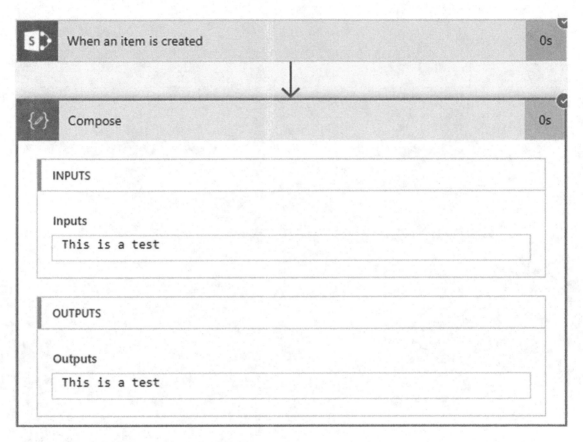

Figure 11-17. *Reviewing run history*

In this chapter, you learned about the types of different triggers and how to specifically create event-based triggers. Furthermore, you learned how to check the run history to validate that the flow executed as intended. Future chapters will continue to build on this example.

CHAPTER 12

Working with Flow Expressions

Power Automate ships with a staggering number of actions that allow for near limitless automation capabilities. However, there are times when you simply want to perform some basic operations like concatenating two strings together, returning the current date and time, or simply formatting a date value. These operations and much more are possible by leveraging the built-in expression language. Power Automate, like Azure Logic Apps, takes advantage of the Workflow Definition Language for writing expressions.

Power Automate facilitates an effortless approach to building automated workflows with a rich UI design experience. Unfortunately, the expression editor does not yield this same experience, far from it in fact. Power Automate is designed for the citizen developer, and as a result, it is a "no-code" or "low-code" tool, and the expression editor reflects this thinking. If you find yourself needing to write expressions in Power Automate, then you might find yourself writing the expression in Notepad or some other text editing tool and then copying that expression back into Power Automate.

Functions in Power Automate

Power Automate provides an extensive list of available functions that can be used when writing expressions. The list of functions is distributed by categories which include string, collection, logical, conversion, math, date and time, referencing functions, workflow functions, URI parsing functions, and manipulation functions. When reviewing the available functions, remember to click "See more" to see a larger list of available options. See Figure 12-1.

© Mitchell Pearson, Brian Knight, Devin Knight, Manuel Quintana 2020
M. Pearson et al., *Pro Microsoft Power Platform*, https://doi.org/10.1007/978-1-4842-6008-1_12

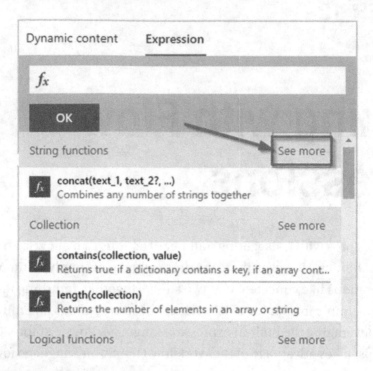

Figure 12-1. *See more available functions*

When using a function, you will be provided with a nice description and the syntax on how to use the function. See Figure 12-2.

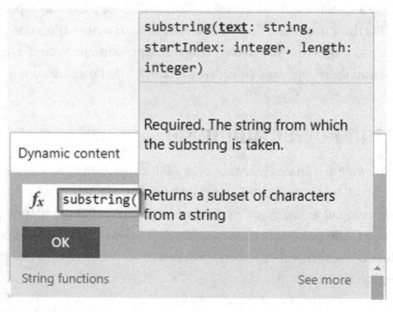

Figure 12-2. *Function tooltip*

Dynamic Content

Another thing Power Automate does exceptionally well is allow easy access to outputs from triggers and actions. Instead of having to write an expression that references the JSON output from a previous action or trigger, the developer can simply select the dynamic content. For example, imagine your flow triggers whenever a new item is added to a SharePoint list, then you may want to use information from that item in your workflow. With Power Automate, that information is stored in the dynamic content window for easy access.

To access dynamic content, click "Add dynamic content"; this link is found below configurable objects. Similar to functions, not all dynamic content is immediately exposed; click "See more" to view the full list of available content. See Figure 12-3.

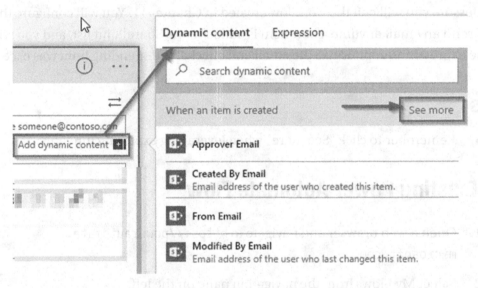

Figure 12-3. *Dynamic content to reference output from triggers and actions*

Expression Language

Expressions in Power Automate are designed through a combination of functions, variables, and dynamic content. As mentioned previously, writing an expression can be challenging considering the editor does not offer a rich design experience; in fact, you have a single line to build your expression on. It is common for Power Automate developers to write their code in a text editor like Notepad and then paste the code back into the expression editor.

113

Try It Out

In this section, you will explore the dynamic content and expression language available within Power Automate. You will need the following items to complete this section:

- Power Automate account

- SharePoint list created previously

  - (https://<your company>.sharepoint.com)

- Email account required (www.outlook.com)

Lesson Requirements

In this lesson, you will edit the workflow created in Chapter 11. You will configure the flow to send an email anytime a new item is added to the SharePoint list, and you will also use expressions to prioritize the email and check if the spending limit was exceeded.

Hints

- Remember to click "See more" when leveraging exploring functions.

Edit Existing Power Automate Flow

1. Open a web browser and navigate to https://powerautomate.microsoft.com.

2. Select My Flows from the navigation pane on the left.

3. Select the flow created in Chapter 11: Chapter 11 – Event Based Flow.

4. This will open up your administration pane; we will discuss this window in more depth later. For now, select "Save As" from the toolbar across the top; refer to Figure 12-4.

Figure 12-4. *Saving a copy of the flow*

5. Selecting "Save As" will open up a new dialog box; name the new flow Chapter 12. See Figure 12-5.

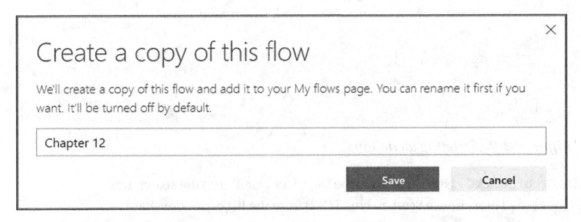

Figure 12-5. *Naming the flow*

6. Now it's time to open the Power Automate Editor for the new flow. Select My Flows from the navigation pane and then select the ellipsis, and you will see a drop-down menu with additional options appear. Select "Edit" from the drop-down; see Figure 12-6.

Figure 12-6. *Editing a flow*

7. Next, you want to add an email action which will send you an email anytime a new item is added to your SharePoint list. First, delete the compose action from the flow. See Figure 12-7.

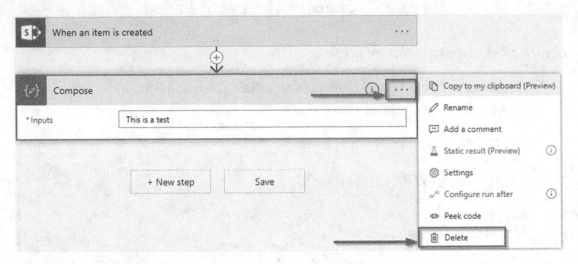

Figure 12-7. Deleting an action

8. Click "+ New Step" and type "Send an email" into the search box. Then choose Send an email (V2) from the list of options that appear; see Figure 12-8.

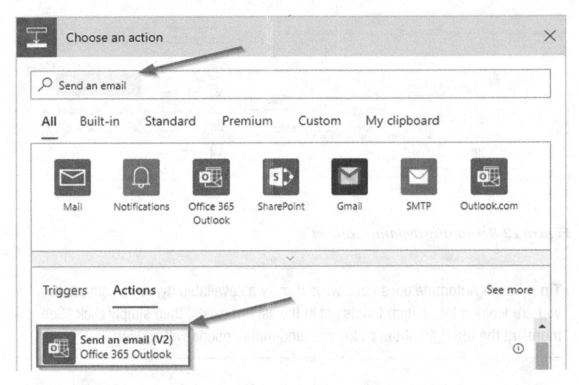

Figure 12-8. Creating a new action

9. To configure the email action, the first property to configure is the "To" property. You have the option to hardcode an email address into the text box provided; however, you can also make this more dynamic and automated by using the dynamic content.

10. The dynamic content box does not automatically appear; place your mouse cursor into the text box provided, and then the option for dynamic content will appear as a hyperlink at the bottom right of the corresponding box. Select Approver Email from the dynamic content options provided. See Figure 12-9.

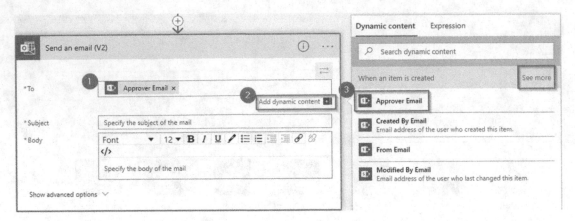

Figure 12-9. *Adding dynamic content*

Tip   Power Automate does not always display all available dynamic content. If you are looking for an item that is not in the list but exists, then simply click "See more" at the top right of the dialog box, and more options will appear!

11.   For the subject, you will combine a literal hardcoded string with dynamic content. Type into the text box:

Review the new expense for approval:

12.   Make sure to leave a space on the end of the string; next select Title from the dynamic content list. See Figure 12-10.

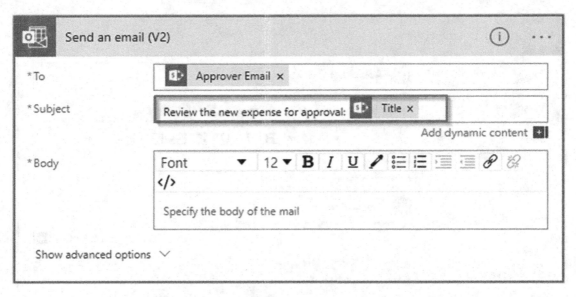

Figure 12-10. *Combining a literal string and dynamic content*

13. Now it's time to build the body of the email; once again, this will be a combination of text and dynamic content. Type the following into the body of the email:

    ```
    Please find the expense report here:
    ```

14. Hit enter and then insert the dynamic content Link to item below. Link to item provides a link directly to the item in SharePoint, making it easy to review. See Figure 12-11.

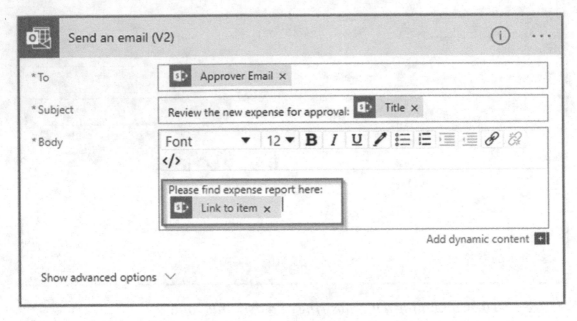

Figure 12-11. *Combining a literal string and dynamic content*

15. Next, add an expression that determines if the spending limit was exceeded. While still in the body of the email, hit enter to proceed to the next line and then type the following:

Was amount Exceeded?

16. Select the expression tab from the dynamic content window. In this window, you will see a large number of functions available in the Power Automate that you can leverage to automate your flows. In this example, you will check to see if the amount was greater than $10; if it was, then yes, the amount was exceeded, else no.

17. Find the function greater() under the logical function category and add it to the expression bar; remember to click "See more" to view additional options available. See Figure 12-12.

Figure 12-12. *Adding a function to the expression*

18. Next, click the dynamic content tab and select total; this will input the code into the function bar.

19. Then finish off the expression by typing , 10 in the following code. The final code is seen as follows. See Figure 12-13. Make sure to click OK to add your expression to the body of the email.

```
greater(triggerBody()?['Total'], 10)
```

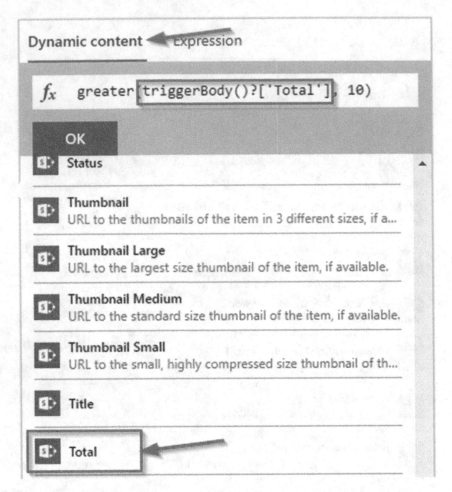

Figure 12-13. Adding dynamic content to the expression

20. The current expression simply returns true or false. The
     expression can be further improved by using if, then, else
     conditional logic. Update the expression to look like the following
     code, changes highlighted in bold:

if(greater(triggerBody()?['Total'], 10)**, 'yes', 'no')**

Code   The completed code for this "Try It Out" section can be found in the course
files downloadable at the following location:

https://github.com/Apress/pro-microsoft-power-platform

21. The expense limitation of $10 is only applicable if the expense category is equal to Meals. Therefore, the expression should read "If the category is equal to meals and the total is greater than $10."

22. You will use the `equals` along with the `and` function to finish off this example. Each of these functions is found under the logical function category. See Figure 12-14.

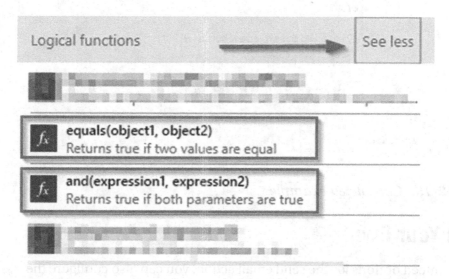

Figure 12-14. Logical functions

23. At the time of this writing, the box provided for editing expressions can be a little difficult to work with. The final expression for this example can be found in the following; modifications to the code have been highlighted in bold. See Figure 12-15.

```
if(and(greater(triggerBody()?['Total'], 10),
equals(triggerBody()?['Category'], 'Meals')), 'yes', 'no')
```

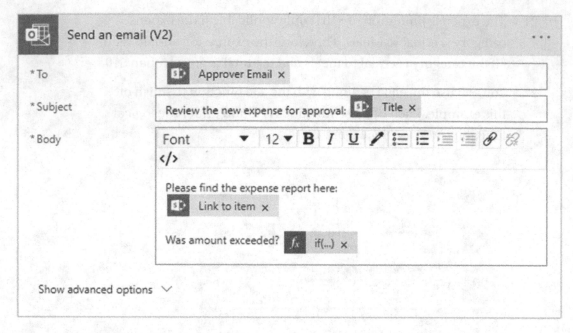

Figure 12-15. *Completed example*

Try on Your Own!

In the advanced options for the send email action, you can also configure the importance level to be low, normal, or high. Configure the importance to be high priority if the spending limit was exceeded.

Hints

- Select "Enter custom value" from the drop-down.

- The values for importance are low, normal, or high.

- Copy and modify the code created in the email body.

Testing Your Flow

1. Save your flow and then navigate back to the administration view.

2. Make sure the flow is turned on; when a flow is copied, it is disabled by default. Click "Turn on" found on the toolbar; see Figure 12-16.

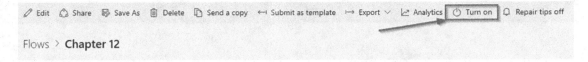

Figure 12-16. Enable flow

3. Enter some sample data into your SharePoint list titled Expenses;
    you can perform this task manually or by using the Power App
    created previously. The data you enter should exceed the limit of
    $10 and have a category of Meals.

4. You will receive an email with the completed email.

CHAPTER 13

Building Conditional Flows

In the previous chapter, conditional logic was used to make the flow automated and dynamic; in this chapter, you will explore the conditional actions available in Power Automate.

Previously, building complex conditional logic into a flow was not easy to implement; it involved a lot of expression writing in advanced mode and nesting conditional actions. However, the condition action recently underwent some major changes, and now there is an advanced condition builder available. In this chapter, we will dissect this action specifically and focus on what is possible with the advanced condition builder.

Implementing Conditional Logic in Flows

Occasionally, it's necessary to build advanced conditional logic in an automated workflow and, optimally, implement this conditional logic through the rich UI experience rather than writing complex and unwieldy expressions. For example, in the previous chapter, an expense was considered exceeded if the category was meals and the price was greater than $10. Now expand the conditional logic to also check for other scenarios, for example, if category is transportation and expenses are greater than N dollars or if category is hotel and expenses exceeded N dollars. You can quickly see how this logic would get very difficult to formulate within the expression language.

© Mitchell Pearson, Brian Knight, Devin Knight, Manuel Quintana 2020
M. Pearson et al., *Pro Microsoft Power Platform*, https://doi.org/10.1007/978-1-4842-6008-1_13

Anatomy of the Advanced Condition Builder

In this section, we will break down the various components that make the new condition builder uniquely equipped for authoring more complex conditional logic. First, let's look at how to find the condition action. See Figure 13-1.

- **+ New step**

- Search for "condition"

- Select condition from the list of actions available

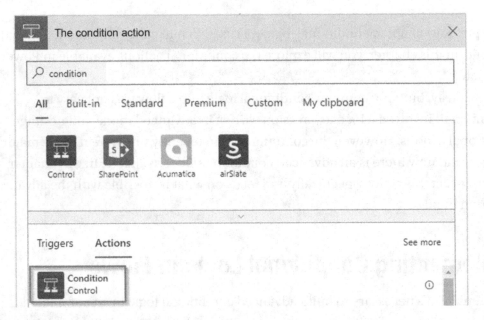

Figure 13-1.   The condition action

At first glance, the advanced condition builder looks quite docile, but don't miscalculate the true potential here. Adding a second condition immediately exposes the capabilities of the builder.

The first option you are presented with is to add a row or to add a group; these are two very distinct and different options. Adding a row will add an additional row to your current conditional logic, for example, if category is equal to meals and total is greater than $10. See Figure 13-2.

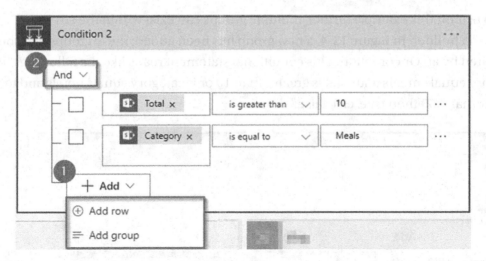

Figure 13-2. *Adding new rows or groups*

Adding a new row will allow the two rows to be evaluated together inside of either an OR or AND condition. To switch the context, click the drop-down represented by step 2 in Figure 13-2.

Understanding Groups

Groups allow for complex logic to be easily written and maintained. Rows can be explicitly added to a group by using the ellipsis (...). Furthermore, the ellipsis menu will allow you to delete a row and move rows up or down. To group two rows, first select their check boxes, then click the ellipsis, and then select Make group. See Figure 13-3.

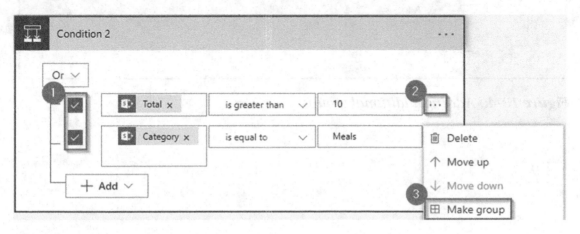

Figure 13-3. *Grouping rows*

To extend this example further, multiple groups can exist within the advanced condition builder. In Figure 13-4, a new group has been added; these groups have been separated by an Or condition. This conditional statement reads like the following: "If category equals meals and total is greater than 10 or if category equals hotels and total is greater than 250 then true, else false."

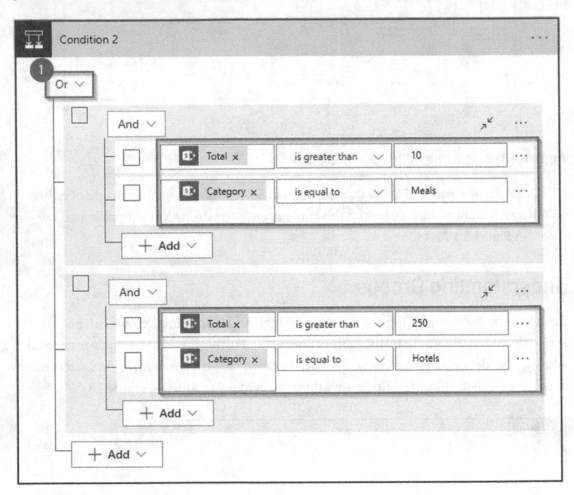

Figure 13-4. *Adding additional groups*

Advanced Condition Builder – True and False Conditions

The advanced condition builder will conclusively return a result of true or false once the logic has been evaluated; the next step is to resolve which actions are performed if the condition evaluates to true and, likewise, what actions are performed if the condition evaluates to false.

For example, if the expression in Figure 13-4 evaluated to true, then the flow might email the manager notifying them of the exception; however, if no exceptions were found, then the flow might immediately approve the expense in SharePoint without manager approval. In Figure 13-5, an action has been added to the true and false evaluations to depict the example presented earlier.

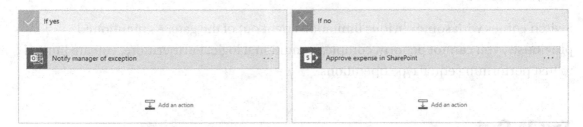

Figure 13-5. *Configuring actions for true and false evaluations*

Switch Action

Another option for implementing conditional logic is the switch action. The switch action does not offer the same robust conditional logic builder you get with the condition action; however, it has its own unique attributes and use cases.

Switch is similar to a case statement; for example, imagine you are importing documents, you may want to perform different actions depending on what type of document file you are importing. This type of logic can be accomplished easily with switch from a single step. For example, if the file type is an Excel file, then upload the file to OneDrive, or if the file is a JSON file, then load that file into Azure Blob Storage. See Figure 13-6.

Switch also comes with a default case; any values that do not meet any of the stated case statements will be redirected to the default option; the default option is not shown in Figure 13-6.

Figure 13-6. *Switch action*

Limitations

Switch comes with some obvious limitations right out of the gate. As mentioned previously, you cannot perform complex conditional logic. Furthermore, you are limited to just performing equal type operations.

Try It Out

In this section, you will explore and familiarize yourself with the condition action and the advanced condition builder in Power Automate. You will need the following items to complete this section:

- Power Automate account

- SharePoint list created previously

  - (https://<your company>.sharepoint.com)

- Email account required (www.outlook.com)

Lesson Requirements

In this lesson, you will edit the workflow created in Chapter 12. You will configure the flow to send an email anytime a new item is added to the SharePoint list and it exceeds the spending limits.

1. Build a conditional logic to determine if expense category was
    exceeded; the spending limit is exceeded if

    -   Category = Meals and Total > $10

    -   Category = Hotels and Total > $250

    -   Category = Transportation and Total > $125

2. Send an email notifying the manager if expense was exceeded.

3. Update the comments section for the item in the SharePoint list
    to reflect if the expense was exceeded and if the manager was
    notified.

Edit Existing Power Automate Flow

1. Open a web browser and navigate to `https://powerautomate.`
    `microsoft.com`.

2. Select My Flows from the navigation pane on the left.

3. Select the flow created in the previous chapter: Chapter 12.

4. Save a copy of this flow and name it Chapter 13.

5. Launch the new flow in the Power Automate Editor.

6. Next, add the condition action before the send email action; this
    is accomplished by hovering over the arrow separating the trigger
    and action. See Figure 13-7.

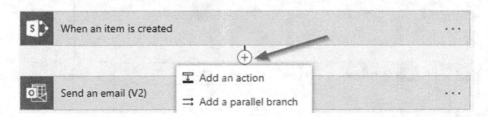

Figure 13-7. Add intermediate action

7. Type condition into the search bar and then select condition from the list of available actions. Reference Figure 13-1 for screenshot.

8. Now it's time to leverage the built-in advanced condition builder. Choose "Category" from the dynamic content, "is equal to" for the comparison operator, and "Meals" as the value. See Figure 13-8.

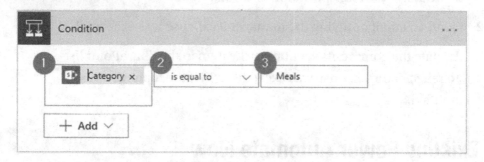

Figure 13-8. *Add conditional logic*

9. Next, click "+ Add"; this will provide a drop-down with two options; choose "add row."

10. Choose "Total" from the dynamic content, "is greater than" for the comparison operator, and "10" as the value. See Figure 13-9.

11. Next, these two rows will need to be grouped explicitly in a group before adding additional conditions. Click the check box to the left of each condition and then select the ellipsis (...) to the right of the category and choose "Make group."

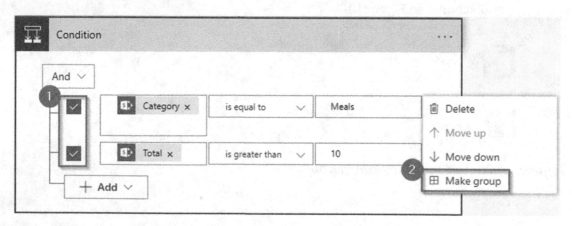

Figure 13-9. *Grouping conditions*

134

12. The first group is complete; next, you will add a second group, and the two groups will be separated by an OR condition. Click the outer "+ Add" and select "Add Group" from the drop-down. See Figure 13-10.

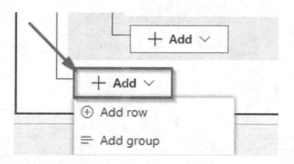

Figure 13-10. *Adding new groups*

13. Add the following two conditions, seen in Figure 13-10, to the new group that has been added; keep in mind that you will need to add one additional row to the new group.

14. Once the new group has been added, change the condition to an OR condition. See Figure 13-11.

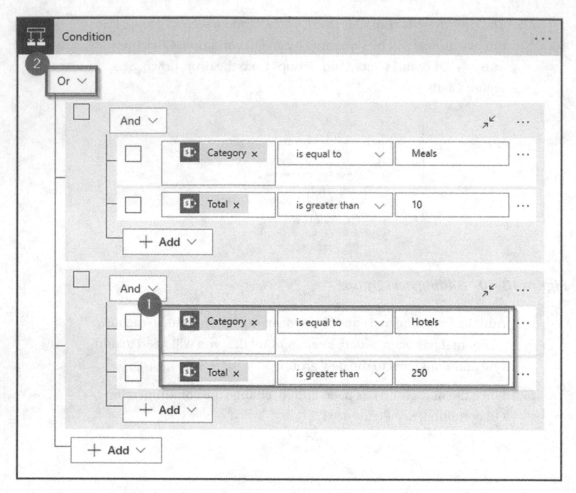

Figure 13-11. *Adding new groups*

15.   Repeat steps 12 and 13 to add one more conditional group. The
category for this group will be Transportation and the Total will be
125. See Figure 13-12.

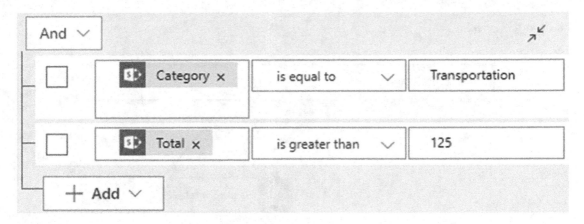

Figure 13-12. Adding grouped condition

16. Next, rename the condition action to be more descriptive. Click the (...) to the right of the action and select rename. Name the action "Check if expense category was exceeded." See Figure 13-13.

Figure 13-13. Renaming an action

17. Now that the conditions have been set, it's time to configure which actions will be executed upon a true evaluation and which actions are run for false evaluations.

18. If the expense was exceeded, then an email needs to be sent to the manager informing them of the exception. The email configured in Chapter 12 can be reused for this example by moving the email action into the "If yes" condition. Simply select the header of the email and drag and drop it into the box provided. See Figure 13-14.

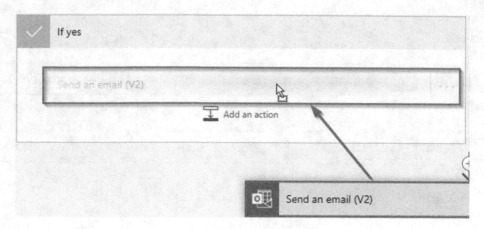

Figure 13-14. *Moving actions*

19. Next, after sending an email, we want to add a comment to the
    item in SharePoint stating that an email was sent to the manager.
    Click "Add an action," search for SharePoint, and then select
    "Update item" from the list of available options. See Figure 13-15.

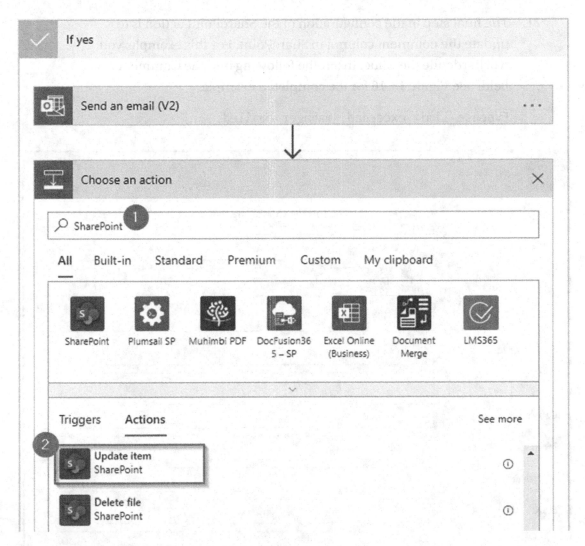

Figure 13-15. *Update item in SharePoint*

20. Similar to the SharePoint trigger, you will need to choose your
     SharePoint list and list name to get started. Next, populate the
     Id column with "ID" found in the dynamic content; this is a
     unique identifier, and this step will ensure that the correct item
     is updated. Likewise, for the title column, select "Title" from the
     dynamic content.

21. The final step in the configuration of the SharePoint action is to
     update the comment column in SharePoint. For this example, you
     will hardcode the value. Insert the following into the Comment
     field. See Figure 13-16 for the completed example.

     `Expense limit exceeded, manager emailed.`

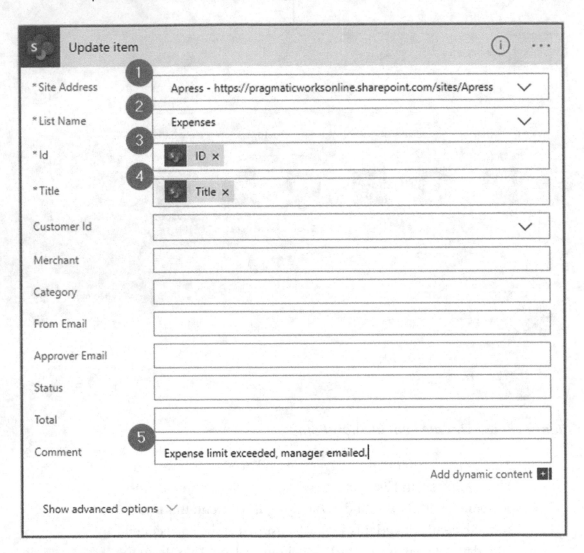

Figure 13-16. SharePoint action configuration

Try on Your Own!

The current automated workflow only performs actions if an expense exceeds predetermined limits. However, you may want to build this flow out further by performing actions for expenses that do not exceed limits.

Design the flow to update the SharePoint list with a comment if the expense falls within acceptable boundaries. The following code could be used as an example:

```
The expense did not exceed limits, manager not notified.
```

Hints

- Update the "If no" portion of the condition activity.

- Use the action "Update Item" found in the SharePoint category.

- The configuration is similar to Figure 13-15, except for the comment, of course.

CHAPTER 14

Designing Approval Flows

In this chapter, we explore one of the most exciting actions and design flows in Power Automate. Approval flows are among the most common flows designed. At its core, approval flows really epitomize what Power Automate is designed for: turning repetitive tasks into automated workflows that are intelligent, dynamic, and flexible. These well-designed workflows save time, improve consistency of processes, and eliminate delays or errors.

This chapter takes a deep dive into the approval action and completes the flow that you have been developing in the last few chapters. The approval action is very rich in functionality and features, as you will see.

Approval Flows

Approval flows are popular and widely adapted because their application is industry agnostic. Regardless of your industry or business, there is undoubtedly a place where an approval flow can be leveraged. Some common use cases for approval flows might include creating a process for approving presentation materials, approving documents, approving proposals for new projects or even for budgets, approving vacation time, and approving expense reports. The list of possible approvals is quite large.

Types of Approval Actions

Power Automate currently ships with three actions available for approvals. The approval action has undergone many iterations over the years and will likely experience more in the future, and therefore one day there may be more actions available.

The three actions currently available are Start an Approval, Wait for an Approval, and Start and Wait for an approval. The available actions are seen in Figure 14-1. Start and

© Mitchell Pearson, Brian Knight, Devin Knight, Manuel Quintana 2020
M. Pearson et al., *Pro Microsoft Power Platform*, https://doi.org/10.1007/978-1-4842-6008-1_14

wait for an approval is the most common of these actions and is the one that will be used in the "Try It Out" section. The other two options are derived from the "start and wait for an approval" action and offer more flexibility and customization.

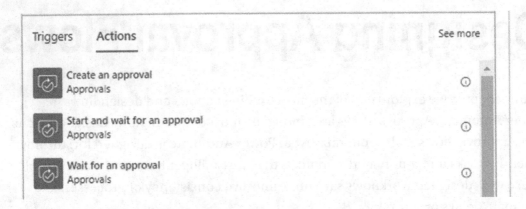

Figure 14-1. *Available approval actions*

Start and Wait for an Approval

The approval action is rich with features and customization options. The first decision is determining what type of approval will be required. There are two primary options available here; the first is "Approve/Reject," and this allows the approver to simply approve or reject the request. Second, you can choose "Custom Response." This option is much more exciting because it offers near limitless flexibility. This long requested and anticipated feature triumphantly emerged, with much fanfare, from the most recent iteration of the approval action.

The option to "approve with edits" is one example of a common use case for custom responses. For example, the approver may look at the document or proposal, make necessary edits, and then select "Approved, but with edits." When creating a list of custom responses, there are two options available. The first option is you can hard-code available responses, and the second is you can pass in a dynamic list of responses.

Typing out a distinct list of available responses is easy and very intuitive; however, the ability to create the list of responses dynamically is often overlooked and missed. What do we mean by dynamically? Dynamically here means retrieving the list of response options from a database, Excel file, SharePoint list, or any other location where data may be stored. Therefore, if the source changes, the list of options available in the workflow will also update, simplifying the maintenance process. The feature that allows the approval action to create a dynamic list of custom responses is called "Switch to input entire array." See Figure 14-2.

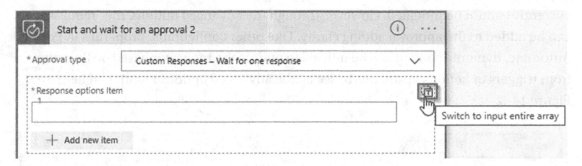

Figure 14-2. *Switch to input entire array*

Markdown Language Supported

Another very exciting feature of approval actions is the availability of Markdown when building out the details of your approval. The details section is what is seen by the approver and has all the necessary elements enabling the approver to make a quick and decisive decision.

What is Markdown? Markdown is a simple, lightweight language that enables you to add formatting to plain text. This simple yet intuitive language is now available in the approval action so that the approval details can be formatted for a better and cleaner approval representation. Markdown allows you to add line breaks, paragraphs, headers, bolding, bulleted list, links to resources, and more. To find out more about the Markdown features currently available in Power Automate, please refer to the following link:

```
https://aka.ms/approvaldetails
```

Advanced Options

The advanced section of approvals makes available additional configuration options. These features are somewhat hidden but can be found by expanding the advanced options menu. In this section, we will discuss those additional features in detail.

Requestor

The first of these advanced options is the option to add the requestor to the approval request. By default, approval requests always originate from "Power Automate"; this currently cannot be modified. However, through the advanced options, the "requestor" can be added to the approval adding clarity. Like other configurable properties in Power Automate, dynamic content can be utilized to update the requestor based on the values from triggers or actions upstream. To see all the advanced options mentioned here, see Figure 14-3.

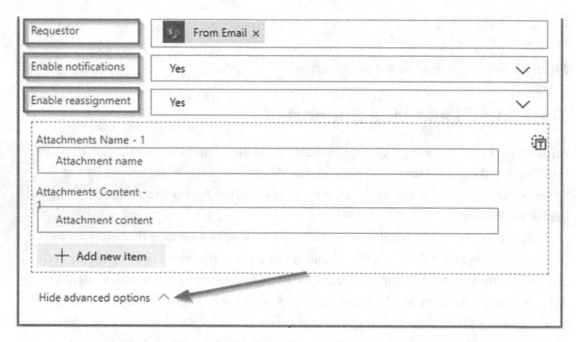

Figure 14-3. *Approval advanced options*

Disable Notifications

Another advanced feature is the ability to disable notifications. Currently, notifications arrive via email and the Power Automate app. Unfortunately, the ability for customizing the delivery method of approvals does not exist within the approval action. Notifications can be disabled to prevent an excess of emails from being sent via a workflow approval. Later in this chapter, we will discuss the different methods available for responding to approval requests.

> **Tip** Users in the community have authored creative workflows that allow them to send notifications via means not natively available within an approval action. Please visit the following link to see an example of a notification through a Microsoft Teams channel: `www.youtube.com/watch?v=5NDy3tGyigI`

Reassigning Flows

If the approval request has been directed to the incorrect approver, then the approver receiving the request can reassign the approval request to another individual. The ability to reassign flows is turned on by default but can be disabled in the advanced options section of the approval flow.

Reassigning an app can be accomplished from the approval center at `www.powerautomate.microsoft.com` or from the Power Automate app. To reassign an approval from the portal, log in online, expand action items, select Approvals, and then click the ellipsis (…) to reassign the flow. The next step is to provide the email address of the user that you want to handle the approval on your behalf. After the approval has been reassigned, the new approver will receive a notification. Reassigning an approval flow is seen in Figure 14-4.

To reassign an approval request from the Power Automate app is a very similar process. Navigate to the activity section and then select approvals, select the approval and click the ellipsis (…), and select reassign from the drop-down menu.

Responding to Approvals

Once an approval has been sent, an approver can respond through the Power Automate portal, directly from the email received or from the Power Automate app.

To respond to approval requests online, log in to `https://powerautomate.microsoft.com` and expand "Action items" from the navigation pane. This view offers a comprehensive view of approvals received, approvals sent, as well as a history of approvals. Refer to step 2 in Figure 14-4.

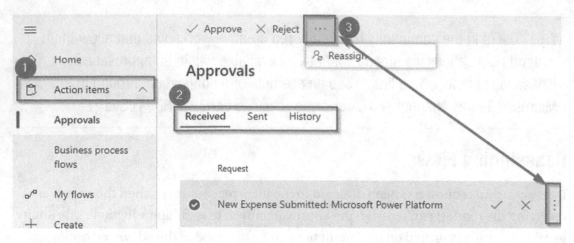

Figure 14-4. *Approvals in the portal*

Response Options

When responding to an approval request, the approver has multiple options available. If a link to the item requesting approval was provided, then the approver can navigate to the link, review, and in some cases even modify the item. For example, the approver may edit a document or a proposal before approving the request.

The next step and most obvious is to approve or reject the approval request. If a custom list of approval options was provided, then the list would include those options in lieu of the standard approve and reject options. To elaborate on our example in the previous paragraph, after editing the document, the approver would select "Approved, but with edits…" from the custom list of options provided. Once an approval option has been chosen, the approver can provide any comments or feedback. Keep in mind the approval response and the comments provided will be available for other actions to utilize downstream in the workflow.

Tip   Comment responses are read by Power Automate as an array, and as a result, whenever comment response is chosen in another action, that action will be wrapped in an Apply to each. This is the natural occurring behavior of this type of dynamic content: leave the Apply to each action in place and continue developing as normal.

Try It Out

Create an approval flow to streamline the process of expense approvals. This example will build from the completed example in the previous chapter. The approval flow will use the Markdown language for text formatting as well as the person requesting the approval. By the end of this "Try It Out" example, you will feel confident working with the approvals in Power Automate! You will need the following items to complete this section:

- Power Automate account

- SharePoint list created previously

    - (https://<your company>.sharepoint.com)

- Email account required (`www.outlook.com`)

Lesson Requirements

In this lesson, you will edit the workflow created in Chapter 13. You will configure the flow to send an email anytime a new item is added to the SharePoint list and it exceeds the spending limits.

1. Use the Markdown language to format the text in the details of the approval request.

2. Add the "requestor" to the approval for clarity.

3. Add and use variables to store if the expense limit was exceeded.

Edit Existing Power Automate Flow

1. Save a copy of the flow created in the previous chapter as Chapter 14 and launch the new flow in the Power Automate editor.

2. Add the action "Initialize Variable" between the SharePoint trigger and the Condition action. When using variables in Power Automate, the variable must first be initialized, and this must occur at the top level, not nested in an action. See Figure 14-5 for the initial configuration.

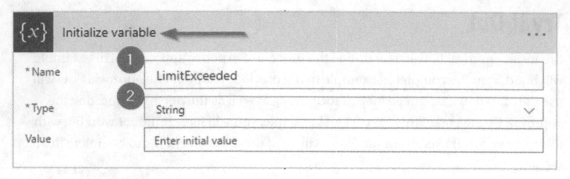

Figure 14-5. *Initialize variable*

3. Next, it's time to do a little cleanup. Delete all actions from the "If yes" and "If no" responses of the condition activity. The send email and SharePoint updates will occur further downstream in the workflow. Remember, to delete an action, click the ellipsis (...) and then select delete from the menu.

4. Now add the action "Set Variable" to the "If yes" and "If no" condition. See the configuration of each action in Figure 14-6.

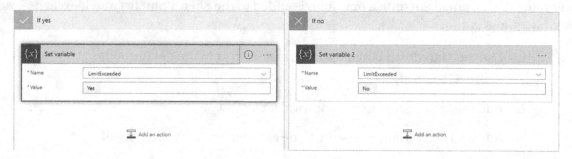

Figure 14-6. *Set Variable action*

5. Add a new step below the condition action. This new action will be "Start and wait for an approval." Remember this action will be outside the condition.

6. The first configurable property is the approval type. Select Approve/Reject – First to respond. See Figure 14-7.

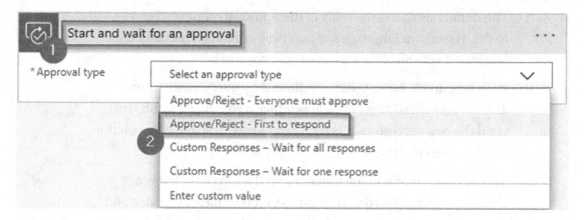

Figure 14-7. *Approval type*

7. Configure the title; the title will be the subject line in the email. Type the following in the Title field: `New expense submitted:` followed by Title from the dynamic content. See the title configuration in Figure 14-8.

8. The Assigned to field determines who the approver is, and this is the person who will be notified of the approval request. Select the approver email from the dynamic content. See Figure 14-8.

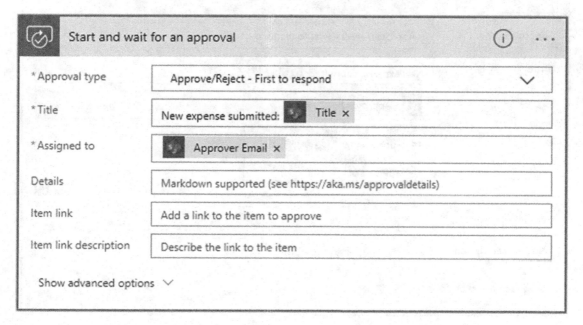

Figure 14-8. *Title and Assigned to fields*

9. The details section is the body of the approval request. Thanks
    to the Markdown language support now available, this can be
    formatted very nicely once you get the hang of it.

10. First, type in `## Report Name:` followed by the dynamic content
    Title. The two hashtags (##) will produce a Heading 2 result. To
    yield the desired results, it is required to leave a space between the
    two hashtags and the text.

11. The next step is to add the Category on the next line. To enter a
    line break using Markdown language, hit the space key twice and
    then hit enter to proceed to the next line. Once again, this key
    sequence must be very precise to work correctly.

12. On the next line, type `- Category:` followed by the dynamic
    content Category. The dash (-) here will create a bulleted list;
    remember to leave a space between dash and Category. Hit the
    space key twice and then hit enter to proceed to the next line. See
    Figure 14-9 for the progress thus far.

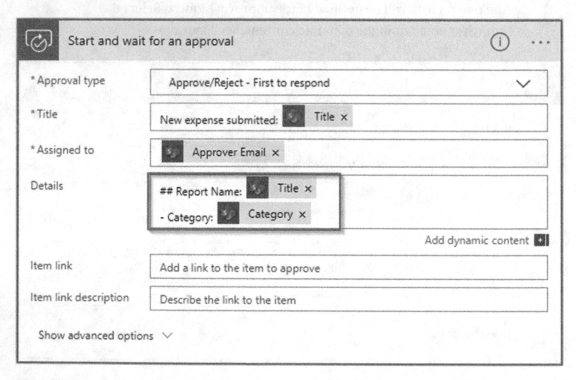

Figure 14-9. *Add conditional logic*

13. Next, add the items Merchant and Total to the list, repeating steps 11 and 12.

    – Merchant: [Merchant]

    – Total: [Total]

14. The final piece to add here will notify the approver if the expense limit was exceeded. First, hit enter twice to start a new paragraph.

15. Type `Was expense limit exceeded?` ** followed by the variable LimitExceeded and then ** at the end. The double asterisks on each side of the text will make it bold. See Figure 14-10 for the final configuration of the Details field.

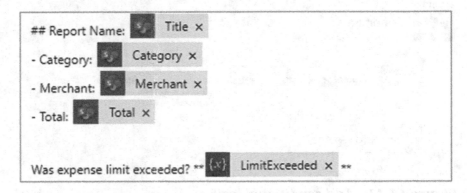

Figure 14-10. *Details configuration*

16. Select the dynamic content "Link to item" for the Item link field. Note, only people with permission to the item will be able to open the link.

17. For the "item link description" type: `Click here to see item details`, this description is the hyperlink seen in the approval request.

18. Now select Show advanced options to see additional configurable properties.

19. For the requestor field, select From Email from the dynamic content.

20. Leave enable notifications and enable reassignment set to true.

Now that the approval action has been configured and is in good shape, the final step is to add a condition action; this will determine which actions are performed if the request is approved and which actions are performed if the request is rejected.

21. Add a new step below the approval, and select the condition action from the list.

22. The approver response has been stored in the dynamic content of Outcome; therefore, the condition step will check to see if the outcome was equal to approve. See Figure 14-11.

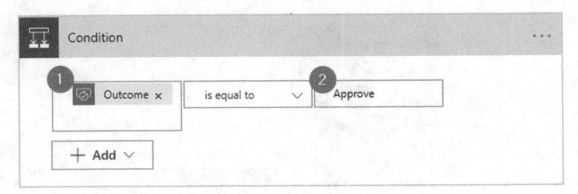

Figure 14-11. *Add conditional logic*

23. Next, add the action "Send an email (V2)" to the "If yes" response of the condition. Configure the To and Subject fields as seen in the following:

To: [From Email]

Subject: Your expense has been approved! [Title]

24. The next step is to configure the Body field; type Your expense has been approved with the following comments:, hit enter, and then add the dynamic content [Response Comments].

Remember, Power Automate reads Response Comments as an array and therefore will wrap the send email action inside of an Apply to each action. This is perfectly normal and the flow will work as intended. See Figure 14-12.

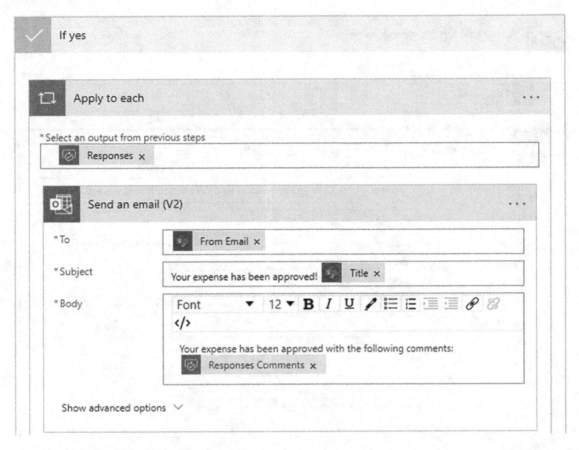

Figure 14-12.   Send an email

25. The next step is to update the status in the SharePoint list with the outcome and the approver's comments.

26. Minimize the Apply to each action; this will help eliminate confusion when adding new actions, then click add an action. Select the SharePoint action Update Item.

27. Select the Site Address, List Name, ID, and Title just like we did in the previous chapter.

28. For the Status field, select Outcome from the dynamic content.

29. For the Comment field, select Responses Comments; again the action will be wrapped inside an Apply to each action. See Figure 14-13.

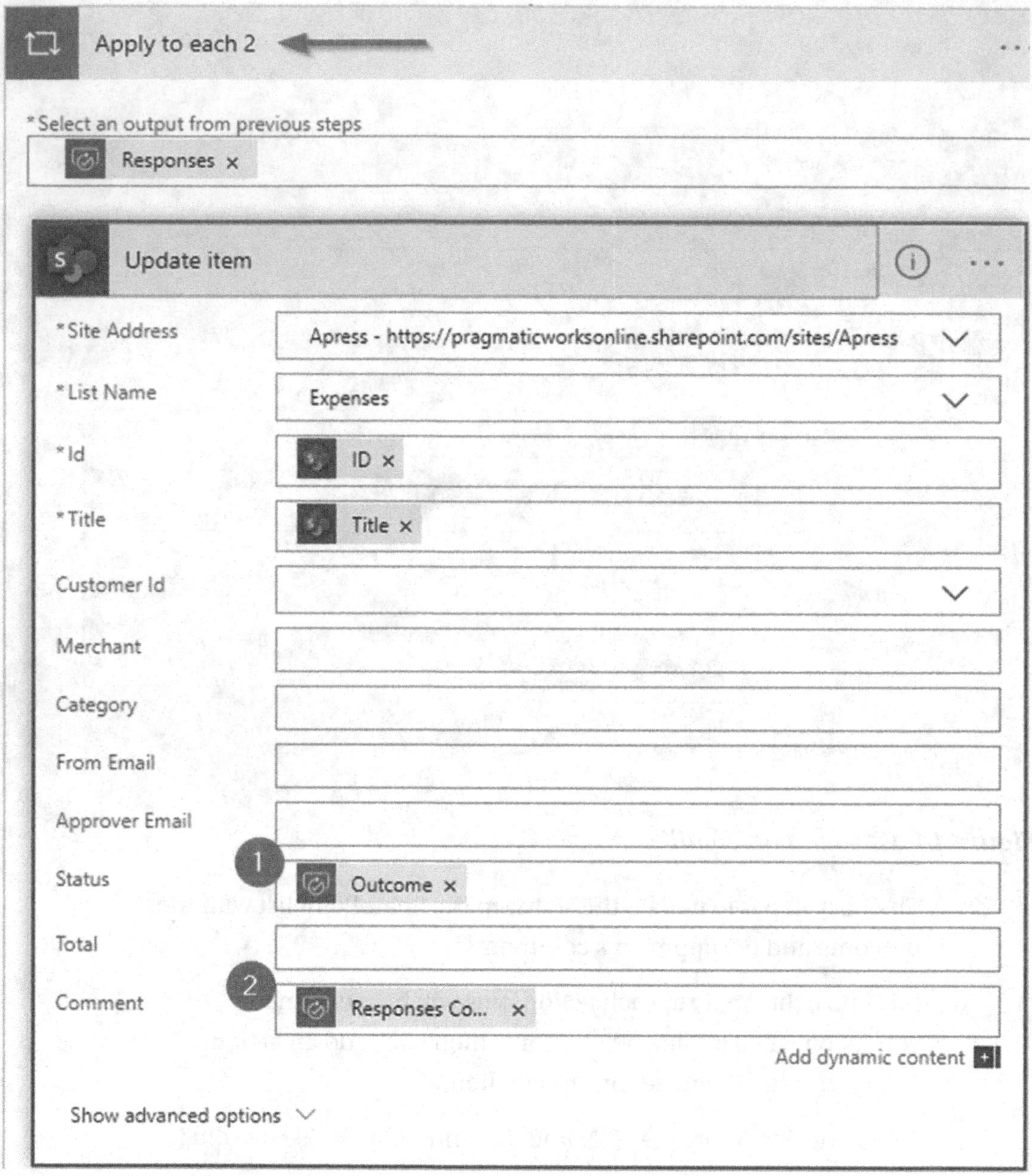

Figure 14-13. Update item

30. The "If yes" response is now complete. If the approval request
     was rejected, then corresponding actions would also occur in the
     "If no" response, and therefore actions also need to be added for
     rejections.

31. You could choose to manually add each of these actions for the "If no" response; alternatively, you could simply copy existing actions and then reference them from the clipboard.

Tip Actions in Power Automate can be copied to the clipboard, and then they will appear under the "My clipboard" category when adding new actions. This can significantly speed up developer efforts while reducing the opportunity to make errors. See Figures 14-14 and 14-15.

---

32. To copy an item, click the (...) and then select "Copy to my clipboard (Preview)." See Figure 14-14.

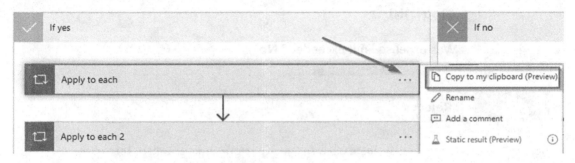

Figure 14-14. *Copy action to clipboard*

33. To paste an item, select "My clipboard" when adding new actions, and that's it! See Figure 14-15.

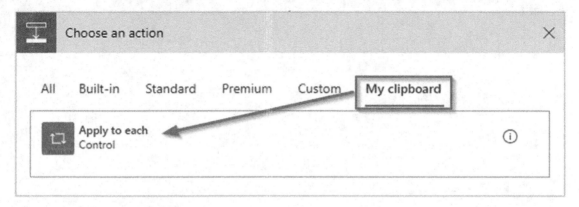

Figure 14-15. *My clipboard*

34. Insert a new record into your SharePoint list and test your flow.
See the final email approval request in Figure 14-16.

Figure 14-16. *Pending approval request*

CHAPTER 15

Administering Power Automate

This final chapter on Power Automate will be centered around administration. The topics will include sharing and collaboration, exporting flows, and installation and configuration of a data gateway. Much of the administration discussed in this chapter will be done via powerautomate.microsoft.com. However, some administration tasks can be performed through the Power Platform admin center as well.

The Power Platform admin center is a central location to perform administrative tasks for Power Platform tools mentioned in this book (Power BI, Power Apps, and Power Automate). To explore the admin portal mentioned here, navigate to `https://admin.powerplatform.microsoft.com`. This view provides an in-depth look at run and usage statistics for flows. More specifically, the Power Platform admin center displays flow runs, usage, creation, errors, shared flows, as well as connectors. See Figure 15-1.

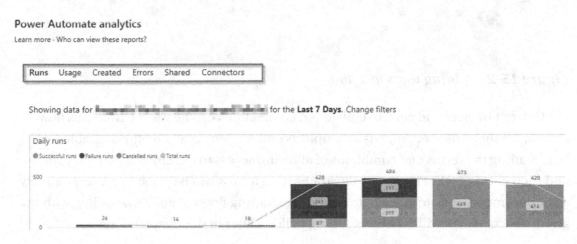

Figure 15-1. *Power Platform admin center*

© Mitchell Pearson, Brian Knight, Devin Knight, Manuel Quintana 2020
M. Pearson et al., *Pro Microsoft Power Platform*, https://doi.org/10.1007/978-1-4842-6008-1_15

Sharing Flows

The sharing of automated workflows is generally performed to add additional developers to a project. Users can be added as either owners to a flow or, in rare circumstances, as read-only users.

Granting Owner Access

Sharing automated workflows is typically between developers. Sharing a flow with a fellow developer is accomplished by adding a user as an owner to the flow. Owner access grants permission to edit, update, and delete a flow. Owners may also access the run history and add or remove other owners. Therefore, be careful with whom owner access is shared!

When a user is added as an owner, they also automatically receive access to all the connections being leveraged in that specific workflow. Keep in mind that this access will only be applicable when using the flow.

Sharing a flow with other users is a very straightforward process; from www.powerautomate.microsoft.com, select an existing flow. Once on the admin screen, find the owner's section and select edit, as seen in Figure 15-2.

Figure 15-2.   *Adding users to a flow*

Current owners and current embedded connections can be viewed from this new screen. Adding a user or group is as simple as entering an email into the available text box, reading the terms and conditions of allowing access to the embedded connections, and then clicking OK. Figure 15-3 illustrates what access will be given to owners; equally as important is the note at the bottom about exporting flows to edit flows offline without granting access. We will discuss exporting of flows later in this chapter.

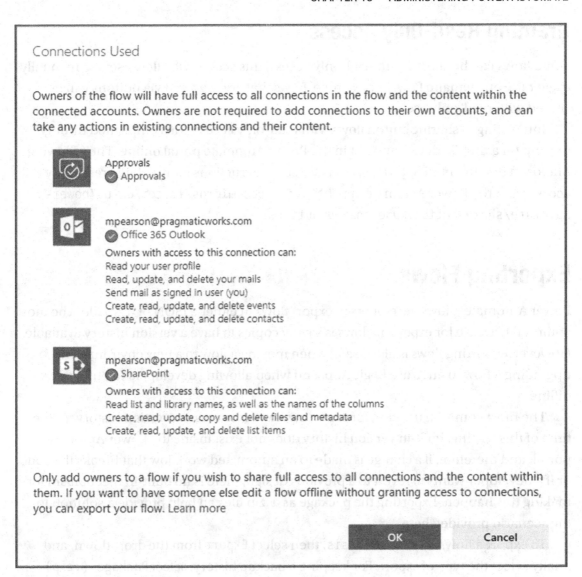

Figure 15-3. Accepting conditions of adding owners

Note   As a best practice, customarily there should be more than one owner assigned to a flow. Therefore, if an owner is sick, on vacation, or otherwise unavailable, changes can be made, and updates can be performed as necessary to keep business-critical flows online.

Granting Read-Only Access

Some flows can be shared with read-only access; this access will allow users to manually trigger the on-demand flow. For example, flows that are triggered via buttons can be shared with read-only access.

Interestingly, sharing button flows with read-only access is accomplished through the app on a mobile device and not in the Power Automate portal online. The following Microsoft documentation provides step-by-step instructions for providing read-only access from the Power Automate app: `https://docs.microsoft.com/en-us/power-automate/share-buttons#use-shared-buttons`.

Exporting Flows

Power Automate allows developers to export flows in either a JSON or a zip file. The most common use case for exporting flows is saving copies to have a version history available. However, exporting flows is also useful when moving a flow to a new environment, upgrading a flow to an Azure Logic App, and when allowing developers to build flows offline.

The most common use case for exporting flows is to create a version history. At the time of this writing, built-in version history does not exist inside the Power Automate portal, and therefore, if a change is made to an automated workflow that breaks the code or if a developer wants to revert to a previous design, there is no built-in mechanism for making this happen. Exporting the package as a .zip file can help provide a solution to the scenario provided here.

To export a flow, click the `ellipsis`, then select `Export` from the drop-down, and finally select the type of export. For keeping a backup history, select `Package (.zip)`. See Figure 15-4 for reference.

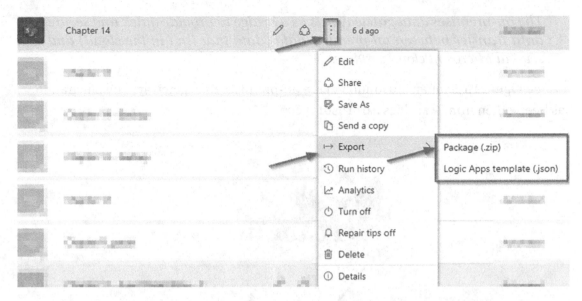

Figure 15-4. *Exporting flows*

As mentioned in the introduction, Power Automate flows are a simplified version of Azure Logic Apps. Azure Logic Apps can offer a richer design experience, higher level of scalability, and even potential cost savings depending on your flow subscription plan and the current design of your flow. In Figure 15-4, one of the export options available was the `Logic Apps template (.json)`. Exporting a flow as a Logic Apps template will create an ARM template that can then be deployed to Azure Logic Apps.

Note   The following link provides step-by-step instructions for deploying an ARM template: `https://flow.microsoft.com/en-us/blog/grow-up-to-logic-apps/`.

On-Premises Data Gateway
What Is a Data Gateway?

The data gateway is the mechanism used by the Microsoft public cloud service for accessing data in your on-prem private network; this enables hybrid deployment-type scenarios where not all data is required to live in the cloud to be relevant or accessible. The following is the official data gateway description via Microsoft Docs:

The on-premises data gateway acts as a bridge to provide quick and secure data transfer between on-premises data (data that isn't in the cloud) and several Microsoft cloud services.

See Figure 15-5 for an illustration of the on-premises data gateway. The illustration has been taken from www.docs.microsoft.com.

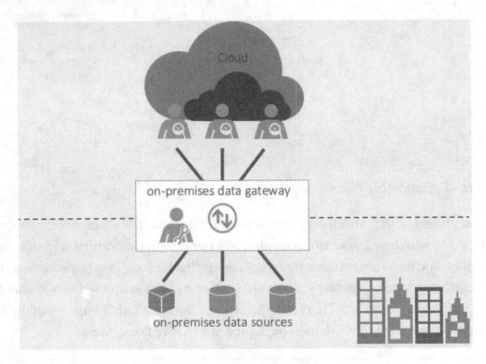

Figure 15-5. *Accepting conditions of adding owners*

Data Gateway Setup and Installation

When installing the on-premises data gateway, there are two modes available; these modes are the enterprise and personal modes. The personal mode only works for Power BI and is limited to a single individual. As a best practice, it is strongly recommended that organizations install the enterprise data gateway. The following is a list of advantages that the enterprise gateway provides, and these features are not available when installing the gateway using the personal mode:

- Installs a stand-alone gateway or multiple gateways in a cluster for high availability

- Can be shared and reused by multiple users, simplifying administration

- Can be used by Power BI, Power Automate, and Power Apps

- Supports Schedule refresh and Live queries for Power BI

When installing the data gateway, there is a list of minimum requirements and recommended requirements. Both are listed as follows:

Minimum Requirements

- .NET Framework 4.6 (Gateway release August 2019 and earlier)

- .NET Framework 4.7.2 (Gateway release September 2019 and later)

- A 64-bit version of Windows 8 or a 64-bit version of Windows Server 2012 R2

Recommended

- An 8-core CPU

- 8 GB of memory

- A 64-bit version of Windows Server 2012 R2 or later

- Solid-state drive (SSD) storage for spooling.

There are certain requirements when installing a data gateway:

- Installed on a Server, not personal laptop

- 64-bit machine

- Only one gateway per machine

The installation and setup of the data gateway is generally a pretty smooth and straightforward process; however, there are some complications that can arise, and it's recommended that your network team perform the installation and configuration or be present during this process. The actual process of installing a data gateway is not covered in this book; however, Microsoft has provided a thorough walkthrough online. See the following link for guidance:

```
https://docs.microsoft.com/en-us/data-integration/gateway/service-gateway-install
```

Note   To further assist in this process, Microsoft has provided documentation for troubleshooting as well as an FAQ page. For convenience purposes, both links have been provided as follows.

Troubleshooting the data gateway:

`https://docs.microsoft.com/en-us/data-integration/gateway/service-gateway-tshoot`

FAQs:

`docs.microsoft.com/en-us/data-integration/gateway/service-gateway-onprem-faq`

Data Gateway Configuration

Once the data gateway has been installed, Power Automate can leverage the data gateway to connect to on-prem data sources. The data gateway will automatically appear in Power Automate when creating new connections to on-prem data sources.

Note   The data gateway will only appear to users who have been added as administrators to the data gateway.

In this example, an action to create a file on a local file system has been added to the workflow. To create a new connection, `click the ellipsis (...)` and then select `+ Add new connection` from the drop-down as demonstrated in Figure 15-6.

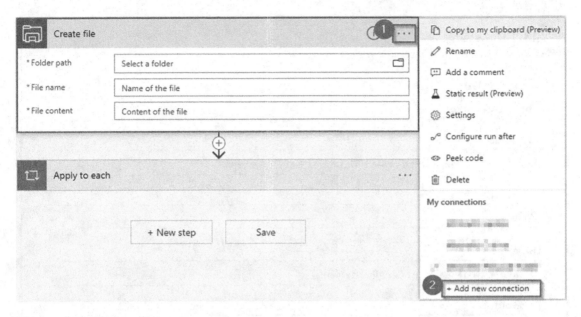

Figure 15-6. *Creating new connections*

A new screen is opened for creating the new connection. The screen provides a list of configurable features; most importantly, at the bottom of this list is a drop-down list where the data gateway can be selected (see Figure 15-7). The data gateway is required when connecting to on-premises networks, and if a data gateway does not appear in the drop-down list, then a data gateway needs to be installed, or you do not have access to create new connections on an existing gateway.

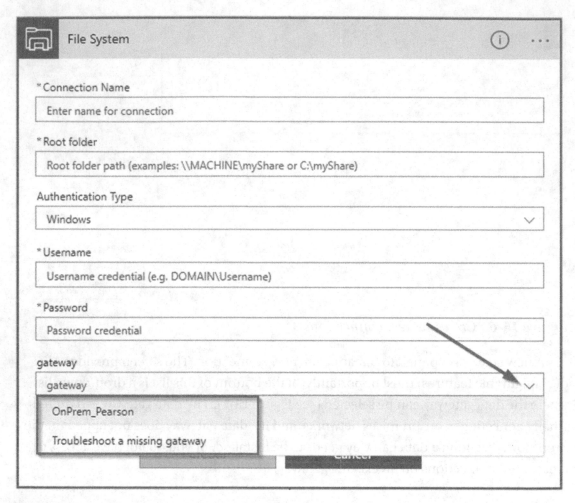

Figure 15-7. *Creating a new connection*

High-Availability Clusters and Load Balancing

As mentioned previously in this chapter, only one data gateway may be installed on a single machine; however, multiple data gateways can be installed on a network. By installing multiple data gateways on the network, a strategy can be implemented that employs high availability and load balancing.

High availability provides durability and consistency of your applications. For example, if one server were to go unresponsive for any reason, the traffic can be routed to another server with a data gateway installed, ensuring that single point of failure does not derail the process.

Another important aspect of a gateway cluster is the ability to implement load balancing. By default, gateways in a cluster are chosen at random when requests are made to access on-prem data. However, a gateway admin can configure the gateway cluster to perform load balancing based on CPU and memory thresholds. Please refer to the following Microsoft documentation to learn more about the setup and configuration of gateway clusters:

https://docs.microsoft.com/en-us/data-integration/gateway/service-gateway-high-availability-clusters

Try It Out

Unlike previous sections, this will be a quick "Try It Out" section. In this section, you will export the flow from Chapter 14, so that you will have a version history to revert to if necessary. Like previous chapters, the following items are required:

- Power Automate account

- SharePoint list created previously

    - (https://<your company>.sharepoint.com)

- Email account required (www.outlook.com)

Lesson Requirements

In this lesson, you will work from the workflow created in Chapter 14.

1. First, select the ellipsis for the flow named Chapter 14 and select export ➤ Package (.zip); see Figure 15-4 for reference.

2. Exporting a package as a .zip file will provide a new screen of configurable options. There are two categories for configuration.

3. The first category is Package Details, and this is where you configure the name and description. First, provide a name; this can be the same name as the current flow. The name of the zip file, once exported, will be the current flow name along with a date and timestamp appended to the name.

4. Next, give it a description that is representative of the current design and configuration.

The second category is `Review Package Content`, and this is where the flow and the connections are configured. There are two decisions to make for each resource type. The first is would you like to add any comments, and the second is will this be a new item or an update. For version control, this would be an `update` as these flows are imported back into the same environment; however, if moving to a new environment, then the configuration would be `create as new`. See Figures 15-8 and 15-9.

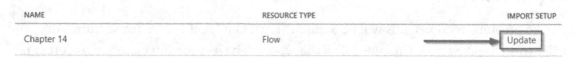

NAME	RESOURCE TYPE	IMPORT SETUP
Chapter 14	Flow	Update

Figure 15-8. *Export setup*

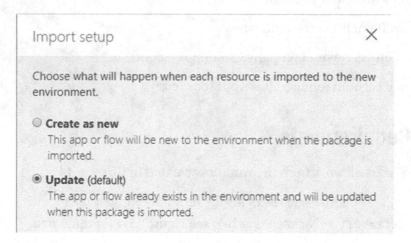

Figure 15-9. *Choosing Create as new or Update*

5. Choose the defaults for the section review package content and then select Export.

6. Choosing export downloads a zip file to the local machine. This zip file contains all the necessary information about the flow, and therefore, that version of the flow has been saved and can be imported in the future if necessary!

PART III

Dashboards, Reporting, and Analytics with Power BI

CHAPTER 16

Introduction to Power BI

Power BI has been around since 2014, and before that, there was growing popularity using the "Power" features within Excel to analyze our organization's data. Years later, Power BI finds itself on the top tier of data visualization tools, and if you go by the Gartner report, it is the number 1 tool! Power BI gives users the capability to import data from a variety of different sources. From there, we can take advantage of features to clean and massage the data to our needs. Once this is done, we can then model and leverage visuals to deliver impactful messages to our end users by sharing reports. In this chapter, we will explore who should be using Power BI, how to subscribe to the service, and get a brief overview of the desktop tool.

What Is Power BI?

Power BI is a collection of software applications, connectors, and apps that allows users to bring data together in order to get a better understanding of that data by analyzing trends and patterns via robust visualizations. It allows access to many different data sources and has the capability to clean up that data if necessary. Throughout the following chapters, we will be using the Power BI Desktop tool to create reports from data and then using the Power BI service to share those reports with other users in, or possibly outside, our organization.

Power BI Desktop

This is the free application that can be downloaded and installed to create Power BI reports. It is within this interface that we can choose what sources we want to connect to and possibly transform or clean the data if required. It is also here where we can combine data sources together which is often referred to as data modeling. The ability

173

© Mitchell Pearson, Brian Knight, Devin Knight, Manuel Quintana 2020
M. Pearson et al., *Pro Microsoft Power Platform*, https://doi.org/10.1007/978-1-4842-6008-1_16

to create visualizations from our newly modeled data can be accomplished within this application but also from the Power BI service. It is quite common for most users to use the Power BI Desktop tool to create visuals and primarily use the Power BI service to share reports with other users. It is important to understand that there are two versions of the Power BI Desktop application; we will discuss them here:

- **Power BI Desktop Optimized for Cloud Service** – This is the application we will be using throughout this book for our examples. This version is meant for creating reports which will utilize the most up-to-date features available within the Power BI service. It should be noted that there are two options for download for this version. The first is that you can go to the Microsoft download page, then install the program on your desired Windows machine. This option will require you to manually update the application when new versions are released. The second option is to visit the Microsoft App Store and install the program from there. By using this method, the Microsoft App Store will manage the updates automatically and update the product when a new release is available. At the end of this chapter, we will walk through the process of downloading and installing Power BI Desktop. One of the biggest items that differentiates these two versions of the tool is the one optimized for the Cloud Service receives updates roughly every 3-4 weeks. Figure 16-1 shows what this version of the tool looks like at the time of this book's publishing. Notice the icon in the upper right-hand corner; it has a yellow background with the Power BI logo in black font. This is one way you can quickly tell which version of Power BI Desktop you are using.

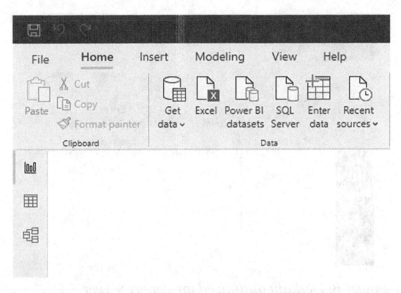

Figure 16-1. *Power BI Desktop optimized for cloud service*

- **Power BI Desktop Optimized for Report Server –** This version of the application effectively grants access to the same capabilities as the Cloud version, but its features are generally 3–4 months outdated. This version is meant for creating reports with the intent to deploy to the Power BI Report Server which is an on-premises solution. In 2019, it was announced for the first time that this version of the Power BI Desktop would receive three updates a year. These updates are scheduled for January, May, and October of every year, but this schedule is subject to change. Figure 16-2 illustrates how this version looks slightly different. You will notice that the icon in the upper-left corner has a black background and yellow font for the Power BI icon. Also, the version that is meant for Report Server always states the month and year version in the title bar.

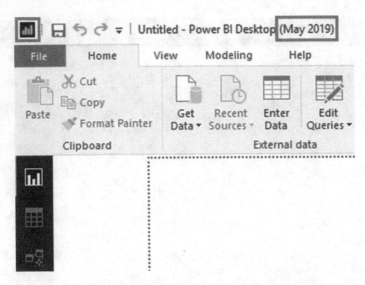

Figure 16-2. *Power BI Desktop optimized for Report Server*

Power BI Service

The Power BI service is often called Power BI online, and you may see it referenced as such throughout this guide. This part of Power BI is known as a Software as a Service (SaaS) and is where we can create workspaces, publish and share reports, create dashboards, publish apps, and schedule refreshes. In order to access the Power BI service, you will need a Power BI account. We will go over the process of acquiring an account at the end of this chapter. Figure 16-3 shows the home page of the Power BI service once logged in.

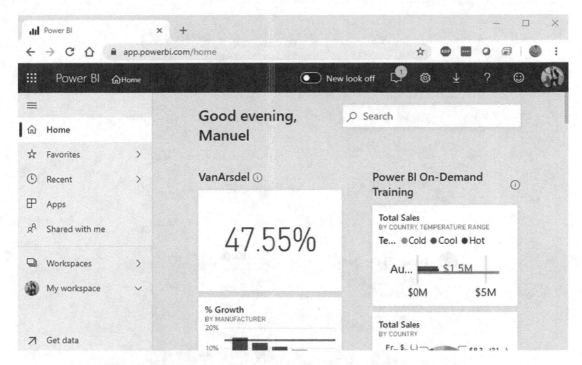

Figure 16-3. *View of the home page of Power BI service*

Workspaces

Think of workspaces as virtual directories within the Power BI service where we can store our Power BI reports along with their datasets. Workspaces are also the places where we can collaborate with other report creators and share our reports with users. There are various roles and permissions available within workspaces, and we will cover these later in the guide. Workspaces are also the location where we can create dashboards as well as apps. Figure 16-4 showcases the various items that comprise a workspace as well as where you can see all workspaces you have either created or have been invited to.

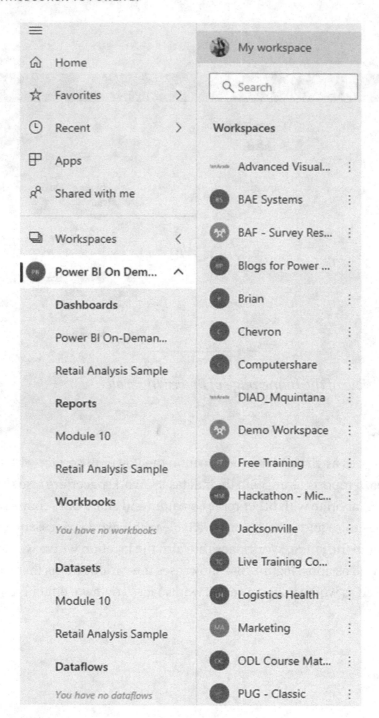

Figure 16-4. *The various areas of a workspace*

Reports and Datasets

When you deploy a report from the Power BI Desktop, it is separated into two parts, the report and its dataset. The report contains all the pages and visualizations that make up the report. The dataset is the finalized model that the report is dependent on. It should be noted that once a dataset has been published to the Power BI service, users can connect to it like any other data source as long as they have been granted access. Figure 16-5 shows the option that is available from the Power BI Desktop. This source requires you to be logged in to your Power BI account to be able to see all accessible datasets.

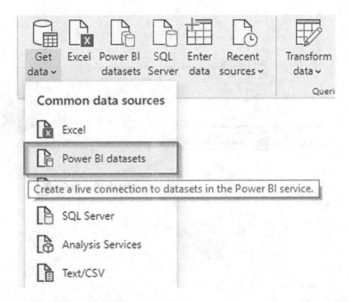

Figure 16-5. *This option allows you to use any dataset published to the Power BI service*

Dashboards

Dashboards are a feature only available to the Power BI service and allow users in a workspace to pin visuals from reports to a single page. Because dashboards are only a single page, they are meant to give highlights relating to the detailed information held in the reports from that same workspace. Dashboards are meant to serve as entryways to the other reports available within the workspace that the dashboard was created in.

A dashboard has no limitation on the number of visuals that can be pinned from various reports. Moreover, you can create as many dashboards as you would like. Figure 16-6 shows an example of a dashboard in which you can see that each visual is represented as a "tile" which can be resized. The default behavior upon selecting a tile is to take the user to the underlying report which contains the visual.

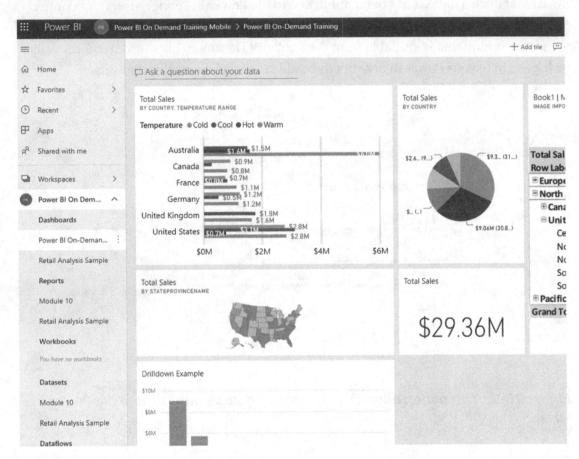

Figure 16-6. *Example of a dashboard with "tiles" pinned from reports*

Who Should Use Power BI?

Power BI is known as a self-service or personal BI solution. These sets of tools should be used by business analysts who understand the business and have a subset of skills with technology. This idea of allowing business users to access data and create visuals began with Excel and the "Power" add-on features and now continues with Power BI. These individuals should be subject matter experts and know where the data resides that needs to be analyzed. The only real involvement that is required by the IT department is in the process of granting access to the relevant sources. Once permission has been granted, these business analysts can start to bring their data into the Power BI model and create visualizations that deliver impactful messages to the consumers of the data.

Subscribing to Power BI

When it comes to using the Power BI tools, a Power BI account is only needed for certain features which we will talk about in this section. Regarding the Power BI Desktop tool, no account is needed, and the basic features can be used indefinitely for free. The only times you will be required to log in to your Power BI account is when you are attempting to access the custom visual marketplace, or you would like to deploy a report to the Power BI service. The Power BI service is quite the opposite. The first thing you must do when wanting to explore the service is to log in to your Power BI account.

When it comes to Power BI accounts, there are two options available for users. We will talk about these options in the context of users who are part of a larger organization leveraging the Power BI tools. The two different options are a Power BI Free account and a Power BI Pro account; we will break down the differences in the following.

Power BI Free Account

This type of account allows users to connect to 70+ data sources. You can use the publish to web option (more on this later), and you can export to Excel. Users are also not limited to the visualizations they can choose from which is quite fantastic. The Free account falls short though when you need to share your report with others through the Power BI service and want to create a workspace. The bottom line is that if you are just looking to do your own analysis and don't need to share with other users, then the Free account will work for you.

Power BI Pro Account

The main reason for needing a Pro account is so that you can share data with other users within your organization. It is important to note that the users you are sharing your report with also need to have Pro accounts. Individuals who have Power BI Pro licenses can also create workspaces to organize their reports and create dashboards. Figure 16-7 quickly showcases the differences between Free and Pro licenses. The cost of a Pro license starts at $9.99 per month.

	Free	Pro
Connect to 70+ data sources	✓	✓
Publish to Web	✓	✓
Export to PowerPoint, Excel, CSV	✓	✓
Enterprise distribution		
Apps	✗	✓
Email subscriptions	✗	✓
Embed APIs and controls	✗	✓
Collaboration		
Peer-to-peer sharing	✗	✓
App workspaces	✗	✓
Analyze in Excel, analyze in Power BI Desktop	✗	✓

Figure 16-7. *A quick comparison between a Power BI Free and Pro account*

Power BI Premium

There is another option available to organizations when looking to license many users for Power BI, and it is known as Power BI Premium. Organizations that do not have Power BI Premium use the Cloud service in what is called a multitenant environment. This means that there are a specific number of computational resources within the Power BI Cloud service, and these are shared between different organizations. So, without Power BI Premium, multiple organizations share the same pool of resources within the Cloud Service. Power BI Premium, or "Dedicated Capacity," removes this multitenant environment and gives the organization access to its own private pool of computational resources. There are many more benefits granted when an organization opts into purchasing Power BI Premium, but the current cheapest option will run you $4995 a month! We will talk more about Power BI Premium later in this guide.

Exploring the Power BI Desktop

We have already discussed how the Power BI Desktop is used to create our Power BI reports. This is the interface where we collect data, clean up that data, model it, and create visualizations that showcase trends and patterns within that data. In this section, we will break down some of the core areas within this desktop application so that you start to feel more comfortable using the tool.

There are really two areas to talk about when using this tool, the Power BI Desktop and the Power Query Editor. The Power BI Desktop can be split into three main parts: the Report View, the Data View, and the Model View. Figure 16-8 indicates which icons within the Power BI Desktop represent each view.

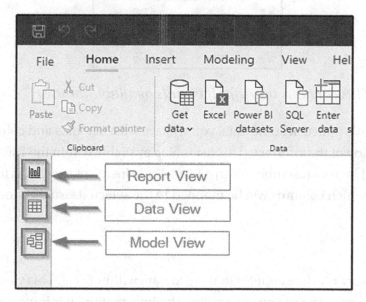

Figure 16-8. *Each of these areas allows for different tasks to be accomplished*

Each of these views allows report creators different pieces of functionality depending on their needs. You can also see from Figure 16-8 that the options available to report creators are held within the ribbons available for selection near the top of the tool. Here we can find the Home, View, Modeling, and Help ribbons. These ribbons contain different pieces of functionality, and depending on what View we are in, these options will change or disappear entirely. Let's take the time to break down the various areas mentioned earlier.

Report View

This is the default view when you start a new Power BI report, and it is where you choose which visualizations you would like to use. It is here where we see the main canvas area for deciding the layout for the visuals we have selected. The Report View also shows (see Figure 16-9) the available visualizations.

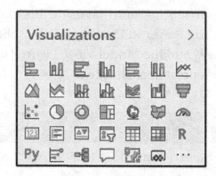

Figure 16-9. *This contains the default visuals available for use*

Once you have pulled in some data, you will see a list of tables and columns on the far right-hand side of the interface. This list is also available within the Data View and Model View and bears a resemblance to a Pivot Table inside of Excel. It is from this list that we choose which columns will be mapped to the selected visualization.

Data View

The Data View very much resembles looking at data within Excel. This view allows you to filter and sort your data so you can explore the information. It is important to note that any filtering done here will not impact any of your visualizations. It is also best practice to use the Data View when creating calculated columns to validate your code. As you can see in Figure 16-10, the Data View offers very simple options but can be very helpful when needing to explore the data to become more familiar with it.

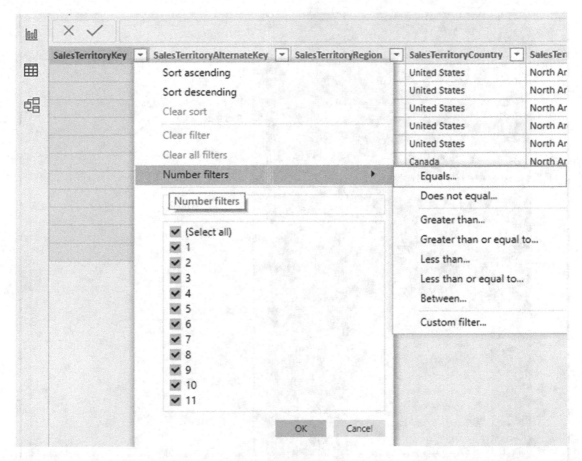

Figure 16-10. *Different filter options will appear depending on a column's data type*

Model View

The last view within the Power BI Desktop is the Model View. It is here where we can view, edit, delete, and create relationships between tables. Users also have the capability of creating new layout windows to narrow down their view of the model. This is a wonderful function if you want to just focus on a few tables within a very complex model. Also, as you can see in Figure 16-11, there is easy access to modify properties for one or multiple columns at the same time.

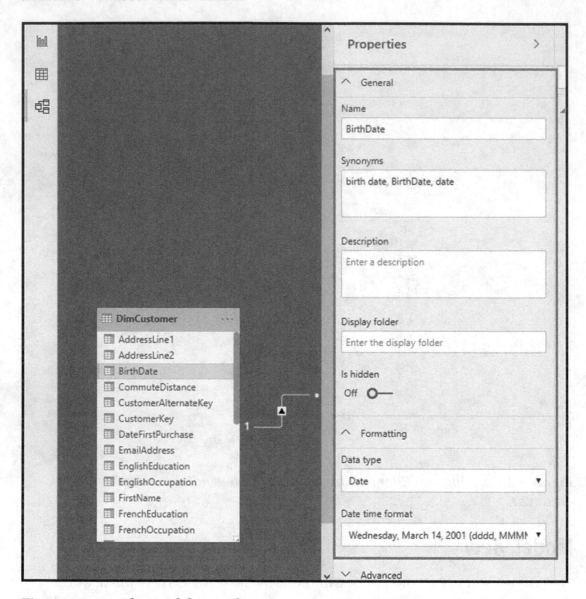

Figure 16-11. *The model provides an easy way to modify properties for multiple columns at one time*

Power Query Editor

The last area we will discuss in the chapter is the Power Query Editor. This area is accessible in two ways. The first is when connecting to a data source, a user can choose the "Transform Data" option to launch the Power Query Editor as an additional Power BI screen. Figure 16-12 shows this option which will be available every time a user connects to a new data source.

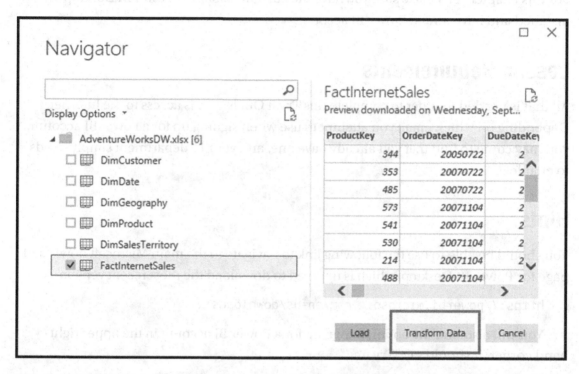

Figure 16-12. *Click Transform Data to access the Power Query Editor*

The second way to access the Power Query Editor is through the "Edit Queries" option that you can find within the Home ribbon. The Power Query Editor is where users will come across the M-query language, which is what Power BI uses to apply any and all changes a user decides to make against a dataset. All the changes and modifications that a user performs against their dataset will be seen in an area known as the "Applied Steps" which can be found on the far right side when looking at the Power Query Editor. Once a user decides that their dataset meets their standards for quality, they can select the "Close and Apply" option which is found within the Home ribbon. This action will close the Power Query Editor and return to the Power BI Desktop. It will also bring in all the data into the data model considering all of the steps the user defined while in the Power Query Editor. There are many data cleansing features within the Power Query Editor, and users should take advantage of these as much as possible.

Try It Out

For this chapter, let's make sure you have the current version of Power BI Desktop installed and have a valid Power BI account.

Lesson Requirements

All that is needed in order to complete this Try It Out lesson is access to the Internet. Depending on which email you attempt to use when signing up for a Power BI account, you may come to find that you already have one, and your IT department simply needs to enable it.

Hints

You should be able to use the following link to navigate to the main Microsoft download page for Power BI Desktop, which is updated to download the most recent version:

https://powerbi.microsoft.com/en-us/downloads/

You will also find the option to sign up for a Power BI account in the upper right-hand corner; it should say "Try free."

Step by Step

Follow the steps in this section to sign up for a Power BI account in the cloud. Here's what to do:

1. Open the preceding URL and choose the download option for the Microsoft Power BI Desktop product.

2. This should prompt you to open the Microsoft Store.

3. Once there, you should see an option to Install the product, and by following this method, the Microsoft Store will automatically update the tool.

4. If, for some reason, you cannot take advantage of the Microsoft Store option, then you can choose the "Advanced download options" selection.

5. This will take you to a download page where you can download the executable for the product and install it locally on your machine. Following this method will require you to manually update the tool whenever there is a new release.

6. The last step is choosing the "Try free" option in order to set up an account if you do not already have one.

7. On the webpage it directed you to, locate the "Start free trial" option, and it will ask you to input your email address. If you are using your company email address, there is a chance you already have an account. If you do have an account, a message will appear telling you so.

8. With all these steps complete, you should have an updated version of Power BI Desktop and a Power BI account, which means we are ready for anything!

Summary

Power BI is a powerful tool that allows a deep analysis of your data and has the ability to display your findings in meaningful ways. It also provides quick, safe, and easy ways to share the reports you have created with users inside or outside your organization. By using Power BI Desktop, you can take advantage of all the various data source connectors, tap into a plethora of data cleansing features, and choose from a robust collection of data visualizations. After developing a report that you know your end users will love, you can then leverage the Power BI service to deploy your report and easily share it with our organization.

In the next chapter, we will look at the many options we have for connecting to data. We will also look at how best to configure the options that we want to use.

CHAPTER 17

Connecting to Data

Every Power BI report must start with bringing data into our model. Power BI itself has over 80 different connectors that allow users to bring data in from databases, files, cloud resources, and many more. When connecting to some of these sources, you may be presented with various methods on how that connection should be established which will have significant impacts on your report. In this chapter, we will explore some of the various connectors available to users within Power BI and the additional options available depending on the connector chosen. It should also be noted that new connectors are added quite frequently to the tool over time. There is also an option to create your own custom connector which will be discussed briefly in this chapter.

Available Connectors

There are over 80 different connectors available to users inside of Power BI, and this list continues to grow to provide more and more options. You can see a list of the available connectors at the following location: `https://docs.microsoft.com/en-us/power-bi/ desktop-data-sources`. To access the list of connectors, you have two options when working within the Power BI Desktop. The first is illustrated in Figure 17-1 with the red arrow. By selecting the **Get Data** button label or the down arrow, users will be presented with the **Most Common** connectors. Users should be aware that this list does not change based on the frequency in which an individual uses certain connectors. This list of the most commonly used connectors is set by the Power BI team.

© Mitchell Pearson, Brian Knight, Devin Knight, Manuel Quintana 2020
M. Pearson et al., *Pro Microsoft Power Platform*, https://doi.org/10.1007/978-1-4842-6008-1_17

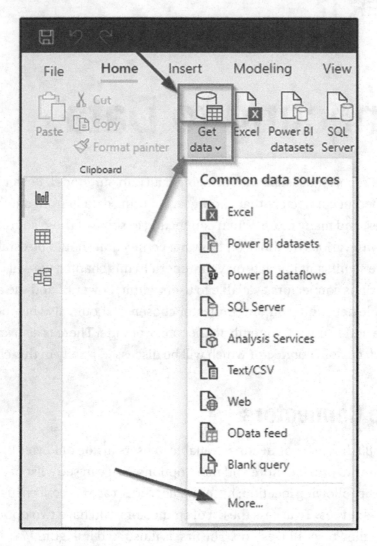

Figure 17-1. *List of the Most Common data sources*

The second method allows users to access the entire list of connectors and not just the **Most Common** list. In Figure 17-1, you will see that there are two blue arrows; choosing either of these options will bring you to the main **Get Data** dialog box which is shown in Figure 17-2. This dialog box has various categories for organizing the plethora of connectors. Next, we will look further into the details for these various categories.

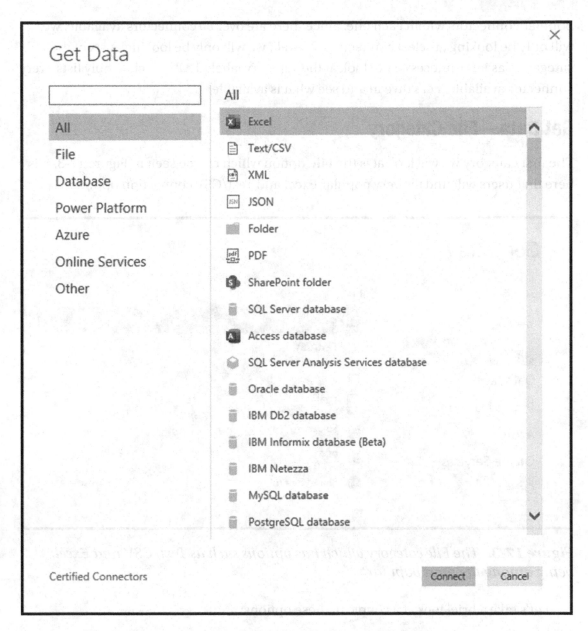

Figure 17-2. Primary Get Data dialog box with various categories

Get Data

At the time of writing this chapter, there are currently seven different categories, as seen in Figure 17-2, used for organizing the various connectors available to report creators. In the following sections, we will look at these various categories and focus on the more popular connectors within each one. Since there are over 80 connectors available, we will only be looking at select connectors. As well, we will only be looking at six of the categories as it is unnecessary to look at the category labeled **All**, which simply lists every connector available. Let's dive in and see what is available.

Get Data – File Category

The first category we will look at is the **File** option which can be seen in Figure 17-3. It is here that users will find the very popular Excel and Text/CSV connection options.

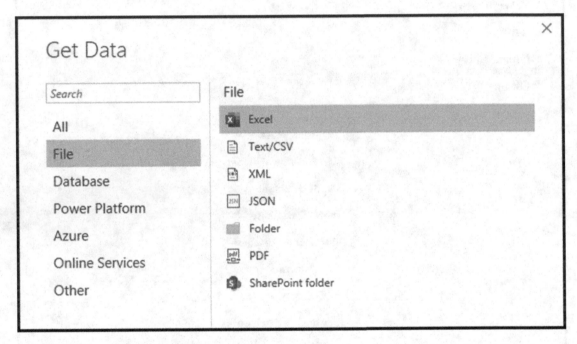

Figure 17-3. *The File category which has options such as Text/CSV and Excel being among the most popular*

Let's take a brief look at a couple of these options:

- **Excel** – When choosing this option, the user will be prompted with a file explorer to navigate in order to select the file to connect to. Once you have chosen the Excel workbook you would like to extract data from, the user will be brought to the **Navigator** experience. It is here that users will see available worksheets as well as formatted tables within the workbook. Each of these items is denoted by different icons, and a user can select as many of these objects as they would like to load into Power BI.

- **Text/CSV** – Similar to the Excel connector, when this option is selected, the user will be prompted with a file explorer in order to select the file that the user wants to load into Power BI. Unlike the Excel connector, the user will not go through the **Navigator** experience. Instead, they will see a preview of the data inside the file and have options to modify the delimiter being used. Power BI will automatically detect the delimiter, so this option is usually not needed to be modified.

- **Folder** – This option also brings up a file explorer where users are prompted to select the folder they would like to load into Power BI. Once a folder is selected, all files in the folder are evaluated as well as any in subdirectories. The user is then presented with a unique option known as **Combine Binaries**; this will be covered in a later chapter. The thing to understand is that this option allows you to combine multiple files from one location into a single table.

Get Data – Database Category

Next on the list, we have our Database category which can mostly be seen in Figure 17-4. There are quite a few more options in this category, so we will only be able to look at a couple. Regardless of the connection you are choosing, users will need to know the server's address and provide credentials that have access to the source.

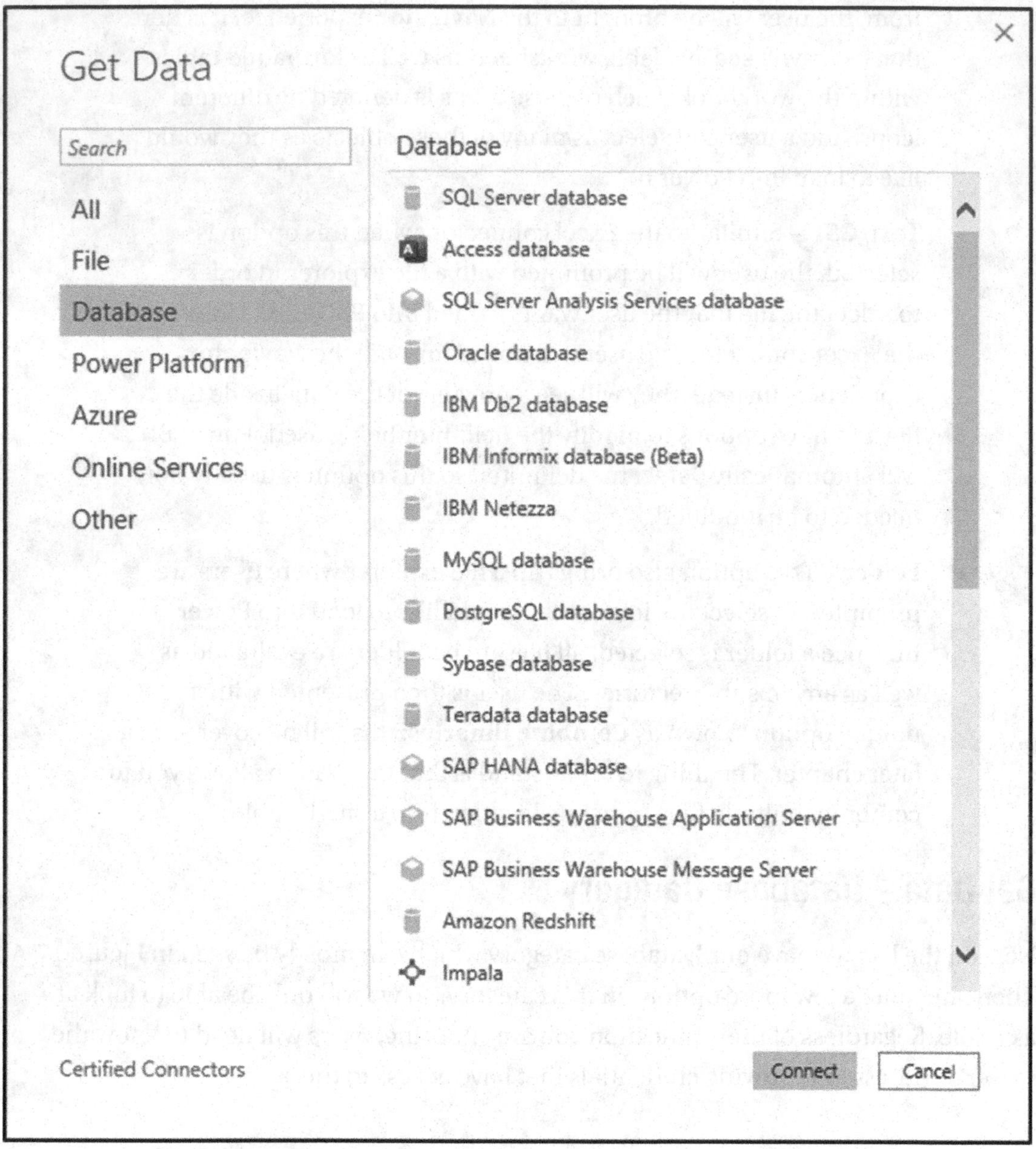

Figure 17-4. *The Database option provides access to many different database platforms such as SQL, Teradata, and Oracle*

Now let's explore a couple of available options:

- **SQL Server** – When connecting to SQL Server, users must provide the server address and optionally may provide a Database name. There is also a choice between **Import** and **DirectQuery**, which we will cover later in this chapter. Users will also find the ability to input a SQL query by expanding the **Advanced options** section. The next step is to provide credentials. Here, users will have the option between Windows, Database, and a Microsoft account. Depending on your setup, simply choose which option suits you, and you will have the ability to navigate through your SQL Server objects and choose which tables, views, or functions you would like to bring into Power BI.

- **SQL Server Analysis Services Database** – Just like the SQL Server connection, users must specify the SSAS server name and optionally define the Database. Once again, there is a decision to be made, but this time it is between **Import** and **Connect Live**; do not worry as this will be covered later in this chapter. For now, let's move forward with the **Import** option selected which will then provide you with the option on how you would like to connect. Once you have provided the correct credentials, you will be able to navigate your SSAS server and choose what you would like to bring into Power BI. This supports either a Multidimensional or Tabular model.

Get Data – Power Platform Category

All the Power Platform options are tied to the Power BI service in some way, and some require additional licensing options that go beyond just Power BI, so this will limit what we will cover at this point in the material. You will see the list of options in Figure 17-5, and we will only talk about Power BI datasets for now.

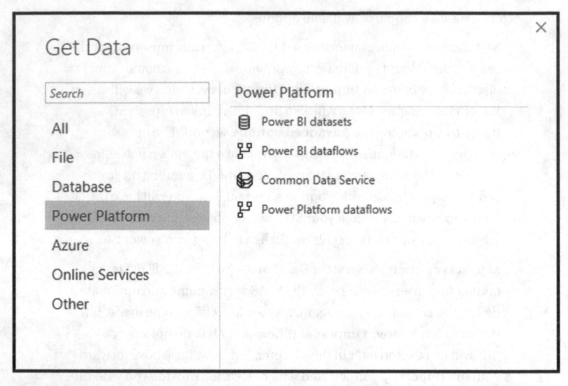

Figure 17-5. *There are limited options here, but all of them relate to the Power BI service in some way*

The one option we'll focus on for now is the following:

- **Power BI Datasets** – The idea behind Power BI datasets is that they are shared datasets that exist in the Power BI service that the organization can connect to. When you choose this connector, it will require the user to log in using their Power BI credentials. Then you will be presented with a list of available datasets from the Power BI service. Access to these datasets is controlled within the Power BI service, and it should be noted that when you create this connection, it is treated as a **Live Connection**, more on this later!

Get Data – Azure Category

With cloud storage and services becoming more and more popular, it only makes sense that Power BI would have quite a few options when it comes to connecting to Azure. As you will see in Figure 17-6, Power BI offers many different options for connecting to data stored in various Azure services.

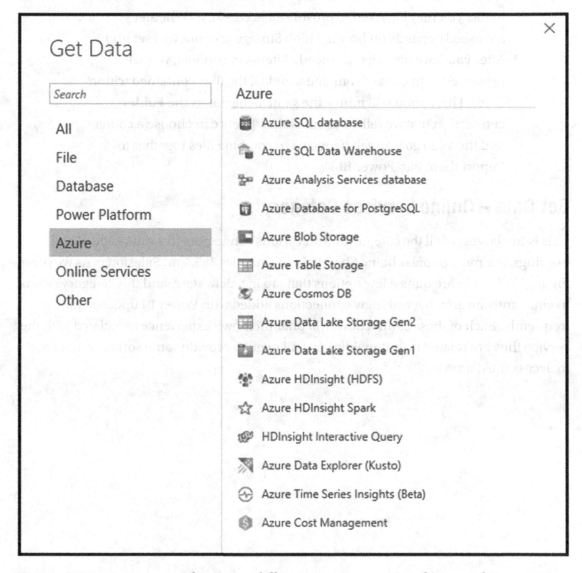

Figure 17-6. *Azure provides many different services to store data, and Power BI ensures that we can extract that data*

Since we have already shown connecting to SQL Server and SSAS, let's look at Blob Storage:

- **Blog Storage** – This Azure service allows users to store unstructured data in the cloud, so think TEXT and CSV files for starters. When you choose this connection, you will be asked to provide the account name or URL for the Blob account. Once the connection has been made, you may be asked to provide an access key. (Whether you are asked depends on how the Blob Storage account was set up.) After you have provided the needed items to connect, you will be presented with a list of containers and all the files contained within them. This option will mimic the same behavior as the **Folder** connection that we talked about earlier. Users can choose a container and then can go through a process to combine files together to import them into Power BI.

Get Data – Online Services Category

This is the largest of all the categories with various connectors to a multitude of online offerings, the most popular being SharePoint, Dynamics 365, and Salesforce. As we see in Figure 17-7, there are quite a few options that are in a Beta state, and this category seems to constantly be growing with new connections added with Power BI updates quite frequently. Each of these connections will offer their own experience associated with the service they are related to, but mainly you will need to provide some sort of credentials to access the data.

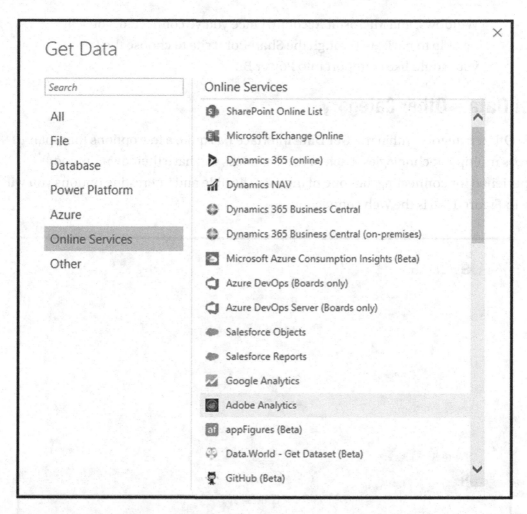

Figure 17-7. *Many different online options here, just find the service that you are looking for and start bringing in that data*

For this example, let's look at SharePoint:

- **SharePoint Online List** – You may have noticed that when we looked at the **File** category, there was an option to connect to a SharePoint folder which allows you to point to a file in a SharePoint library. The SharePoint Online List allows you to navigate through your SharePoint site and pull data directly from a SharePoint list. When this connection is selected, users will need to provide the root URL for the SharePoint site. Then you will need to provide the correct form of credentials, choosing between the options of Anonymous,

Windows, and Microsoft Account. Once you've connected, you will be able to navigate through the SharePoint site to choose the Lists you would like to import into Power BI.

Get Data – Other Category

The Other category within the **Get Data** interface has quite a few options that span across multiple technologies. Each of these choices will have their own unique experience for connecting, but one of the most flexible and interesting options you will see in Figure 17-8 is the Web connection.

Figure 17-8. *Many different options are presented here with quite a few being in a Beta state. This is another section that does seem to get quite frequent updates*

Let's take a quick tour around the Web connection:

- **Web** – This connection is quite versatile in bringing in data from a website. A user simply inputs the desired URL and then may be asked how to connect to the web content. The options here include Anonymous, Windows, Basic, Web API, and Organizational account. If you are connecting to a public URL, then the Anonymous option will most likely be the right choice. After making this decision, Power BI will present any available tables that can be read from the website and preview that to the user. If no option is available that matches what you are looking for, there is a powerful option known as **Add Table Using Examples** available which can help in telling Power BI what information you would like extracted. We will look at a similar feature in a later chapter.

Import

Now that we have covered quite a few connectors available to us within Power BI, let's take a closer look at how that data is brought into Power BI. The most common method of bringing data into Power BI is known as **Import**. When you are connecting to any source and you do not see an option between **Import** and something else, then Power BI will be using the **Import** option by default except for some of the Power Platform connectors which automatically use the **Live Connection** option which will be discussed later. Other options like SQL Server will offer something known as **DirectQuery** which will also be covered later in this chapter.

Any source that is using the **Import** option means that we are effectively downloading all the information from that source and storing it inside of what is known as the Power BI model. Users do have the ability to filter what data is brought from the source, and this is accomplished inside of the Power Query Editor which will be covered in a later chapter. The important thing to note is that **Importing** data into a Power BI report will directly affect the size of that report, and there are limitations around how large a report can be in relation to publishing to the Power BI service. This limitation can vary depending on what type of Power BI solution your organization is paying for, so it is important to research these limitations as they do change over time.

Another important thing about **Importing** data into Power BI is that it gives you full access to the **Power Query Editor** as well as full functionality of the **DAX** language which we will be looking at more in depth in a later chapter. In Figure 17-9, you will see an example of the SQL Server connection which offers a choice between using the **Import** option or the **DirectQuery** option. In contrast, if we explore the Excel connector, we are never presented with a choice which means that the data will use the **Import** option.

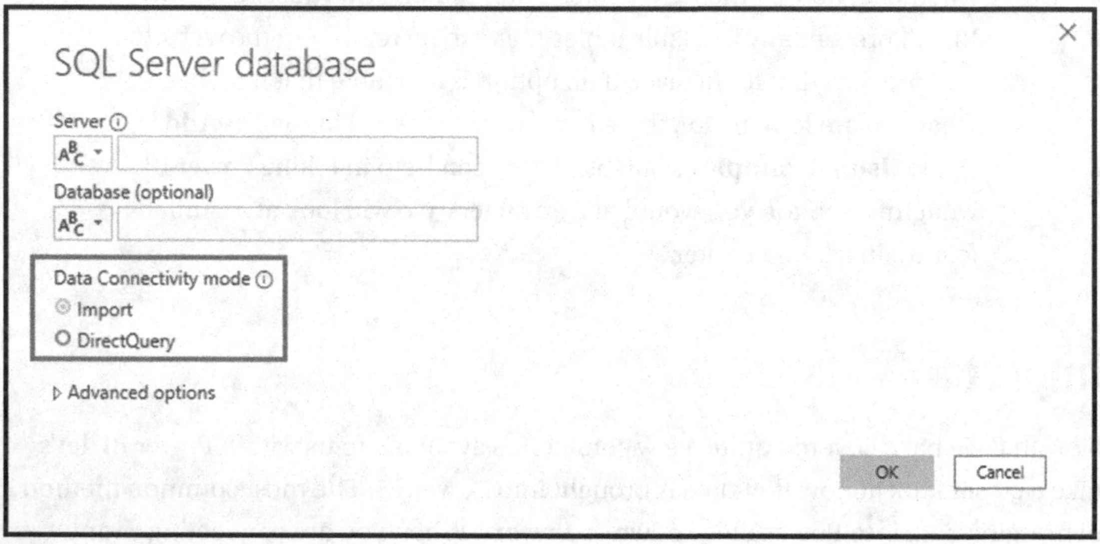

Figure 17-9. *We have a choice when using the SQL Server connector between Import and DirectQuery. Options that do not present this choice mainly will use Import by default*

DirectQuery

As described in the previous section, **DirectQuery** is an option for certain sources such as SQL Server, Oracle, and other various Database sources. Upon choosing one of these sources from the **Get Data** menu, you will be presented with the radial options as seen in Figure 17-9. There are quite a few differences between **Importing** data and using **DirectQuery**; one of the biggest is that a Power BI report that is using a **DirectQuery** connection stores no data within the file. When using the **DirectQuery** option, you effectively have an open connection with the source system to bring in whatever data is being requested by the visualizations in your report. Depending on those requests, there can be some negative impacts. Let us first look at the potential benefits of using **DirectQuery**:

- DirectQuery can let you work with much larger datasets where importing is not an option.

- There is no need to set up a scheduled refresh for your Power BI reports as they will always be looking at the most current data from the source.

Along with these benefits, there are some limitations that users should be aware as well:

- Some options are unavailable within the Power Query Editor, so certain data cleansing options with Power BI are unavailable.

- Certain DAX capabilities are limited such as Time Intelligence; this will be covered in a later chapter.

There are other considerations that should be considered when deciding whether to use **DirectQuery** or not such as performance. Because we are constantly making requests from the source system from our visuals in the Power BI report, we need to make sure that the source system can handle the workload. **DirectQuery** is a very important feature within Power BI, and sometimes this is the only option for certain reports because of the amount of data. It is always important to keep up to date with all potential updates that could be made to this feature as it is sure to get better with time.

Connect Live

The last method of connection we will look at is **Connect Live** which has some similarities to **DirectQuery** in that it doesn't store any data within the Power BI report; it maintains a connection with the source system. At the time of writing this chapter, the Connect Live option is only available for SQL Server Analysis Services Tabular, SQL Server Analysis Services Multidimensional, and Power BI service datasets. You can see the option in Figure 17-10 for an Analysis Services connection.

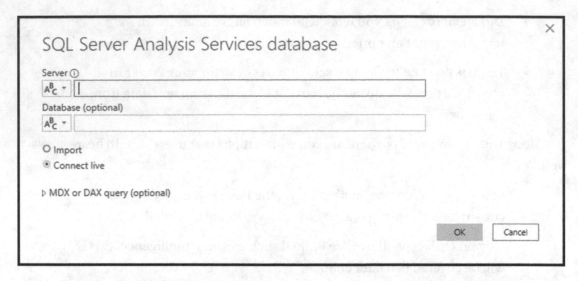

Figure 17-10. *This looks very similar to the DirectQuery option, but it is for sources of a different technology*

One major difference that will be noticed is the potential for better performance when using this option as compared to **DirectQuery** because of the nature of the underlying sources. With that being said, let us look at some benefits of using **Connect Live**:

- The source options you will use this with have the capability of intuitive change control with something like Team Foundation Services.

- A centralized enterprise model which can be used by the organization.

- Some great built-in security features that come with Analysis Services.

There are some other benefits, but like mentioned before, this is a topic that you need to stay up to date with as Power BI will surely be updating the capability of this feature over time. Now let us look at potential limitations:

- The most obvious thing users will see after connecting using **Connect Live** is that there is no longer a **Data View** or a **Model View**. We are effectively placing all the data shaping needs on the source system, which means users will not have access to the Power Query Editor.

- If you connect to a source with this type of connection, you cannot add any additional sources. This might be one of the biggest limitations to **Connect Live** that **DirectQuery** does not have to suffer, but we may see this go away in time using a similar remedy as they have for **DirectQuery**.

Between all these connection types, there is always a time and place for each, so it is important to look at all your options to decide what is best. This also may change over time as your organization grows and the amount of data you are reporting on increases.

Try It Out

In this section, we will go through the process of connecting to an Excel workbook and importing data from various worksheets. In later chapters, we will build upon this dataset that we will be loading during this Try It Out lesson.

Lesson Requirements

To successfully accomplish the lesson, you will need to download the Excel workbook named AdventureWorksDW.xlsx. That file is part of this book's example download on GitHub. You can find a link to the example code from this book's catalog page on the Apress website.

You must also have access to the Power BI Desktop tool which can be downloaded here: https://powerbi.microsoft.com/en-us/desktop/.

Hints

We will be using the Excel data source option and import the data from all the worksheets. The data contained in this worksheet has been cleaned up so we will not need to access the Power Query Editor. See if you can import the data and then save your Power BI report as "Chapter 17 – Connecting to Data."

Step by Step

Time now for some step-by-step practice. Create connection to some data by executing the following steps against the example files given in the lesson requirements:

1. Open the Power BI Desktop and close out the "Getting Started" pop-up if it appears.

2. Because Excel is one of the more popular connectors, there are a few very easy ways to start the Get Data process for this. Either select the **Excel** option visible in the Home ribbon or hit the drop-down option for **Get Data** and select the option Excel from there as seen in Figure 17-11.

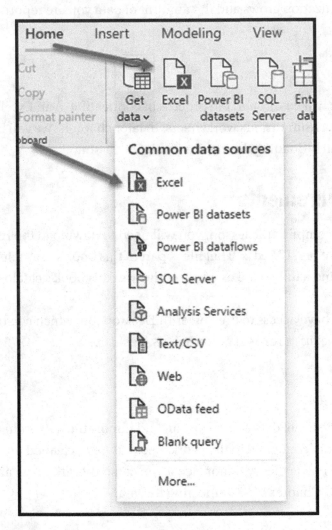

Figure 17-11. *There are three different places we can make the decision to connect to an Excel source*

3. A file explorer will appear, and you will want to navigate to the location where you downloaded the "AdventureWorksDW" Excel workbook and choose "Open."

4. The next screen you will see is called the *Navigator*. Here, you can preview the data that exists in the various worksheets. You will want to select all the worksheets as shown in Figure 17-12 and choose the "Load" option.

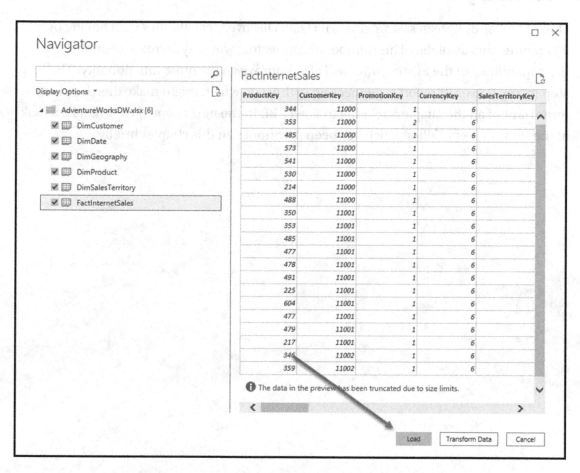

Figure 17-12. *Do not forget that the Excel connector will show any worksheets and formatted tables in the workbook*

5. After a few moments, all the data from the workbook will be loaded into the Power BI model. The final step is to save this Power BI report by choosing the save icon in the upper left of the application or from the File menu. Save the report as "Ch 17 Connecting to Data."

Summary

One of Power BI's greatest strengths is its Data Discovery capabilities with having over 80+ connectors available. This number of connectors will only increase over time, and the capabilities of the existing ones will also improve giving more functionality. The first step in any Power BI report is connecting to the data which might make this the most important of all the chapters relating to Power BI. In the next chapter, we will take a look at the Power Query Editor which has been mentioned in this chapter briefly.

CHAPTER 18

Defining Data Cleansing Business Rules with the Power Query Editor

As we saw in the previous chapter, there are many different connectors available within Power BI. Depending on what sources we are connecting to, we may run into data that needs to be cleaned up or transformed before building our reports. When this situation arises, we need to turn to the Power Query Editor to solve our data cleansing needs. In this chapter, we will take the time to explore the Power Query Editor, understand what basic transforms are at our disposal, and have a brief conversation about the M-query language.

Exploring the Power Query Editor

There are two ways to access the Power Query Editor inside of Power BI. The most organic way that users discover the Power Query Editor is when they are connecting to any data source. The last step when connecting to any data source in Power BI is to decide from one of the following three choices:

- **Load** – This option skips the Power Query Editor and loads the data in its current state into the Power BI data model. Once this process has completed, there is still a way to launch the Power Query Editor if you realize that you do need to perform some data cleansing.

© Mitchell Pearson, Brian Knight, Devin Knight, Manuel Quintana 2020
M. Pearson et al., *Pro Microsoft Power Platform*, https://doi.org/10.1007/978-1-4842-6008-1_18

- **Transform Data** – This is the option that will launch the Power Query Editor. A second window will appear, and this is where we can define our data cleansing business rules.

- **Cancel** – This option is self-explanatory and will neither load data into the Power BI data model nor launch the Power Query Editor.

The other method to launch the Power Query Editor is located within the "Home" ribbon and is labeled **Transform data** which you can see in Figure 18-1.

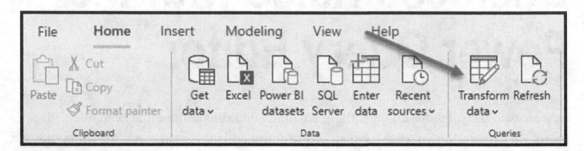

Figure 18-1. *This Transform data option allows you to launch the Power Query Editor*

This will launch the Power Query Editor in a second window, and users can start creating any business rules that they would like. The Power Query Editor has four main parts: Query Pane, Ribbon Area, Data Area, and the Query Settings. Let us take a quick look at each of these sections (see Figure 18-2 for reference):

- **Query Pane (A)** – This area will display your various queries/tables. You can only have one object in this pane selected at a time, and whatever you have selected will be shown in the Data Area (C) and the Query Settings (D).

- **Ribbon Area (B)** – This area is very similar to the ribbon area we see in the Power BI modeling side when Power BI first launches. We will be exploring the ribbon area of the modeling side of Power BI in a later chapter. The ribbon area of the Power Query Editor has various tabs which contain numerous transforms that can be used against the currently selected query.

- **Data Area (C)** – Here we will see a tabular representation of the query selected in the Query Area (A). Users can also access various transforms in this area relating to tables and columns, but all these options can also be found in the Ribbon Area (B).

- **Query Settings (D)** – This area contains an ordinal list of all the business rules that have been applied to the query selected from the Query Pane (A). This is probably the most important area of the Power Query Editor.

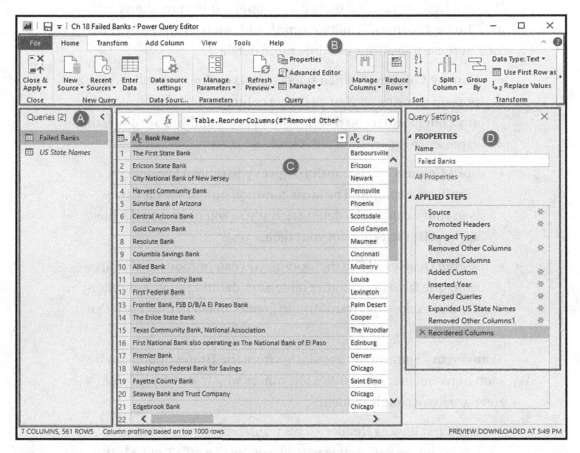

Figure 18-2. *It is always beneficial to maximize the size of this Power Query Editor window so that you do not confuse the ribbon area from this window with the ribbon area from the Power BI modeling side*

Basic Transforms

Inside of the Power Query Editor, there are too many transforms to cover in just one chapter, so we will explore some of the more commonly used options from within the Ribbon Area (B). There are seven tabs inside the Power Query Editor, each with their own transformations. Let us look at each of these tabs and a couple of their most popular transforms:

- **File** – This tab is mainly just accessed to save your Power BI report.

- **Home** – Here we can find quite a few popular transformations such as "Choose Columns," "Split Column," and "Merge Queries." Let us look at these transforms in a little more detail:

  - **Choose Columns** – When selecting this option, you will receive a pop-up showing all your available columns. You simply uncheck any columns that you do not want to keep, and you are done; this experience is very similar to Excel.

  - **Split Column** – This transform gives you quite a few options to split up a column. The most common option selected here is to split a column by delimiter, but you will need to make the appropriate selection for your data.

  - **Merge Queries** – With this option, you can introduce columns from one table into another table after defining a join condition. We will explore this transform in greater detail in the "Try It Out" section.

- **Transform** – Some of the transforms from the **Home** ribbon can be seen here, but there are quite a few others which are very helpful. Here are just a couple of them:

  - **Use First Row as Header** – This transform is quite often used when you are connecting to a file source like a TXT or CSV. It allows you to promote your first row of data to the header.

  - **Replace Values** – With this transform, you can search for a character and replace it with something of your choosing.

- **Add Column** – As labeled, this tab will give you various options to add new columns to your selected query.

  - **Column From Examples** – When you choose to use this transform, it will change the UI and you will be prompted to input values to serve as the **Example**. Power BI will take your example and attempt to derive a pattern from that data that exists in the query. We will be looking at this feature in the "Try It Out" section.

- **View** – This tab does not contain any transformation options, but there are quite a few user interface items which can be toggled on or off. If you ever accidentally close the **Query Settings** pane, this is the tab where you can relaunch it.

- **Tools** – Here you can start a diagnostics session to investigate any potential performance issues you are experiencing. It is important to note that when you start a diagnostics session, it will consume quite a bit of your system resources.

- **Help** – Various help and support options are in this tab. You can also come here to see what version of Power BI you are using by selecting the **About** button.

What Is M?

When it comes to the Power Query Editor, it is important to understand that every transformation option that is used generates code which is written in the background for you. This is why Power BI is known as a low-code/no-code application. All of the actions you take while in the Power Query Editor act as a code generator, and this code is called the M-query language. The "M" stands for Mashup, and this serves as the transformative language used within Power BI. Even though you never have to write M-query, Power BI gives you access to the code if you want to customize it. The primary way to access the "M" code of a Power BI report is to select the "Advanced Editor" option which can be found within the Power Query Editor inside of the **Home** ribbon as seen in Figure 18-3.

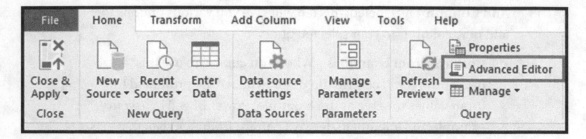

Figure 18-3. *By selecting this option, a window will appear showing all the "M" code for the currently selected query*

If you plan to either edit existing code or write your own from scratch, keep in mind that the Mashup query language is case sensitive. Power BI has built-in code completion for the Mashup query language which really helps ensure proper syntax. However, writing your own M-query code is a bit more advanced than what we will be covering in this book.

Try It Out

Now that we have explored areas of the Power Query Editor, we can dive in and use some of the transforms we have talked about. In this example, we will use two different data sources, clean them up, and then merge them together.

Lesson Requirements

To complete this exercise, you will need access to the Internet as both of our sources will be online. Open the following two sites, and you will be directed on how to use them in the steps that follow:

FDIC Failed Banks: `https://catalog.data.gov/dataset/fdic-failed-bank-list`

List of US States: `https://en.wikipedia.org/wiki/List_of_U.S._state_abbreviations`

Hints

The idea behind this example is to create a dataset that will contain a list of failed banks in the United States to help in deciding where the best place to set up a new brick-and-mortar location would be. So, we need to import both sources and clean up the dataset so that we can eventually create visualizations to help us with the decision-making process.

Step by Step

1. Open the Power BI Desktop and close out the "Getting Started" pop-up if it appears.

2. We will first start by connecting to the web source to bring in the FDIC Failed Bank list. Select the drop-down option for the Get data button and choose the *Web* option as seen in Figure 18-4.

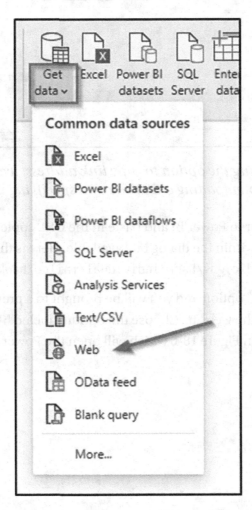

Figure 18-4. *The Web connector offers a broad range of capability for connecting to many different sources*

3. Leave Power BI open and go to the FDIC Failed Bank list site listed in the "Lesson Requirements" section. You will then right-click the "Download" option and select "Copy link address" as shown in Figure 18-5.

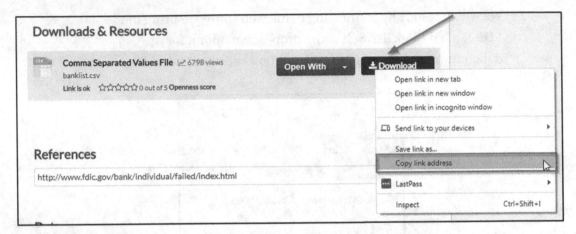

Figure 18-5. *By choosing the option to copy link address, we can use the Web connector instead of downloading a CSV file and specifying the location of the file*

4. Head back over to Power BI and paste in the URL copied in the previous step within the dialog box available. Here is the URL:
    `http://www.fdic.gov/bank/individual/failed/banklist.csv`

5. Select the "OK" option and you will be brought to a preview of the data from the website. Choose the option labeled "Transform Data" as seen in Figure 18-6 which will open the Power Query Editor.

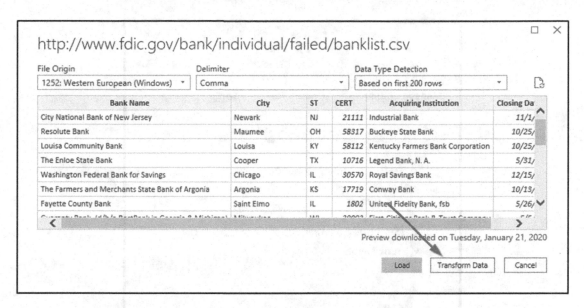

Figure 18-6. *This preview is actually the same experience a user will have if they choose the Text/CSV connector*

6. A good practice is to first rename the table/query to something more friendly. In our case, we will rename the query to "Failed Banks" by modifying the "Name" field in the Properties area to the right.

7. With this type of source, one of the first things we should do is remove any column that we know will be unused for reporting purposes. For this source, we will only eliminate the "CERT" column. There are various ways to accomplish this task, but the method we will use is to select the "Choose Columns" option located in the ***Home*** ribbon. This will launch a screen that presents all the available columns, and we simply remove the check mark from the "CERT" column and select OK as seen in Figure 18-7.

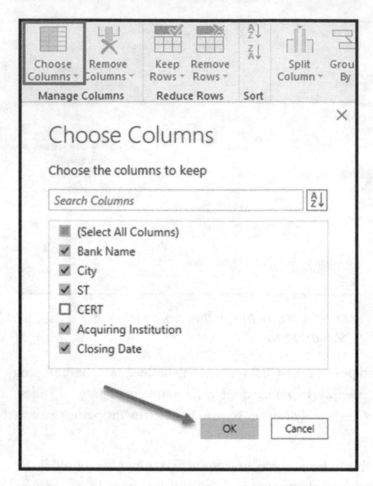

Figure 18-7. *The option to remove columns is presented in various locations; you just need to choose the option that best suits your preference*

8. Next, we should rename any columns to provide the highest degree of clarity for the end users. We will really want to give names to columns that are as friendly as possible. Do not fear having spaces in the name! The only column we will rename is the "ST" column, and we will change it to "State." You can either double left-click the column name and just put in the new name, or you can right-click and select the "Rename" option within the menu that is presented as seen in Figure 18-8.

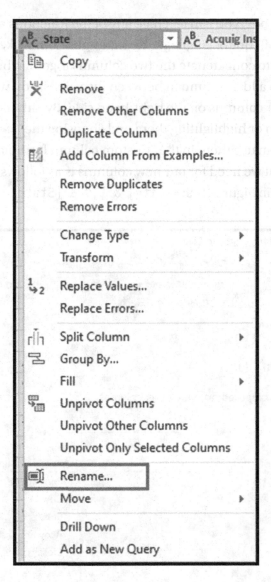

Figure 18-8. *When you right-click a column, you get quite a robust list of options to choose from. You can find all these options under various ribbon tabs*

9. Now we will create a new column which will be the result of combining the "City" and "State" columns together. This will prove beneficial when we get to the visualization section of the book. Near the top, choose the "Add Column" to change the ribbon choices. In this new ribbon, select the "Custom Column" option, and a pop-up should appear in the center of your screen.

In the dialog box, you can leverage any of the functions available within the "M"-query language. To accomplish our task, we simply need to concatenate the two columns together, but we also would like to add a column in between the values. You will see a list of all your columns on the right-hand side. By either double-clicking them or highlighting them and choosing the "<< Insert" option, we can use them in the "Custom column formula" section. The code that we need for our new columns is as follows and can also be seen in Figure 18-9: =[City] & "," & [State]

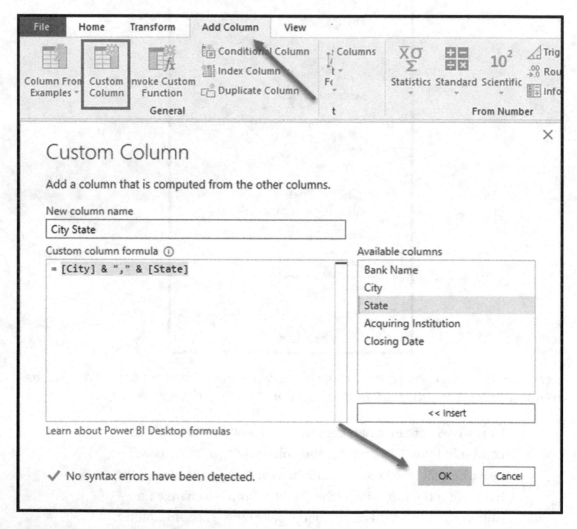

Figure 18-9. *Another way this step could have been accomplished is by using the "Column From Examples" option as you will see shortly*

10. The last transformation we will do with this dataset is to create a new column that contains just the Year value from the "Closing Date" column. While still on the "Add Column" ribbon, select the "Column From Examples" option which will slightly modify the user interface of the Power Query Editor. A new blank column appears labeled Column1. Now we must give Power BI an example of what we would like to populate this new column. This example must be something from within the same row that we are using to give an example. As you will see in Figure 18-10, my first row has a year value of 2020, so this is what I will type in the same row within the blank space under the new column. After inputting the example, simply hit the Enter key on your keyboard, and Power BI will attempt to populate the rest of the empty rows within the new column based on the example given. As seen in Figure 18-10, you can examine the "M" language expression that Power BI is using to fill in the rest of the data. If everything looks good, you can select "OK" and we now have a new column.

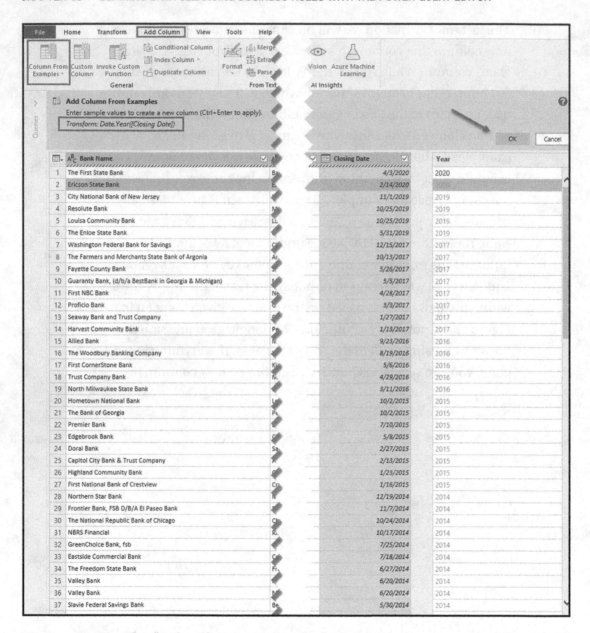

Figure 18-10. *The "Column From Examples" option is a very user-friendly way of doing transformations within the Power Query Editor*

11. Currently, our **Failed Banks** table has US State abbreviations, but we would like to have full US State names. This information is stored in a second web source which we will now bring in. Change to the "Home" ribbon and select the "New Source" option.

12. In the drop-down menu, select the Web option like we did
     in step 2 and use the following URL and hit "OK": https://
     en.wikipedia.org/wiki/List_of_U.S._state_abbreviations

13. From the *Navigator* menu, select the table that contains the data
     from the website as seen in Figure 18-11.

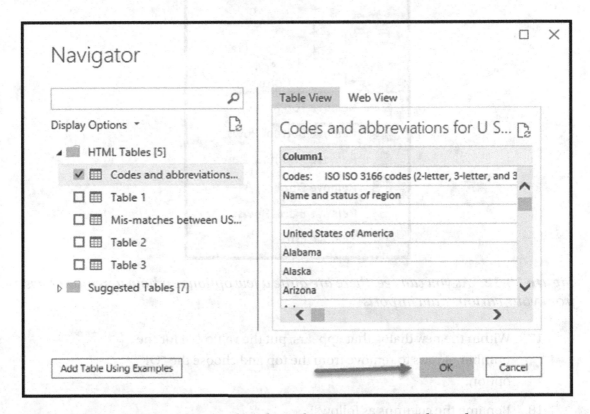

Figure 18-11. *Because we are already in the Power Query Editor, there was no
need to make a choice between "Load" and "Transform Data"*

14. The first thing we should do is rename the table to something
     more friendly like **US State Names**.

15. Now we need to remove any extra rows and columns. While in the
     "Home" ribbon, we will once again select the "Choose Columns"
     option. Currently, our column names are poorly labeled which
     we will fix soon. For now, make sure to have only "Column1" and
     "Column2" selected. Then hit the "OK" button.

16. Next, we will remove the top four rows of data as they are
     unnecessary. In the "Home" ribbon, select the option labeled
     "Remove Rows" which will give you a couple of options. Choose
     the "Remove Top Rows" option as seen in Figure 18-12.

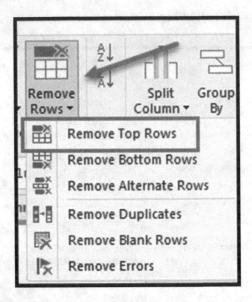

Figure 18-12. *As you can see, there are quite a few options on how to remove rows
from your various data imports*

17. Within the new dialog that appears, put the value of 4 for the
     number of rows to remove from the top and choose the "OK"
     option.

18. Rename the columns as follows:

     Column1 → State Name

     Column4 → Code

19. Now we can merge the two tables together using the columns that
     contain the State abbreviations. Select the **Failed Banks** dataset and
     select the "Merge Queries" option which is in the "Home" ribbon.

20. A couple of decisions need to be made within the dialog box that
     appears. First, we must select the query that we will be merging
     into the **Failed Banks** query, which of course will be the **US State
     Names** dataset.

21.   We must also decide what Join Kind we would like to use. In our case, we
select the drop-down and use the "Inner (only matching rows)" option.

22.   Lastly, we need to select the columns which will be used for the
Inner Join. From the **Failed Banks** query, choose the column
labeled "State," and from the **US State Names** query, choose the
column labeled "Code," as seen in Figure 18-13. Should a "Privacy
levels" dialog appear, check the "Ignore Privacy Levels…" option
and hit the "Save" button and then hit "OK."

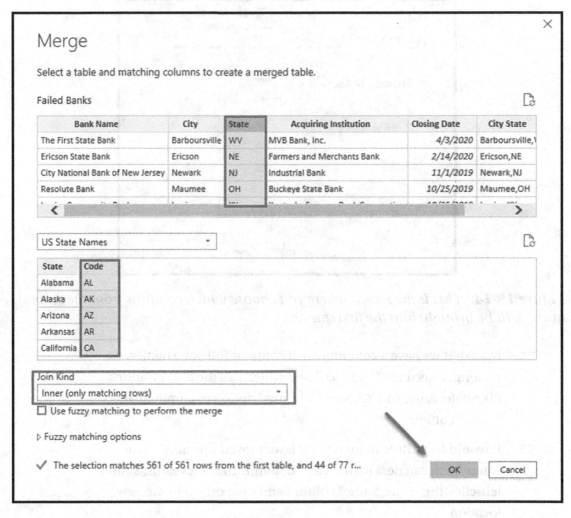

Figure 18-13. *Choosing the right Join Kind is very important as each one can have
a different effect on what rows will be in the final query*

23. The result of the merge is a packed column which has the name of **US State Names**. We must choose which columns we want from this query, and in our situation, it is only one, the "State Name" column. In this new column, you will see an icon that looks like two arrows pointing away from each other. This is known as the "Expand" option. Select this option, make sure to put a check mark for the "State Name" column, and hit the "OK" button. See Figure 18-14 for reference.

Figure 18-14. *This is the screen where you choose which columns from the second query will be brought into the first query*

24. Now that we have a column which contains full State names, we no longer need the "State" column which has the abbreviations. Like before, use the "Choose Columns" option to eliminate the "State" column.

25. It would feel a little more natural if we moved this new "State Name" column next to the "City" column. To achieve this, simply left-click the "State Name" column and then drag it to the new location.

26. Now that our **Failed Banks** query has all the data we need, there
     is no reason to load the **US State Names** query into the Power BI
     data model. We cannot delete this query because it is required for
     the merge process we are using, but if you right-click the **US State
     Names** query, you will see an option labeled "Enable Load" which
     is currently checked. If we just select this option, it will remove the
     check and now that query will no longer be loaded into the Power
     BI model which is exactly what we want.

27. We can now choose the "Close & Apply" option to load our **Failed
     Banks** query into the Power BI model. Go ahead and save the
     Power BI report as **Ch 18 Failed Banks**.

Summary

Power BI is well equipped to handle many different data cleansing needs, but this will
really be dependent on what data source you are working with. Some users will be able
to connect to a source that has already been cleaned up by IT which will require very
minimal use of the Power Query Editor, and this is not a bad thing. Should the situation
arise though and you are working with data that is not cleaned up, you can rely on the
depth of the Power Query Editor. The Power Query Editor allows you to set your business
rules to shape the data to your needs. In the next chapter, we will look at the Power BI
data model and how we can make enhancements in order to maximize usability for
report consumers.

CHAPTER 19

Data Model Design

Now that we have finished learning what capabilities exist within the Power Query Editor, it is time to discuss data model enhancements. The Power Query Editor is there to shape the data, but once we hit **Close & Apply**, we need to begin modeling the data. Primarily, when in this phase of creating a Power BI report, you will find yourself in the **Model View** of Power BI. This view gives us the capability of achieving almost everything we need from a modeling perspective. It is in this chapter that we will discuss various aspects of the Power BI data model such as defining relationships, creating hierarchies, hiding columns, and other usability enhancements that will make the end-user experience the best it can be.

What Is a Power BI Data Model?

The Power BI data model is comprised of the tables, columns, and relationships that exist within our Power BI report. It is in this phase that we can connect multiple data sources together where normally they would have no relationships because they exist in different external systems. Not only do we need to create relationships between our tables, but we also need to make decisions around certain behaviors for columns such as if they need to be aggregated or not. There are quite a few processes that Power BI will attempt to do automatically, but it is up to us to ensure that these decisions fall in line with our understanding of the model. There are quite a few data modeling tasks that should be done, but it is always good to start with relationships.

Defining Relationships

A relationship in Power BI is defined by specifying one column from one table and another column from a second table. By default, Power BI automatically attempts to detect relationships between tables. If columns have the same name and compatible

231

© Mitchell Pearson, Brian Knight, Devin Knight, Manuel Quintana 2020
M. Pearson et al., *Pro Microsoft Power Platform*, https://doi.org/10.1007/978-1-4842-6008-1_19

data types, Power BI will create a relationship for you. The relationship may not always be correct, so it is very important to inspect any and all relationships that may have been made by going to the **Model View**. Relationships within Power BI allow tables to "talk" to each other which will be very important when it comes to filtering visualizations. There are four types of relationships that can be made. Those four types are One to Many, Many to One, Many to Many, and One to One.

We will be focusing on the One to Many or Many to One in this book, which are the typical type of relationship that you will work with. The great thing is that when a relationship is created between two tables, Power BI will examine the columns that have been specified and create the appropriate relationship type which is known as the cardinality. In a One-to-Many relationship, the column from the first table that is used within a relationship contains a unique list of values (one), while the column in the second table will be comprised of the same values but can and will be duplicates.

As an example, let us take the idea of having two tables. The first is a customer table that contains a list of unique customers. In this table, there is a column called CustomerID that is used to identify each customer. The second table is a Sales table which lists all the sales that a company gets. As part of each transaction that is recorded, we record the CustomerID for each purchase. Assuming that the company makes lots of sales, it is easy to assume that one customer may have many transactions. Therefore, the two tables can be related and will be defined as a One (Company table) to Many (Sales table) relationship within Power BI.

Another important thing to understand when it comes to relationships in Power BI is filter direction. By default, the filter direction is set to **Single** when a One-to-Many relationship is created. This means that the "One" side of the relationship can filter the "Many" side, but not the other way around. From an introductory perspective, users should leave this default setting and only change the filter direction if they have knowledge of Many-to-Many relationships as there may be adverse effects on visualizations when changing the filter direction. At the end of this chapter, in the "Try It Out" section, we will see that sometimes Power BI does not always make the correct decisions when automatically defining relationships.

The last concept that we will discuss regarding relationships is the ability to define a relationship as either active or inactive. The default behavior within Power BI is that the first relationship created between two tables will always be set as the active relationship, and there can only ever be one active relationship between two tables. The active relationship defines the columns that will be used when filtering tables. Even though you can only have one active relationship, you may have as many inactive relationships as you would like. Inactive relationships have no effect on the model until they are explicitly referenced in a DAX expression which we will cover in the next chapter.

Relationships are one of the first things that should be looked at from a modeling perspective, but there are more items that must be addressed. Let us continue to explore more topics.

Creating Hierarchies

As discussed earlier, when defining a relationship, you specify one column from one table and another column from a second table. Hierarchies in Power BI allow us to define relationships between columns within a single table which will give performance benefits when using those columns in a visual. Hierarchies within Power BI are experienced from within visualizations.

We can create visualizations that allow users to "Drill Down" into the data to get a greater degree of detail. A very common example of a hierarchy would be the relationships between a Year column, Quarter column, Month column, and Day column. When we put all four of these columns into a visualization, a user can choose what level of detail they would like to report on. By defining this hierarchy in the model, we can maximize the performance of this exploration. At the end of this chapter, in the "Try It Out" section, we will create a hierarchy, but we will not be able to fully experience the benefit until we create a visualization to showcase this "Drill Down" capability. This of course will be done in a later chapter.

Other Usability Enhancements

There are other usability enhancements to be aware of. These are described in the subsections that follow.

Hiding Columns

In the previous chapter, we saw the ability to remove columns within the Power Query Editor. Sometimes though, we require columns within the data model that will never be visualized. These columns are needed to define relationships within the data model, but since they will never be used in visuals, they also take up unnecessary room in the **Report View**. This is where the ability, **Hide in report view**, comes in handy. We report creators can right-click any column, and we will be presented with the option of **Hide in report view**, and that option accomplishes exactly what it says. The column in question can still be viewed from the **Data View** and the **Model view**, but not the **Report View**. These hidden columns may still be used as parts of relationships as well as in DAX expressions. The only benefit is that the list of columns as seen in the **Report View** is trimmed down to only those that will be used as part of visualizations.

Sort by Column

Another issue that occurs quite commonly in Power BI data models is the ability to change how a column is sorted. If a column is of a numeric data type, it can be sorted descending or ascending based on the values. When a column is sorted that is of a Text data type, it can be sorted either from A to Z or from Z to A. Sometimes it makes more sense to see the Text values within a visualization, but have it sorted by some numeric representation in the background. A very common example would be a column that is populated with month names. If we were to use the Month Name column in a visualization, the sorting options would be A to Z or Z to A, which really does not make sense. Users will want to see these values sorted January to December or December to January. That's not an alphabetical sort, but it sure does make sense from a sorting perspective.

If a column exists within the table to numerically represent each month, we can use the feature **Sort by column** to accomplish this very objective. This is something we will showcase in the "Try It Out" section.

Default Summarization

Within Power BI, if a column is of a numeric data type and it is not part of a relationship, it will automatically receive a default summarization indicated by a sigma symbol next to the column. When this occurs, the column will be summed when placed in a visualization.

As you can expect, automatic summarization is not always correct. It is very important to inspect every column in the data model and remove any default summarization that does not make sense. It is very common for this to be a problem with tables that contain information around dates. Columns that contain data such as years, quarters, or month numbers will be summarized, and this is incorrect.

Power BI does give us the capability to remove summarization where it is not needed and potentially adjust the summarization from sum to other aggregations like min, max, average, and count if it makes sense. When you select a column from the **Report View**, then the **Column tools** ribbon will be made available. It is here that you will find the summarization option, and we will explore this in the "Try It Out" section.

Try It Out

We now know that there are quite a few usability enhancements that can be made to make the end-user experience much better. Not only do some of the enhancements have performance impacts but also some great navigational experiences. We will now open the Power BI report we created in Chapter 17 called **Ch 17 Connecting to Data** and add some of the enhancements that we talked about in this chapter.

Lesson Requirements

To start this exercise, locate the Power BI report we created in Chapter 17 called **Ch 17 Connecting to Data** and open it in Power BI Desktop.

Hints

The data that we are working with is meant to mimic working with data from a well-formed data warehouse, so we do not need to worry about using the Power Query Editor. For the data model, we need to explore the **Model View** in order to verify any relationships that Power BI has automatically created and potentially fix any that are in error as well as create any relationships that are missing. As well, we need to look at renaming tables and columns so that they are more user-friendly. Then we can look to enhance our model by creating a user-defined hierarchy on the Date table. Lastly, we will want to take advantage of the **Sort By** feature so that the column inside the **Date** table which has the month names will sort correctly when used inside of a visual.

Step by Step

Work this chapter's example by executing the steps that follow:

1. With the **Ch 17 Connecting to Data** report open, the first thing
   we should do is access the **File** menu and select the option of
   Save As. This will allow us to isolate the work we are doing in each
   chapter. The name you should use for this report will be **Ch 19
   Data Model Design**.

2. To start, we will focus on renaming the tables we have in our
   model. There are a couple of ways to achieve this, but we will go to
   the **Model View** to perform most of our model enhancements as
   seen in Figure 19-1.

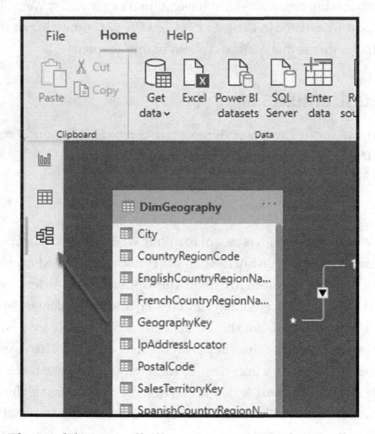

Figure 19-1. *The Model View will allow us to perform almost all model
enhancements*

3. Now that we are in the Model View, we can select any of the tables, and this will populate the **Properties** pane. One of the options that can be modified is the **Name** property, and this is what we will do first for all our tables. You should rename all the tables as seen in the following:

DimDate → Date

DimProduct → Product

DimSalesTerritory → Sales Territory

DimGeography → Geography

DimCustomer → Customer

FactInternetSales → Internet Sales

4. Next, we need to examine the relationships which have been created by Power BI. In our model, we need to make three adjustments. The first is to create a relationship between the ***Date*** table and the ***Internet Sales*** table. There are a couple of columns available to us within the ***Internet Sales*** table to choose. As an organization, we have decided to use the ***OrderDate*** column. Left-click the ***FullDateAlternateKey*** column from the ***Date*** table and drag it on top of the ***OrderDate*** column in the ***Internet Sales*** table which will define a relationship between the two as shown in Figure 19-2.

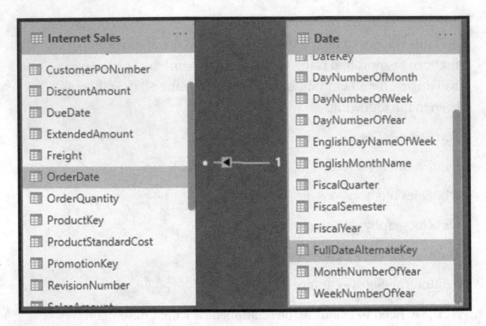

Figure 19-2. *By hovering over the line between the two tables, it will highlight which two columns are part of the relationship*

5. The second adjustment we need to make for our model is to delete the relationship that exists between the **Geography** table and the **Sales Territory** table. To achieve this, hover over the line that represents the relationship and right-click. Choose the **Delete** option and a dialog will appear confirming if you would like to delete, select the **Delete** option, and the relationship will be removed.

6. The last update we need to make in the *Model View* will be to change the relationship between the *Sales Territory* table and the *Internet Sales* table from inactive to active. Right-click the line that represents the relationship and choose the *Properties* option. In the dialog box that appears, we will need to check the option labeled "Make this relationship active" as seen in Figure 19-3.

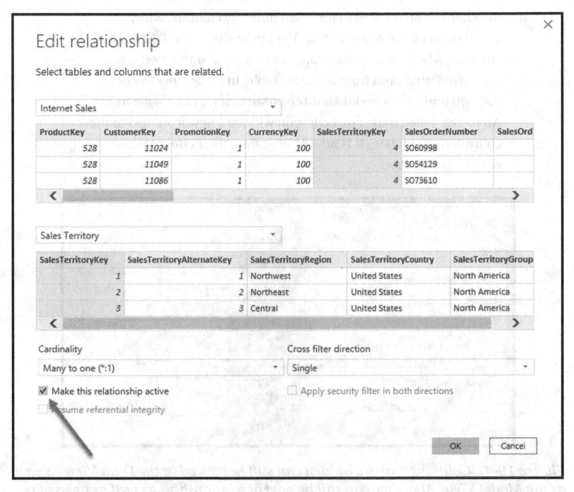

Figure 19-3. In this Edit relationship area, we can make various adjustments to existing relationships such as changing from active to inactive and changing the columns that are part of the relationship

7. The next item we will look at is renaming columns. For this step, you can update as many columns as you would prefer because this step is just for making the columns understandable for end users. In a full production report, you would take the time and update all the columns. For this exercise, we will only update the name of one column from the **Date** table, the **FullDateAlternateKey** column. Highlight the column in question and simply update the **Name** property to the following:

FullDateAlternateKey → Date

239

8. Another important step to take is to hide any columns which are not needed for the *Report View*. For our model, we will hide all columns which contain the word "key." We will start by selecting the *DateKey* column from the *Date* table. In the *Properties* pane, you will find an option labeled *Is hidden* that we can toggle from *No* to *Yes*. When done correctly, you will see a new icon next to the column that indicates it is now hidden from the *Report View* as seen in Figure 19-4.

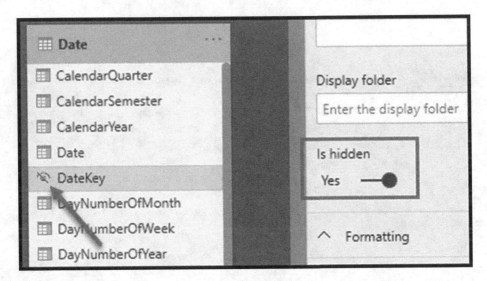

Figure 19-4. *Columns that are hidden can still be viewed in the Data View as well as the Model View. Also, they can still be part of relationships as well as be used in DAX expressions which we will see later*

9. You should perform the previous step for every column that has the word "key" in it. It should be noted that you can multiselect columns by holding down the **Control** key on your keyboard.

10. Now we will create a user-defined hierarchy within the **Date** table. We will begin by right-clicking the **CalendarYear** column and choosing the **Create hierarchy** option. Once completed, you will see the hierarchy is created, and we have an option to add additional columns to the hierarchy.

11.   In the *Properties* pane, there is an option called *Select a*
       column to add level. This drop-down shows all the columns
       that are part of the *Date* table. Select the drop-down and choose
       the *CalendarQuarter* column to add this underneath the
       CalendarYear within the hierarchy as seen in Figure 19-5.

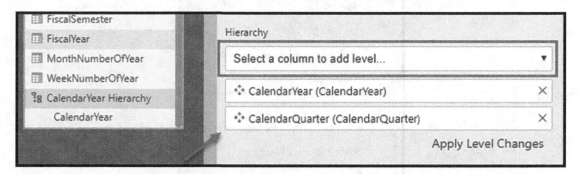

Figure 19-5. *Users do have the capability to move columns either up or down*
within the hierarchy in case they have been added in the wrong order

12.   In the same fashion as the previous step, add the
       EnglishMonthName and **Date** columns to the hierarchy and
       select the **Apply Level Changes** option.

13.   The final thing we should do with this new hierarchy is to give it a
       better name. With the hierarchy selected, change the value within
       the **Name** property as follows:

       CalendarYear Hierarchy → Date Drilldown

14.   Repeat steps 10–13 for the *Geography* table and create a hierarchy
       named *Geography Drilldown* as shown in Figure 19-6.

Figure 19-6. *Hierarchies will be very useful when we create visualizations within our report*

15. The next enhancement we will make to our model will be to the **EnglishMonthName** column inside the **Date** table. If we were to use this column in a visualization, it would be sorted alphabetically which is not what our users want. To fix this issue, we will need to update the **Sort By Column** option for this column. Select the **EnglishMonthName** column and expand the **Advanced** category within the **Properties** pane.

16. Here you will see an option called *Sort By Column* which is automatically set to the same column that is selected which is the default behavior. Use the drop-down list and select the *MonthNumberOfYear* column as seen in Figure 19-7. This will now allow the *MonthNumberOfYear* column to be ordered as we would expect.

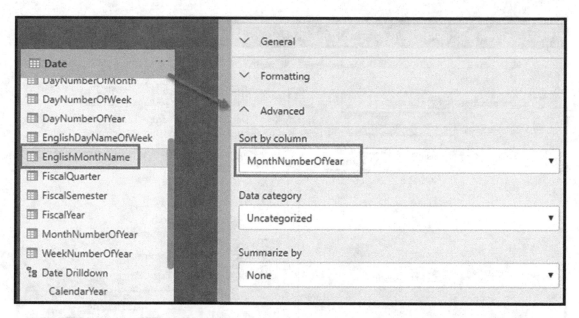

Figure 19-7. *Every column within the Power BI model will automatically be sorted by itself. It is very common to use the Sort By Column option when sorting alphabetically is not what you want. To achieve this sorting, you will need a column which represents the numeric ordering of your values*

17.   The last enhancement we will make to our model is to remove any default summarization that should not exist. This occurs for any column that is of a numeric data type and is not part of a relationship. For this exercise, we will focus on the **Date** table and remove the default summarization for all columns that it would apply to. Go to the **Report View** for this task, because that view makes it easy to identify columns that are being summarized. Just look for the sigma symbol next to them.

18.   The first column in the table is *Calendar Quarter*. Highlight this column and you will be presented with the *Column tools* ribbon. In the *Properties* section, you will see the drop-down for *Summarization*. Select the option of *Don't summarize* as seen in Figure 19-8.

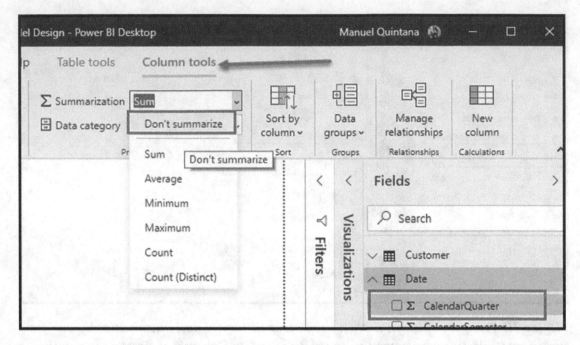

Figure 19-8. *You can also change the summarization from the Model View, but it is much easier on the Report View because you can see the sigma symbol next to the columns that are being summarized*

19. Repeat step 18 for the rest of the columns inside the **Date** table so that no columns are being summarized.

20. Save your report and you have now completed this exercise.

Summary

Model enhancements are crucial for maximizing performance within the Power BI model. Not only is performance a factor, but some of the usability enhancements we explored in this chapter will allow for some awesome exploratory capabilities once we start visualizing data. An effective and simple model will allow users to fully explore the data being provided to them in a clean and understandable way. In the next chapter, we will look at another item for extending our data model, the DAX expression language.

CHAPTER 20

Extending Your Data Model with DAX Calculations

As part of the data modeling process, Power BI gives us access to a language called DAX or the Data Analysis Expression language. DAX allows us to expand the analytical power of our data model with the creation of calculated columns, calculated measures, and calculated tables. Each of these items is created using DAX which is a user-friendly language that has parallels to the Excel formula language. In this chapter, we will gain an understanding of the differences between calculated columns, calculated measures, and calculated tables. In the "Try It Out" section, we will extend the model we have been working with by adding calculated columns and calculated measures.

Calculated Columns

Calculated columns allow users to add new data to a table already in your model. This differs from adding a column in the Power Query Editor because calculated columns will be based on data that you have already loaded. It should also be noted that you cannot see your calculated columns inside the Power Query Editor. Both calculated columns and calculated measures are generally used to perform some sort of arithmetic operation on top of the data we already have in the model. The biggest difference between calculated columns and measures is that a calculated column is evaluated for each row in the table that it is created in by default; this is known as the evaluation context.

It takes up more space in the model since it is a physical column that is added to that table. Quite often, we will create calculated columns to add additional information

© Mitchell Pearson, Brian Knight, Devin Knight, Manuel Quintana 2020
M. Pearson et al., *Pro Microsoft Power Platform*, https://doi.org/10.1007/978-1-4842-6008-1_20

to a table which will give users more options to filter the metric value which is the focus of the Power BI report. An example of this would be using DAX to create a new column which combines the first and last name of customers within a table. This new column which would contain the customer's full name in one field would be a much better way to look at the breakdown of sales by our customers.

Another use for calculated columns would be as a method for connecting disparate data sources with multiple key columns. In the previous chapter, we discussed how you can only have one active relationship between tables, and that relationship can only be defined between a single column from each table. We can use DAX to combine data from multiple columns, potentially columns which are not even in the same tables, to create a column that can be used to define a relationship. You can create a calculated column from the **Report View** by selecting the **New Column** option from the **Modeling** ribbon or from the **Data View** by choosing the **New Column** option in the **Home** ribbon. It is preferred to use the **Data View** because we will be able to immediately see the results of the DAX used in the calculated column. To identify calculated columns more easily inside the data model, a special icon is placed next to the column name as seen in Figure 20-1.

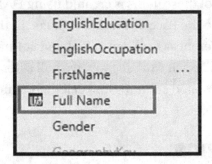

Figure 20-1. *By selecting calculated columns, you can bring up the formula bar which allows you to see the DAX expression that was used to create it*

Calculated Measures

To create a calculated measure, you would want to select the **New Measure** option which can be found in both the **Report View** and the **Data View**. Unlike calculated columns, it is preferred to create measures while in the **Report View** because you need to use your measures inside of a visual in order to validate those measures. This means that calculated measures take up less room inside of our data model, but require more resources when they are processed as part of visualizations.

We will be using measures to calculate aggregates like the sum or average of a column. Also, we can take advantage of certain DAX functions to create **Time Intelligence** measures to compare sales from one year to another. Calculated measures are sometimes referred to as explicit measures because they are defined by the users. Meanwhile, Power BI will automatically aggregate any columns in our data model that are of numeric data type and are not part of a relationship; these are called implicit measures. Implicit measures are indicated by a sigma symbol, while explicit measures have a calculator icon as seen in Figure 20-2.

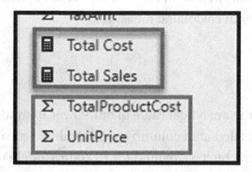

Figure 20-2. *The items in blue represent calculated measures also known as explicit measures. The items in red are known as implicit measures created by Power BI*

Quick Measures

At the end of this chapter, we will be creating calculated columns and measures by writing DAX on our own. To assist those who are newer to DAX, Power BI has a library of common DAX expressions to perform powerful calculations quickly and easily. This feature is known as **Quick Measures** and can be accessed via the **Report View** or the **Data View**. The **Quick Measures** library has various categories of DAX expressions and includes descriptions of what they will accomplish and how to use them. The nice thing is that you do not have to write any DAX as it will be done for you in the background based on the input you provide within the dialog box that appears.

Calculated Tables

Normally, you will create tables in Power BI by importing data in your model from a source. By using DAX and creating a calculated table, you add a new table into your model based on the data that is already loaded. You can create calculated tables from both the **Report View** and the **Data View**, and you can use any DAX functions you would like. Calculated tables are created when the data in the model is refreshed which is like calculated columns. Calculated tables will mainly be used to create tables that are derived from data that already exists in the data model or to possibly create a new Date table which can be used with calculated measures.

Try It Out

It is now time to expand the analytical value of our Power BI model by adding some DAX into it. We will be adding calculated columns and calculated measures to the report we created in the last chapter which we named **Ch 19 Data Model Design**. At the end of this exercise, you should have a good introductory grasp on how to write various DAX expressions and the versatility of the DAX language.

Lesson Requirements

To start this exercise, locate the Power BI report created in Chapter 19 called **Ch 19 Data Model Design**, and open that report in Power BI Desktop.

Hints

First, we will be creating calculated columns that will do the following:

1. **Full Name** – A combination of the First and Last Name columns

2. **Age** – The difference between the customer's birth date and the current date

3. **Age Breakdown** – Place customers in age brackets of 55+, 45–54, 35–44, and 18–34

Then we will create a couple of calculated measures that will do the following:

1. **Total Sales** – Get the sum of the SalesAmount column

2. **Total Cost** – Get the sum of the TotalProductCost column

3. **Profit** – Figure out the difference between the Total Sales and Total Cost measures

4. **Prior Year Profit** – Display profit values from the year prior to what is being seen in the visual

5. **YTD Profit** – An additive form of the profit measure

Step by Step

Here are the steps to follow in working this chapter's example:

1. With the **Ch 19 Data Model Design** report open, the first thing we should do is access the **File** menu and select the option of **Save As**. This will allow us to isolate the work we are doing in each chapter. The name you should use for this report will be **Ch 20 Extending Your Data Model With DAX**.

2. Select the **Data View** so that we can immediately see the value of our calculated columns as seen in Figure 20-3.

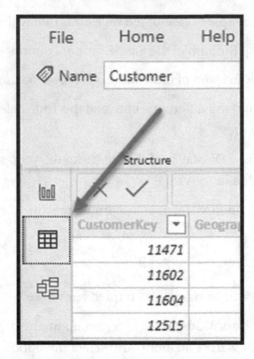

Figure 20-3. *The Data View is the best place to create your calculated columns because we will be able to immediately validate the results of our DAX expressions*

3. Ensure that you have the ***Customer*** table selected and choose the
   New Column option found in the ***Table tools*** ribbon as seen in
   Figure 20-4.

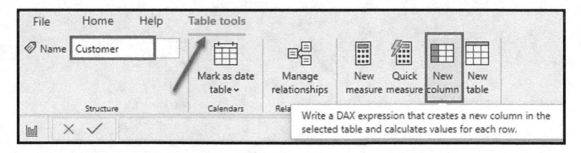

Figure 20-4. *In this one ribbon, we can create calculated columns, measures, or tables depending on our needs*

4. The formula bar will appear which allows us to input our DAX expression. The first calculated column we will create will be **Full Name**. This will be a combination of the **FirstName** and **LastName** columns from the **Customer** table. To concatenate these values together, we will take advantage of the "&" operator which allows the combining of text values. Do not forget about the space we want between the two names. The formula should look like the following:

```
Full Name = 'Customer'[FirstName] & " " &
'Customer'[LastName]
```

5. After confirming the preceding DAX formula, you should have a new column called **Full Name** with values for each row.

6. Repeat step 3 to open the formula bar to create another calculated column.

7. The next calculated column we will create will be called **Age**. This column should calculate how old each customer is by comparing the value from the **BirthDate** column and whatever today's date is. This calculation should be flexible enough to update every time the report is refreshed.

8. To achieve this, we will need to leverage a logical statement that will perform different actions depending on the results of the logical test. We will be using the "IF" and "FORMAT" functions to accomplish our goal.

    a. **IF** – Checks if a condition provided as the first argument is met. Returns one value if the condition is TRUE and returns another value if the condition is FALSE.

    b. **FORMAT** – Converts a value to text according to the format you specify.

9. The logical test that we need to perform is to determine whether a customer's birthday has already occurred within this year. If their birthday has not occurred already this year, then we need to account for that in the formula. The formula should look like the following:

```
Age =
IF(
  FORMAT(TODAY(),"MMDD") >= FORMAT('Customer'[BirthDate],
  "MMDD"),
  DATEDIFF('Customer'[BirthDate], TODAY(), YEAR),
  DATEDIFF('Customer'[BirthDate], TODAY(), YEAR) - 1)
```

10. The last calculated column we created, Age, will serve as a nice bridge column for use in creating another calculated column by which to group our various ages.

11. We will use a new DAX function that can be used in a similar way to the IF condition but looks a little cleaner when used. It will be the SWITCH function.

12. The SWITCH function will evaluate an expression and return a result depending on the outcome of the expression. In our scenario, we would like to create four different brackets or groups in which our customers will fall into. This will be very helpful when we get to visualizations. The names of the brackets we would like to create are as follows: 55+, 45–54, 35–44, and 18–34.

13. The formula will go as follows:

```
Age Breakdown=
SWITCH(TRUE(),
   Customer[Age] >= 55, "55+",
   Customer[Age] >= 45, "45-54",
   Customer[Age] >= 35, "35-44",
   "18-34")
```

14. Now that we have a couple of calculated columns, it is time to extend the analytical capability for our model by creating some calculated measures.

15. The first calculated measure we will create will calculate the sum of the **Sales Amount** column from the **Internet Sales** table. To start this process, highlight the Internet Sales table and select the **New measure** option as seen in Figure 20-5.

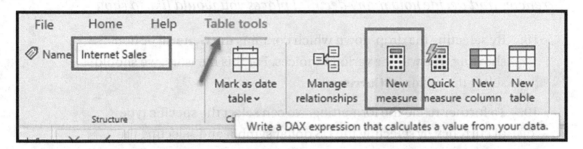

Figure 20-5. *All the choices available will launch the same formula bar, and every DAX function will be available regardless if you are creating a column, measure, or table*

16. The formula for this first measure is straightforward and will use the SUM function which adds up all the values in a specified column. The name of the measure will be **Total Sales** and the formula should look like the following:

```
Total Sales = SUM('Internet Sales'[SalesAmount])
```

17. With this measure created, we should do some formatting. With the measure selected, you will see a **Formatting** section visible with the **Measure tools** as seen in Figure 20-6.

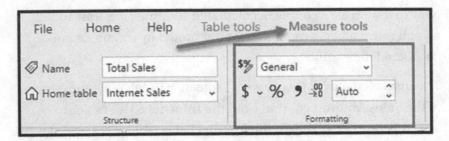

Figure 20-6. *In this formatting area, you can handle thousand separators and currencies and decide how many decimal places you would like to show*

18. By selecting the drop-down which contains the **General** option showing, you will see various choices. For this measure, we should select the option of **Currency**.

19. To further refine the formatting, we can select the specific type of currency by selecting the US dollar symbol and selecting the option of *$ English (United States)* as seen in Figure 20-7.

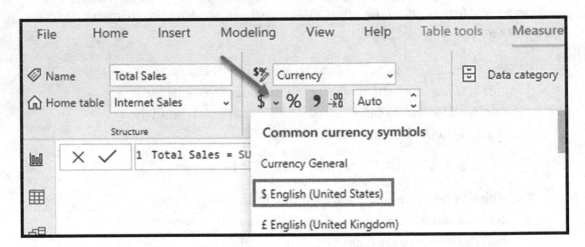

Figure 20-7. *Power BI allows formatting for many different types of currencies from all around the globe*

20. To validate our calculated measure, we cannot use the **Data View** like we could with our calculated columns. Instead, we will need to access the **Report View** and leverage a visualization to show our new measure.

21. The simplest visual to use to validate this measure and all future ones we will be the **Matrix** visual.

22. Select the ***Matrix*** visual and then use our ***Date Drilldown*** for the ***Rows*** and our new ***Total Sales*** measure for the ***Values*** as seen in Figure 20-8.

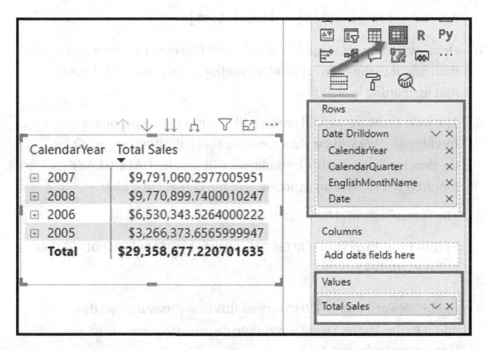

Figure 20-8. *Using this Matrix visual, we can validate all our calculated measures and verify that formatting has been done correctly*

23. Let us continue with our next calculated measure which we will call **Total Cost**. To accomplish this, we will get the **SUM** of the **TotalProductCost** column from the **Internet Sales** table. The formula should be written as follows:

```
Total Cost = SUM('Internet Sales'[TotalProductCost])
```

24. Repeat steps 18–20 to format this new measure and then add it to the same Matrix visual we currently have. We do this to validate the measure and verify that the formatting looks good.

25. Now that we have a **Total Sales** and a **Total Cost** measure, we can create a new calculated measure which will give us our profit. All we need to do is to subtract the **Total Cost** from the **Total Sales** measure.

26. The formula should be written as follows:

```
Profit = [Total Sales] - [Total Cost]
```

27. Once again, repeat steps 18–20 to format this new measure and then add it to the Matrix visual to validate the measure and verify that formatting looks good.

28. The next measure we will create will fall into the realm of Time Intelligence. We will create a measure that will show our profit for the previous year. In this formula, we will use the **CALCULATE** function to evaluate an expression in the context of a filter.

29. The formula should be written as follows:

```
Prior Year Profit = CALCULATE([Profit], SAMEPERIODLASTYEAR
('Date'[Date])
```

30. Again, repeat steps 18–20 to format this new measure and then add it to the Matrix visual to validate the measure and verify the formatting looks good.

31. The last measure we will create will be an additive one that will show us the year-to-date profit. To accomplish this, we will take advantage of one of the built-in Time Intelligence functions, **TOTALYTD**. The measure should be named **YTD Profit** and should be written as follows:

```
YTD Profit = TOTALYTD([Profit], 'Date'[Date])
```

32. The last thing is to format this measure and add it to the Matrix visual to validate the results. With this last measure, we have completed this **Try It Out** lesson.

Summary

By using DAX to create calculated columns and calculated measures, we can extend the analytical capabilities of our Power BI data model. The columns and measures added will give us many more options to choose from when we are creating visualizations for our report. It should also be noted that occasionally new DAX functions are introduced with Power BI updates which could allow you to further extend your data model.

We've now finished modeling our data. In the next chapter, we will explore visualizations so that we can choose the right option to represent our data to end users.

CHAPTER 21

Report Writing Basics

Once all the data shaping and data modeling have been completed, we report writers still have the important task of deciding which visualizations to use to bring our data to life. There are over 30 visualizations built into Power BI. If we do not make the right decision on which to use for displaying certain data, it could lead to confusion or just a general lack of direction when it comes to delivering a message to our end users. In this chapter, we will look at choosing the right visuals for categorical data, showing data trends, visualizing goal tracking, and displaying geographical data. Although it will not be looked at in this chapter, it should be noted that there are also over 260 custom visualizations available from the Microsoft App Store.

Visualizing Categorical Data

When we say categorical data, we mean data that can be divided into groups. In our data model, we have quite a few columns which we will use in the "Try It Out" section later such as EnglishCountryRegionName, Age Breakdown, Gender, and Color from the product table. As you can see from these examples, categorical data is very common in models, which means that it is very likely you will be using one of the visualizations discussed in this section. Let us look at some of the options available to us within Power BI.

Bar and Column Charts

The only difference between these two charts is the axis property. The Bar chart maps the categorical values on the Y axis, while the Column chart maps the categorical values on the X axis. So really the choice is whether you want to have your bars go horizontally or vertically. Both types of charts come in three different flavors: **Stacked**, **Clustered**, or **100%**. The **Stacked** version of these charts allows for a second categorical value to be

© Mitchell Pearson, Brian Knight, Devin Knight, Manuel Quintana 2020
M. Pearson et al., *Pro Microsoft Power Platform*, https://doi.org/10.1007/978-1-4842-6008-1_21

used for the **Legend** property and will present itself in the form of segmenting the bar or column for each category as seen in Figure 21-1.

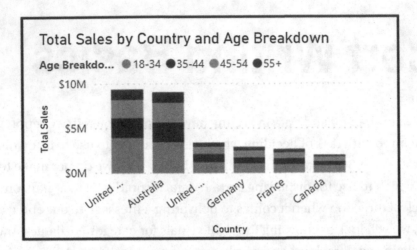

Figure 21-1. *By accessing the formatting options, users have access to many different properties. One such property is the ability to decide what colors will be used for the various categories*

The **Clustered** form of the chart will depict the values from the legend in their own separate bars within the Axis categories as seen in Figure 21-2.

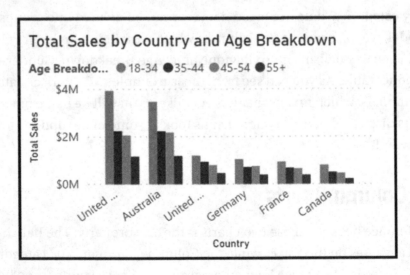

Figure 21-2. *If the column chosen for the legend has a larger amount of categorical values, the Clustered Bar/Column chart can start to look overcrowded very quickly*

The last option available for Bar and Column charts is the **100%** version which looks just like the **Stacked** version except all the bars are of the same exact length, and the emphasis is on the difference between the values coming from the column mapped to the **Legend** section.

Pie and Donut Charts

These two charts are meant to showcase a section of data compared to the whole, rather than comparing individual values to each other. Both charts can be effective ways to allow users to filter other visuals using **Interactive Filtering** which we will talk about more in the next chapter. The main thing to keep in mind when it comes to both the **Pie** and **Donut charts** is that you should have a limited amount of categorical values for the column used in the **Legend** section, and the distribution of data should be as even as possible. If you map a column to the Legend section that has outliers based on the column mapped in the **Values** section, users will have a difficult time interacting with the visual. In Figure 21-3, you will see an example of mapping a column that has way too many categorical values; this should always be avoided.

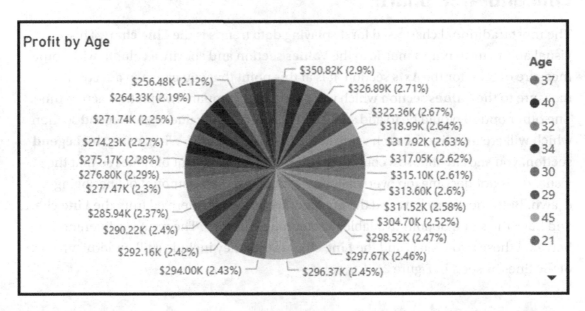

Figure 21-3. *Along with ensuring that you have a limited amount of categorical values, you must also make sure that there is a somewhat even distribution of data between the categories based on the metric used in the Values section*

Treemap Visual

The Treemap visual is another great option to use because when set up correctly, it allows for easy interactive filtering for users. The column that you map to the **Group** section displays as squares/rectangles within the visual and has a very button-like look and feel. In order to make the Treemap an effective visual, you do want to ensure that you have a controlled amount of categorical values in the column used for the **Group** section and that there is an even distribution of data in regard to the metric mapped to the **Values** section.

Visualizing Data Trends

Usually, when you see the term data trends, it means to look at and compare data over time. Power BI offers a few choices that allow us to draw attention to these trends in a couple different ways.

Line and Area Charts

The most traditional chart used for displaying data trends is the **Line chart**. This visual allows us to map a metric to the **Values** section and specify a column with some measure of time for the **Axis** section. It is at this point that you can map a second measure to the **Values** section which will allow us to compare two metrics across time. The other option would be to add some sort of categorical value to the **Legend** section which will create a line for each value in the mapped column. When using the **Legend** section, you should choose a column that has a limited amount of values so that the visual does not become too overwhelming with an excessive amount of lines being drawn. Both the **Area** chart and the **Stacked Area** chart are derived from the **Line** chart and have the same options available for mapping columns. The primary difference between these two visuals and the **Line** chart is that they include a fill underneath each of the lines as seen in Figure 21-4.

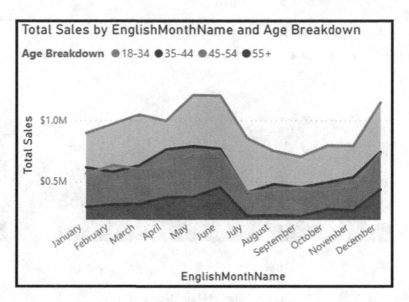

Figure 21-4. *Both the Line chart and the Area chart have an option to allow a second measure to share the same Y axis in the visual, or it can have its own separate Y axis*

Ribbon Chart

The **Ribbon** chart is unique in that it has the capability of showing data over time but also a more pronounced way of showing a change in rank. Initially, when you select the **Ribbon** chart and you only map a field to the **Axis** section and a measure to the **Values** section, the visual looks very much like a column chart. This visual really requires a field to be mapped to the legend which gives us that ribbon look and feel. Basically, what is happening is that the different categories within the legend are connected, and it allows for changes in rank to be more easily identified as seen in Figure 21-5.

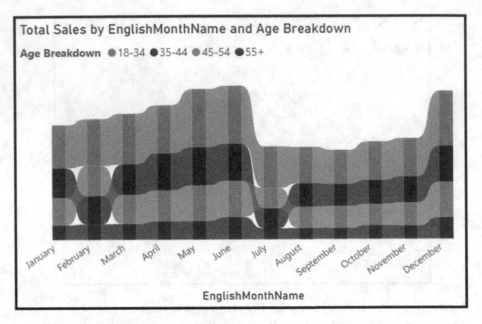

Figure 21-5. *The Ribbon chart has a pleasant flow to the presentation, and the fact that we can see the change over time with a focus on rank change is great*

Funnel Chart

The **Funnel** chart is good at showing trends between different stages of data. The category which has the highest value in relation to the measure used for the **Values** section is set at the top of the **Funnel** chart, and all other values are ranked below it. The interesting characteristic about this visual is that each category will show the percentage difference between itself and the category directly above it as well as the difference between itself and the highest category. The main thing that needs to be done to show values in that order is to ensure that you are sorting the visual on the metric value as seen in Figure 21-6.

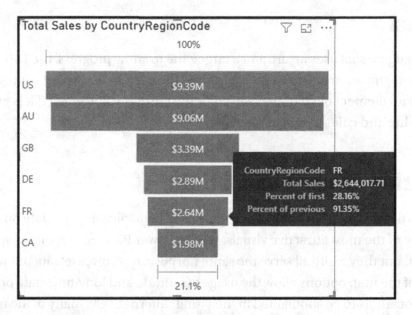

Figure 21-6. *By sorting the visual by the metric value used in the Values section, we can achieve this presentation of a funnel with the highest value on top and lowest on the bottom*

Visualizing Goal Tracking

With goal tracking, the idea is to visualize how close we are to achieving a certain objective. Power BI has only a couple options to showcase data in relation to some sort of target or objective. These visuals are the **KPI** visual and the **Gauge** visual. Both visuals are simple in their design, and both display a single value and its progress toward a specific goal.

Gauge Visual

This visual allows users to map a metric value to both the **Values** section and the **Target Value** section. The **Values** section is looking for a measure which is showing some sort of current metric, while the measure mapped to the **Target Value** section will be represented by a line within the arc inside the visual.

KPI Visual

While the Gauge visual uses an arc and a target line to show progress, the **KPI** visual is a bit more straightforward. The **KPI** visual shows the current and target values in plain text; there is an element of color that will color the current value green if it is greater than the target value and color it red if it is below.

Visualizing Geographical Data

People love maps! When working with geographical data, plotting that date on a map can make for one of the most attractive visuals. Within Power BI, there are four maps available for selection, but they really all serve the same purpose: to showcase data points on a map. Most of the map options allow the usage of latitude and longitude data points to dictate the locations to be spotlighted in the visual. Alternatively, many of the maps offer an online search capability through Bing to map the relevant locations on the map.

Map Visual

This visual is sometimes referred to as the **Bubble Map** as it allows the mapping of a metric value for the **Size** section to influence the size of the bubbles. Users will also find the ability to turn this into a heat map from the formatting options.

Filled Map

The default behavior of the **Filled Map** is to shade in the entire area indicated by the field used in the **Location** section. To showcase a variation in metric values across these locations, users will have to access the **Formatting** pane to set up conditional formatting and map that metric value to the **Tooltips** section.

Shape Map

At the time of writing this chapter, the **Shape Map** visual is still in a "preview" state. What makes this map option unique is the ability to import a map file to visualize any custom map. The file type needed to import must be compatible with the ".json" format. Once the import is completed, you can specify locations on a custom map of your choosing.

ArcGIS Map

This is the only visual that has some optional "paid" features to take advantage of. If you already have an ArcGIS account that you are paying for, this visual allows you to log in and take advantage of the layering options offered by **ArcGIS**. It also should be noted that in order to edit this visualization, users must use the **Focus Mode** option to see the various choices.

Try It Out

Now that we have discussed the various types of visualizations Power BI has, let us add some to the report we have been working on. We will pick a couple visualizations from each of the categories to showcase in our report. In the next chapter, we will add to these visualizations and focus on filtering and interactions between visuals. Feel free to explore the **Pane Filter** to adjust the font style, size, colors, and other options.

Lesson Requirements

To start this exercise, locate the Power BI report we created in Chapter 20 called **Ch 20 Extending Your Data Model With DAX** and open it in Power BI Desktop. As soon as this report is open, choose the **Save As** option in the **File** menu and name the report **Ch 21 Report Writing Basics**.

Hints

For each of the following categories, we will use the following visualizations:

1. Visualizing Categorical Data

   a. **Pie Chart** – Profit by Age Breakdown

   b. **Clustered Column Chart** – Profit by EnglishCountryRegionName and Gender

   c. **Treemap** – Profit by EnglishCountryRegionName

2. Visualizing Data Trends

    a. **Line Chart** – Total Sales by EnglishMonthName

    b. **Ribbon Chart** – Total Sales by EnglishMonthName and Age Breakdown

    c. **Funnel Chart** – Total Sales by CountryRegionCode

3. Visualizing Goal Tracking

    a. **Gauge** – Profit and Prior Year Profit

4. Visualizing Geographical Data

    a. **Map Visual** – Total Sales by EnglishCountryRegionName

    b. **Filled Map Visual** – Total Sales by EnglishCountryRegionName

Step by Step

Here are the steps to follow in working this chapter's example:

1. With the Power BI report open, ensure that you are in the **Report View** and let us rename the report page at the bottom. Call the page **Categorical Data** as seen in Figure 21-7.

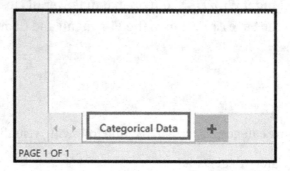

Figure 21-7. *You can create as many report pages as you like, and you will learn how to allow them to communicate in the following chapter*

2. Choose the **Pie chart** visual from the selection area and resize it to your liking.

3. For this first visual, we will show the amount of **Profit** by **Age Breakdown**. Locate the **Age Breakdown** calculated column and drag it to the **Legend** section of the field well.

4. Locate the **Profit** measure and drag it to the **Values** section of the **Pie chart** as seen in Figure 21-8.

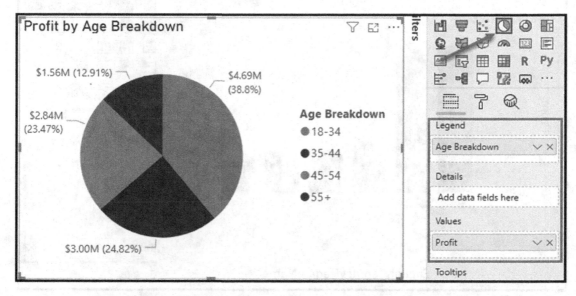

Figure 21-8. *Do not forget that a Pie chart can be effective if there are a controlled number of categories and there is an even distribution*

5. The next visual we will use to showcase categorical data will be the **Clustered Column chart.** To create this new visual, ensure that you have no other visual selected when you choose the **Clustered Column chart**. Select this visual and position it where you prefer.

6. For the **Axis** of this visual, locate the **EnglishCountryRegionName** column and drag it to this location.

7. Next, find the **Profit** measure and drag it to the **Values** section of this visual.

8. Last, we have an option to either add another measure to the **Values** section or to add a categorical column to the **Legend** section to populate the additional columns that make this the **Clustered Column chart**.

9. For this example, we will use the **Gender** categorical column in the **Legend** section of the visual as seen in Figure 21-9.

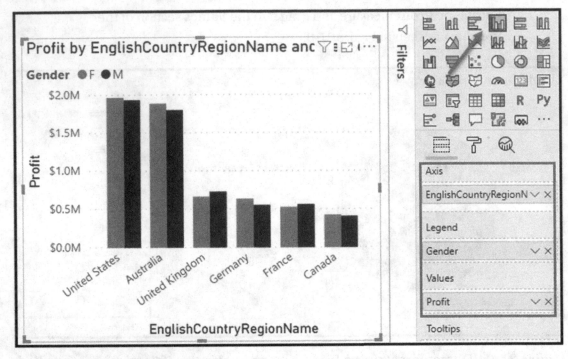

Figure 21-9. *In this example, the number of columns that will appear depends on the number of unique values in the column used in the Legend section*

10. The last visual we will use for this report page will be the **Treemap visual**. Once selected, resize the visual to your liking within the remaining available space.

11. For the **Group** section, we will use the **EnglishCountryRegionName** column, and for the **Values** section, we will bring in the **Profit** measure.

12. The visual will change in presentation depending on the size you specify. Thus, your **Treemap** may not look exactly like in Figure 21-10.

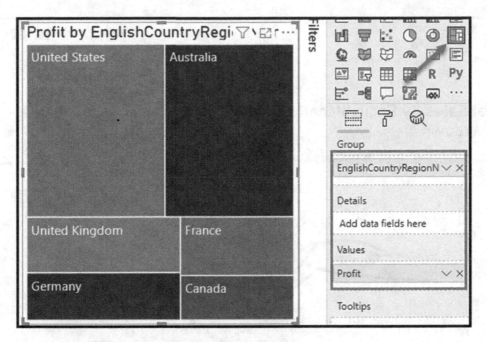

Figure 21-10. *The Treemap visual works nicely with hierarchies which we will explore in the next chapter*

13. Next, we will move on to visualizing data trends. In the bottom left part of Power BI Desktop, you will see a "+" icon which creates a new report page.

14. Select this option and rename the new page **Visualizing Trend Data** as seen in Figure 21-11.

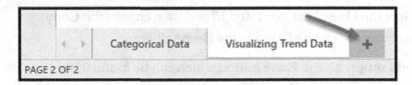

Figure 21-11. *Report pages can be hidden if you do not want your end users to navigate to it*

15. The first visualization we will use is the **Line chart**. For this visualization, we will map the **EnglishMonthName** to the **Axis**, **Total Sales** to the **Values**, and **Age Breakdown** for the legend as seen in Figure 21-12.

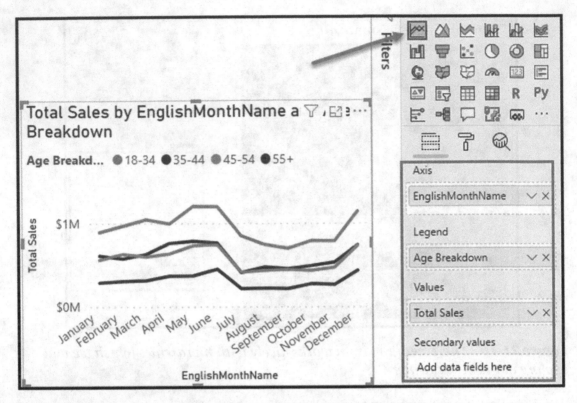

Figure 21-12. *Line charts are great for easily seeing upward or downward trends*

16. The next visualization we will use is the **Ribbon chart**. This visualization not only shows the trending but also has an element of ranking as well. To showcase this, we will copy the previous visual and simply change it to a **Ribbon chart**.

17. Select the **Line chart** from step 15 and then choose the **Copy** option which can be found in the **Home** ribbon.

18. Then simply hit the **Paste** button which can be found in that same section in the **Home** ribbon which will create a duplicate visualization.

19. With the newly duplicated visual selected, choose the **Ribbon chart** visual, and you will see that all the mappings are preserved for you as seen in Figure 21-13.

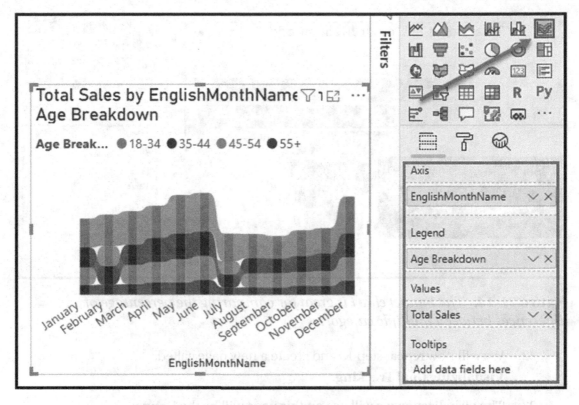

Figure 21-13. *The Ribbon chart is effectively a Stacked Column chart that shows the change in ranking from one category to the next*

20. The last visualization we will create on this page will be the **Funnel chart**.

21. With the **Funnel chart** selected, map the **CountryRegionCode** column to the **Group** section and the **Total Sales** column to the **Values** section as seen in Figure 21-14.

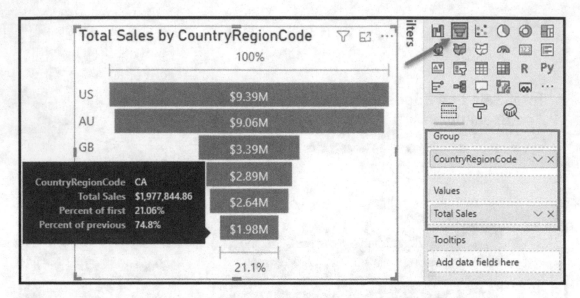

Figure 21-14. *The Funnel chart is great for comparing the percentage of differences between multiple categories*

22. We will now repeat step 13 and create a new page called **Visualizing Goal Tracking**.

23. The visualization we will use on this page will be the **Gauge visual**. This visual only requires the **Values** section and the **Target Value** section to be mapped to render.

24. For this visual, we will be using the **Profit** measure for the **Values** section and the **Prior Year Profit** measure for the **Target Value** section.

25. Even with these two fields mapped, the visual will look a little odd because these measures require some form of date input. We will accomplish this by creating a Slicer visual that uses the **Calendar Year** column.

26. We will cover the Slicer visual more in depth in the next chapter, but for now use the drop-down in the upper right of the slicer to choose the **Dropdown** slicer option and choose the year **2007** which will make the **Gauge** visual function as seen in Figure 21-15.

Figure 21-15. *The Minimum and Maximum sections will always automatically default to 0 and double the Value amount when left unmapped*

27. Once again, we will create a new report page, and we will call this one **Visualizing Geographical Data**.

28. The first visual we will use is the **Map** visual. Select this option and resize it as you see fit.

29. With our dataset, we will have to map the **Location** section since we do not have latitude/longitude information. We will use the **EnglishCountryRegionName** field for the **Location** section, but we do need to set its data category.

30. Highlight the **EnglishCountryRegionName** field and select the drop-down for the **Data Category** option within the **Column tools** ribbon. Choose the **Country** value as seen in Figure 21-16.

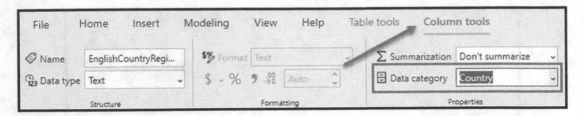

Figure 21-16. *You should always take the time to set the Data Category property for all your geographic columns*

31.   Now we can map the **EnglishCountryRegionName** column to the **Location** section of the **Map** visual which will present bubbles in the correct locations.

32.   Optionally, we can also map the **Total Sales** measure to the **Size** section to distinguish which countries have more total sales than others as seen in Figure 21-17.

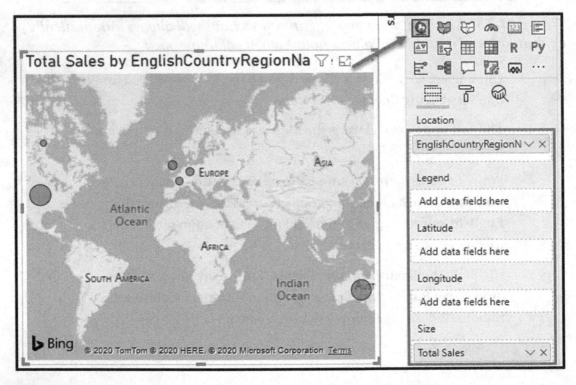

Figure 21-17. *There is an option within the format setting to change this into a heat map visual*

33.   This is the last visual for this exercise so make sure to save
        your report.

Summary

Power BI has many different visualizations available by default to display our data.
Knowing and understanding which visuals are best for displaying certain types of
data is critical. In this chapter, we explored our various options to ensure that we
are picking the very best visual for the message we are looking to deliver to our end
users. In the next chapter, we will add more items to these visuals to give them a more
interactive look and feel.

CHAPTER 22

Designing Interactive Reports

The interactive capabilities of Power BI open a whole new world of exploring data never before available to the non-IT professional. Report consumers today are no longer receiving static printed reports on their desk. Instead, they are receiving interactive and responsive dashboards that give them immediate insights into their data. These new reports and dashboards allow them to drill down further and explore the data in ways never before imagined. In this chapter, you will learn about some of the exciting interactive capabilities available in Power BI, and as you continue your journey with Power BI after this book, you will learn we are just scratching the surface!

Filtering in Power BI

There are many available options for filtering data in Power BI. In the previous chapter, you learned how to filter data from the filter pane. In this section, you will learn how visuals can filter other visuals and how to control that behavior. You will also learn how to use visual filters, also known as slicers, to make your reports exciting and interactive for report consumers.

Filtering Data with Visuals

Visualizations can filter other visuals; this is really awesome and adds a lot of analytical depth to Power BI. This exploratory feature has long been a favorite of Power BI users. In Figure 22-1, the United States has been selected on the Treemap visual, and accordingly the rest of the visuals within the report page are filtered automatically. This filtering is the default behavior of Power BI and can be changed by editing the way visuals interact with one another, but that will be discussed later in this chapter.

© Mitchell Pearson, Brian Knight, Devin Knight, Manuel Quintana 2020

M. Pearson et al., *Pro Microsoft Power Platform*, https://doi.org/10.1007/978-1-4842-6008-1_22

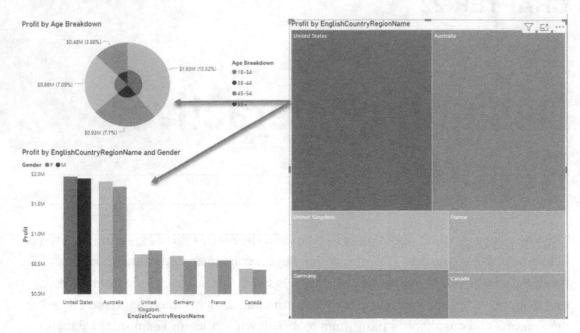

Figure 22-1. *Filter a report from an existing visual*

Slicers

Slicers are visual filters that report consumers can easily interact with. Slicers, unlike filters in the filter pane, are available on the report page with other visuals. Because of their proximity and visibility, the user is always aware of any filters that are currently impacting the results of a report. Their accessibility alone is a big reason why slicers are often used rather than the filter pane.

When developing a report, the developer can choose a few different options for how the slicer will be visualized. Slicers can appear on a report as a drop-down box, as a list of selectable items, as a relative slicer, or as a range slicer. In Figure 22-2, the slicer is represented as a list of available years, and the report has been filtered to only display the data for the calendar year of 2008.

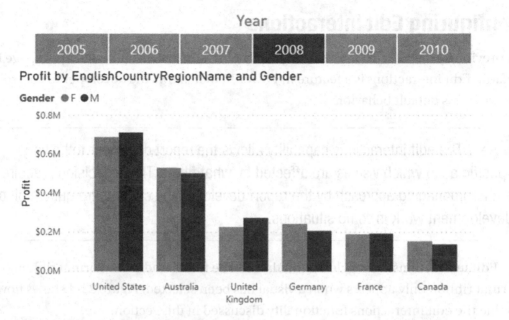

Figure 22-2. Filtering data with slicers

Sync Slicers

By default, a slicer only filters the report page that it has been assigned to. However, sync slicers allow the developer to extend the reach of slicers to other pages within a report.

When syncing a slicer across multiple report pages, you will have two options to choose from. The first option is to choose which additional pages will be filtered by the current slicer. The second option is whether the slicer should also appear and be visible on the pages which will be affected. Enabling the sync slicer functionality is shown in Figure 22-3. To enable this functionality, select "Sync slicers" from the View ribbon, and then a new pop-up pane will appear; once a slicer has been selected, the options within the pane can be modified.

Figure 22-3. Enabling and configuring sync slicer capability

Configuring Edit Interactions

As previously discussed, filters automatically filter all other visuals on a report page by default. Edit interactions is a feature in Power BI that allows the developer to control and override this default behavior.

Note   The edit interactions capability allows the report developer to be very specific as to which visuals are affected by what filters. These decisions require a micromanaging approach by the report developer and can require quite a bit of development work in some situations.

Edit interactions is a toggle button that can be found under the Format ribbon. The Format ribbon only appears when a visual has been selected. Figure 22-4 shows how to enable the edit interactions functionality discussed in this section.

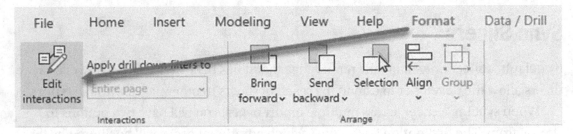

Figure 22-4. *Enable edit interactions*

Once enabled, the report developer can then configure how each individual report will interact with each visualization on the report page. In Figure 22-5, the slicer has been selected, and each of the other visuals now has an option box that appears. Generally, this Filter option will appear at the top right of a visual as seen in Figure 22-5, but not always. There are two options available in Figure 22-5; the first option is to enable filter, which is enabled by default. The second option is to turn off filtering.

Keep in mind that disabling filtering will only turn off filters that come from the visual currently selected. If you want a visual in Power BI to be completely unaffected by all visuals, then you would have to repeat this process for each visual.

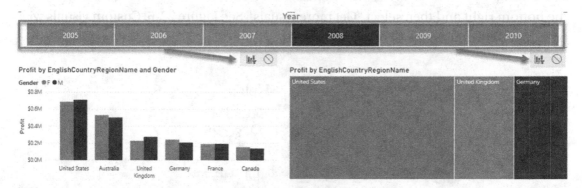

Figure 22-5. *Edit the way visuals interact with one another*

Using Custom Visuals

Custom visuals is the final topic in this chapter on interactivity. Microsoft Power BI ships with a solid collection of default visualizations that are more than capable by themselves. But Microsoft opened up the ability to create visuals to the community, and the results have been staggering. Custom visuals really allow the developer to extend the capabilities of an already incredible tool even further.

Free and Paid Versions

Many custom visuals are free, but there are quite a few that do cost money to use. Information about which ones are free and which custom visuals cost money can be found from the Microsoft Office store.

Certified Custom Visuals

Interestingly, some custom visuals are created by Microsoft. However, most of them are not. When using code developed by a third party, it is always good to be cautious and aware of what risks may exist. To ease your concerns, Microsoft has certified many of the custom visuals by checking the code to make sure that it performs well and is free of any malicious intent.

Using Custom Visuals from the Microsoft Store

Importing custom visuals from the Microsoft store is a very simple process, like most other things in Power BI. From the Visualizations pane, click the ellipsis (…) located at the bottom right and then select "Get more visuals." See Figure 22-6. Custom visuals will be explored further in the "Try It Out" section.

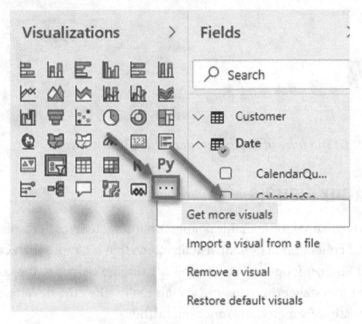

Figure 22-6. *Edit the way visuals interact with one another*

Note   Because custom visuals are created by the community, they can sometimes be difficult to set up and configure. To help with this dilemma, Devin Knight has created a huge series of blogs and short YouTube videos that show setup and configuration of over 100 custom Power BI visualizations. Visit his website at www.devinknightsql.com.

Try It Out

In this exercise, we will add to the Power BI report created in the previous chapter. We will implement a **Slicer** visual and explore the available styles that can be used. We will also look at the different options available that affect the **Edit Interactions** feature and update how our **Treemap** visual will react when filtered. Lastly, we will visit the custom visual marketplace and import a custom visual into our report.

Lesson Requirements

Before you begin the example, make sure that you have the following requirements in place:

1. Access the Power BI report that was created in the previous chapter called **Ch 21 Report Writing Basics**.

2. You will need to be signed in to Power BI Desktop using your Power BI credentials to access the custom visual marketplace.

Building Interactivity in Power BI

Ready? Here are the steps to follow:

1. Let us first open the previous Power BI report and use the **Save As** feature to rename this report to **Ch 22 Designing Interactive Reports**.

2. We will start from the report page labeled **Categorical Data**.

3. On this report page, we are looking at various visuals which showcase the difference in values between different categories. We would like to give our users the ability to apply a filter on our **CalendarYear** column.

4. A great option to accomplish this would be the **Slicer** visual. Select this visual and rearrange your other visuals to allow room for the slicer.

5. There is only one section available for mapping inside the **Slicer** visual, and that is the **Field** section. This area expects a categorical value, and we will select the **CalendarYear** column from the **Date** table.

6. By default, our years are displayed in what is known as a **Numeric Range Slicer**. This option for slicers can be adjusted to specify a range of years on which to filter the results. We would like our users to be able to select a value from a drop-down list.

7. In the upper right-hand corner of the Slicer visual, you will find a tiny down arrow icon. When selected, this arrow will present a drop-down list of slicer styles, and the option we want is called **Dropdown** as seen in Figure 22-7.

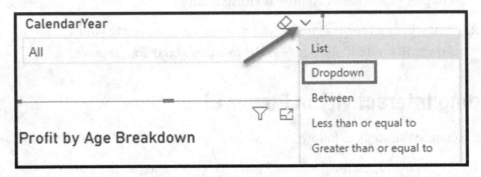

Figure 22-7. *Depending on the data type of the column used in the slicer, certain options may not be available*

8. Now that we have a slicer, users can filter this report page by whatever years they would like to see.

9. On this report page, we also have a **Pie chart** showing the distribution of **Profit by Age Breakdown**. When a user selects one of the pieces of the **Pie chart**, it will filter the other visuals on this page; this is the **Interactive Filtering** option.

10. The default behavior, which can be seen in the **Treemap** visual, is called **Highlight Filtering**. This ensures that the original shape of the **Treemap** will not change because of **Interactive Filtering**. Therefore, the tooltip will display the highlighted amount as well as the total amount.

11. We will now change the interactive filtering behavior for the **Treemap** visual by accessing the **Edit Interactions** feature.

12. While you have the **Pie chart** selected, click the **Format** ribbon, which is only available when a visual is selected, and click the **Edit Interactions** button.

13. You will now notice three new icons located in the upper-right corner of the *Treemap* visual as seen in Figure 22-8.

Figure 22-8. *When you turn on Edit Interactions, you grant yourself the ability to dictate how other visuals will behave when you select a value within your currently highlighted visual*

14. The icon on the farthest left is the **Filter** option. The icon in the middle, which is selected by default, is the **Highlight** option, and the item on the right tells the visual to ignore all filtering.

15. Choose the **Filter** option and then select the "18–34" category of the **Pie chart**. It will be difficult to notice but the structure of the **Treemap** has now changed and is no longer showing the highlight and the total, but only the filtered value amount.

16. The last thing we will add to our Power BI report is a custom visual. To access the library of custom visuals, you will want to navigate to the **Insert** ribbon and select the option labeled **More visuals** and choose the **From AppSource** option as seen in Figure 22-9.

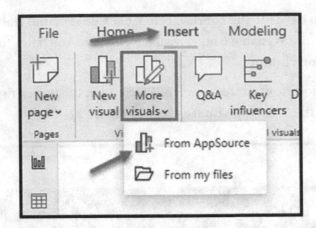

Figure 22-9. *The AppSource is always being updated with new and exciting custom visuals which can be used in Power BI*

17. When the **AppSource** dialog box opens, select the **Search** option, and look for the term "flag."

18. The option we want to choose is called "Enlighten World Flags" slicer. Once you have located this custom visual, select the **Add** option.

19. You will be returned to your report and receive a message that the custom visual has been imported. You will also see a new icon in the Visualizations pane as shown in Figure 22-10.

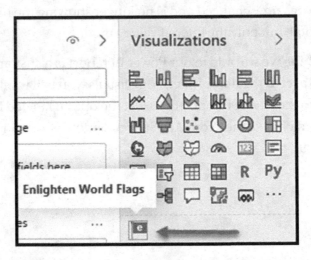

Figure 22-10. *Custom visuals are saved as part of the report. You can choose to add this custom visual to Power BI Desktop, and it will be available for all future reports*

20. Select the **Visualizing Trend Data** report page and rearrange the visuals to make room for this new custom visual.

21. Select the **Enlighten World Flags** slicer and map the **EnglishCountryRegionName** to the **Country** section within the slicer.

22. You will see that we are presented with the flags for each of our countries. This custom visual accepts full country names or the two-letter alpha code to identify the appropriate flag as seen in Figure 22-11.

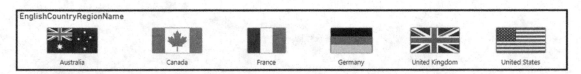

Figure 22-11. *This custom visual makes it very easy to add beautiful images to your report*

23. Save your report and we have now completed this exercise.

Summary

In Chapter 21, we started with basic report visuals, and now with this chapter, we have explored the interactivity available to us within Power BI Desktop. Also, we have seen how we can expand our reports using the custom visual AppSource to import amazing custom visuals. In the next chapter, we will see how we can bring all these features together to tell a story with our data.

CHAPTER 23

Data Storytelling with Power BI

By now you have learned how to use Power BI to connect to, clean, organize, and present data. These are all important skills to have, but to really make your reports stand out and help drive decision-making, they should tell a story. Data is inert unless your audience knows the story it tells. That is why it is up to you to be a storyteller with your data. You can translate your data from having potential value into driving real business outcomes.

So, what makes storytelling so special? Stories have always been one of the most effective tools for sharing information with others. Our brains are built for telling and listening to stories. What occurs biologically when we hear stories is pretty amazing! When listening to a data-driven story, our body releases dopamine into our systems that places emotions behind data, making it easier to remember. Another thing unique to storytelling is our brain tends to turn stories we hear into our own ideas and experiences. You at some point have likely experienced this concept. Have you ever heard a story that you were not actually part of, but when you are listening to it, you can picture yourself there? This is what makes storytelling so effective.

In this chapter, you will learn about several of the features that are built-in to Power BI that can be utilized for storytelling. These features by themselves are not capable of telling stories, but how you use them is what can make an impact on your users.

Using Power BI Drill Through

Often when viewing a report, end users will want to know more details about a specific aspect of the data. To provide that level of detail about a specific attribute, it may make sense to implement a drill-through report page. When report consumers use a drill through, they first right-click a data point. This then gives the user an option to select

© Mitchell Pearson, Brian Knight, Devin Knight, Manuel Quintana 2020
M. Pearson et al., *Pro Microsoft Power Platform*, https://doi.org/10.1007/978-1-4842-6008-1_23

drill through to another page. This drill-through page generally navigates the user to a report page displaying a filtered view of detailed data. The "Try It Out" section of this chapter will cover the details of configuring a drill-through report page.

Report Page Tooltips

Tooltips have long been a method of showing users additional information regarding data points they hover over with their mouse. Almost all visuals in Power BI have this capability. For example, if you were to hover above a Bar chart on a report page, you will see a tooltip automatically appear and look like Figure 23-1.

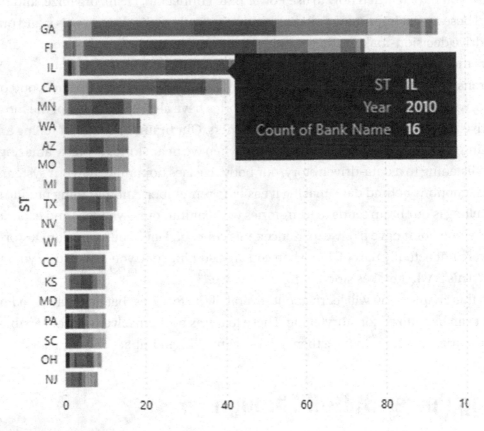

Figure 23-1. *A standard Power BI tooltip*

This is the default behavior of Power BI, but you have the ability to override this default with a more custom approach. That is where Report Page Tooltips come into your design. With Report Page Tooltips, you can replace this standard tooltip with one of your own design. Nearly anything that you can put on a report page can also appear within a Report Page Tooltip. Figure 23-2 shows the same Bar chart as you saw earlier, but now with an upgraded Report Page Tooltip. The tooltip pops up when a user hovers above a particular data point on the chart.

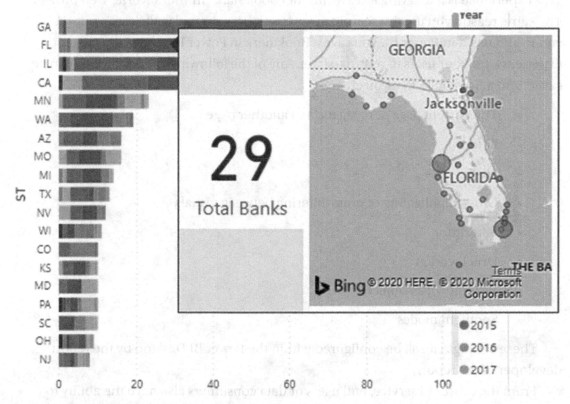

Figure 23-2. An effective Report Page Tooltip

You will learn more configuration steps required to implement your own Report Page Tooltips in the "Try It Out" section of this chapter.

Selection Pane

The Selection pane has a very simple task. It is used to either hide or show visuals, buttons, images, and any other controls you might put on the design surface of the report. This feature by itself may not be incredibly impressive, but when combined with other features like Bookmarks, you can build some exciting interactive features on your report.

Bookmarks

Bookmarks are one of the storytelling features of Power BI that really let you be creative. Using Bookmarks allows you to capture the current configuration state of a report page. This experience is like saving a "Favorite" or "Bookmark" in your favorite web browser. The same reason you use this feature in your web browser is also the same reason why you would use it in Power BI. You save a Bookmark in Power BI to save the current experience for your users to return to later. Any of the following configurations can be saved into a Bookmark that you create:

- The current page or navigation to another page

- Filters

- Slicers

- Cross-highlighting or cross-filtering between visuals

- Sort order

- Drill location

- Visibility of an object

- Spotlight modes

These settings can all be configured within the Power BI Desktop by the report developer of the report.

From the Power BI service, end users or data consumers also have the ability to save Personal Bookmarks. The idea behind Personal Bookmarks is for users to take a report that is meant for hundreds of people and save design features like filters, slicer selections, and the state of visuals. The next time they return to the report, their personal view is made automatically available.

Test this out for yourself! The "Try It Out" section will walk you through building a report that uses all of the storytelling features mentioned in this chapter.

Try It Out

In this "Try It Out" section, you will take the skills that you learned in the previous sections and use them together to build a Power BI solution that tells a story. Doing this will not only make for a more engaging report but one that helps drive decisions in your organizations.

Lesson Requirements

You have been tasked with building a report to show trends in the video game industry for an important presentation your manager is delivering. Your company is considering investing in a video game publisher and wants to make a data-driven decision. You have been provided the data, but it is up to you to design a report that is engaging and helps your company make the best decision.

Hints

- Create a drill-through report page so users can see the details of each video game title.

- Build a Report Page Tooltip that will list top game titles by user scores.

- Use the Bookmark and Selection pane features to create a pop-up for your users to apply filters to the data based on the publisher and video game console.

Step by Step

Connect to the Data Source

1. Launch the Power BI Desktop and select **Get data** to select the data source used for this example.

2. Choose Excel as the source type and click **Connect**. Choose the file Video Games.xlsx from the book files and then select **Open**.

3. The Navigator window will launch where you will select the spreadsheet called Video Game Sales and then click **Load**.

Build Basic Report Visuals

1. Bring a Line chart onto the report design surface and add the Date column to the Axis, Revenue to the Values section, and lastly Game title to Secondary values.

Tip   Using the Secondary values section of a Line chart creates a second Y axis, allowing you to measure multiple types of metrics on the same chart.

---

2. You can rename fields within a chart simply by double-clicking them within the chart configuration. Go ahead and rename Count of Game Title located in the Secondary values to Total Games.

3. Next, select the white background of the report and bring in a Stacked Column chart. Place Revenue into the Values section and Console into the Axis section.

4. For the last visual on this page, select the page background again and bring in a Scatter chart. Place Publisher on the Legend, Game Title under X axis, and Revenue in the Y axis.

5. Select the page background again and modify the page formatting to add a background image. Select the Format paint roller icon and then choose **Page background**. Choose the **Add image** button and select the file named StorytellingBackground.png found in the Apress book files.

6. After you select the image, change the **Transparency** property to 0% and the **Image Fit** property to Fit.

7. Now, select *each* visual individually and turn on the border in the Format section of the Visualization pane. Under the Border section of properties, you should also change the **Radius** setting to 20 px.

8. Add a text box, from the Insert ribbon, to the top of the report header area with the text "Industry Summary." Make the text size 44 and turn off the background in the Format section of the Visualization pane.

9. Use the theme file created for this chapter by going to the View ribbon and expand the default themes to find the **Browse for themes** button. Select the theme file called VideoGameIndustry. json to use for this report.

10. Rename this report page "Industry Summary" and change the size
     and position of each visual on the report so it appears as shown in
     Figure 23-3.

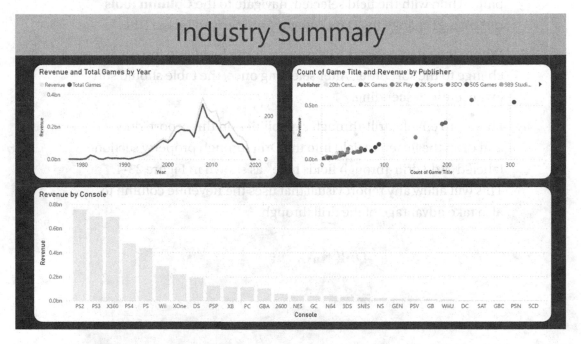

Figure 23-3. *Visuals aligned within the background selected*

Seeing Details with a Drill Through

1. Add a new page to this report and rename it "Game Details."

2. Add the same background image to this new report page that you
    did in step 8. Again, you will need to change the **Transparency** to
    0% and change the **Image Fit** property to Fit.

3. Add a text box to the top of the report header area with the text
    "Drill through." Make the text size 44 and turn off the background.

4. Bring the Table visual on the report design surface and add the
    following fields to it: Cover Art Image URL, Game Title, Publisher,
    Console Image URL, Revenue. Resize the table to take up the full
    page without covering up the header area.

5. Notice that the fields Cover Art Image URL and Console Image URL are links to an image. To make Power BI render the image in your report, select each of these fields individually in the Fields pane. Then with the field selected, navigate to the **Column tools** ribbon and change the **Data category** property to Image URL.

6. Within the table, select the Revenue column header to force a change to the sort order. After selecting once, the table should sort by Revenue descending.

7. Finally, to enable drill-through capabilities on this report, drag and drop the Revenue field into the Drill through property section labeled "Add drill-through fields here" as shown in Figure 23-4. This will allow any report visual that uses the Revenue column to also take advantage of the drill through.

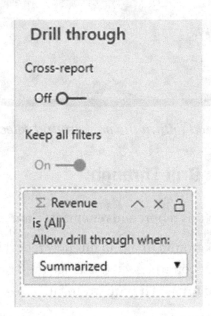

Figure 23-4. *The Drill through property section leveraging the Revenue field*

8. When a field is added to the Drill through property, a back button is automatically added to the top left of the report page. This allows users interacting with the report the ability to easily navigate back to the report they came from.

To make this back button better blend with our report design, select the button. Next, go to the Visualization properties to turn off the background color. If you do not see the back button, you might need to move your table as it could be covering it up.

9. It is unlikely that a user would come directly to any drill-through report you design. It often makes sense to hide drill-through pages from end users. To do this, right-click the page name at the bottom of the screen "Game Details" and select **Hide Page**.

10. Test out the drill through by first selecting the Industry Summary report page previously created. On the chart labeled Revenue by Console, right-click the value labeled XOne and select **Drill through ➤ Game Details**. This will launch the drill-through report with only Xbox One games displayed as shown in Figure 23-5.

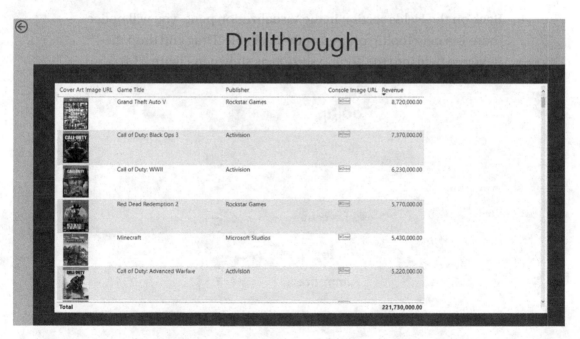

Figure 23-5. *The completed Game Details report page*

11. To go back to the Industry Summary page, do a **Ctrl+Click** on the back button in the top left. The **Ctrl+Click** action is only needed while in the Power BI Desktop. Once this report is deployed to the Power BI service, a simple click will activate the button.

Building Your Own Custom Tooltips

1. Add another new page to this report and rename it "Tooltip." Hide this page in the same manner as you did with the drill through page. You do not want your users to accidentally navigate to this page once published.

2. There are a few page-level settings that need to be modified to use this new page as a tooltip. Navigate to the Format paint roller icon and turn on the **Tooltip** setting found under the **Page Information** section.

3. Next, change the **Type** to Tooltip under the **Page size** section. This will make the tooltip so it is not overwhelming in size when it pops up on the report.

4. Back on the Fields section in the Visualization pane, you will notice there is a new Tooltip property now available. Drag and drop the Revenue field into the Tooltip section as shown in Figure 23-6.

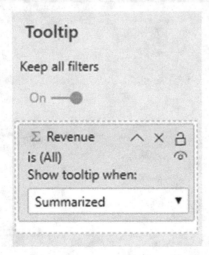

Figure 23-6. *The Tooltip property section leveraging the Revenue field*

5. Place a Multi-row card to the top of the report design surface. Add Revenue and Game Title fields to the visual. Change the name of Count of Game Title to just Total Games. Expand the Game Title in the Fields section to select Count.

6. Next, add a small table to the design surface with the fields Game Title and User Score. Change the aggregation on User Score to Don't Summarize for the visual only. Sort the table's data so the higher values in User Score appear at the top. You may need to resize the table right away as it most likely covered up your Multi-row card.

7. There is a very small design surface to work with but shift around your visuals, so they appear as shown in Figure 23-7.

4,601,930,000.00	2805
Revenue	Total Games

Game Title	User Score ∧
Bully: Scholarship Edition	10.00
Red Dead Redemption	10.00
Star Wars: Knights of the Old Republic	10.00
Forza Motorsport 3	9.80
Metal Gear Solid 4: Guns of the Patriots	9.80
BioShock	9.60

Figure 23-7. The completed Tooltip report

8. To test out the Report Page Tooltip, navigate back to the Industry Summary page and hover above any of the data points on your visuals to see the updated tooltip interaction. You should note that not all games have a value for the user score so you will likely see several blanks depending on what you hover above.

Using Bookmarks and the Selection Pane to Build Interactive Reports

1. Navigate to the View ribbon and select both Bookmarks and Selection buttons to show these panes. Leave these open as you will need them throughout the next several steps.

2. While still on the Industry Summary page, go to the Insert ribbon and select Image. Choose the ClearFilterIcon.png and select open. Resize this image and place it in the top-right corner of the header area of this report.

3. Bring in a second image by going to the Insert ribbon again and selecting Image. Choose the FilterIcon.png and select open. Resize this image and place it in the top-right corner of the header area of this report next to the previous image.

4. Next, you will create a pop-up menu for slicers you would like to make available for your end users. You will use these two images to launch a slicer menu and clear all slicer selections when you are done. Slicers are visuals that can take up a lot of real estate, so this method is an effort to reduce the space they require.

    Under the Insert ribbon, select Shapes and choose Rectangle. Resize the rectangle so the width is 800 pixels and the height is 600 pixels, then place it in the center of the design surface. You can resize your object by expanding the general section under format shape as long as you have selected your shape.

5. Add a slicer on top of the rectangle and place the field Publisher in it. In the top-right corner of the slicer, click **More Options** and select Search. This will allow users to easily find the publisher they are interested in analyzing.

6. Add a second slicer on top of the rectangle and place the field Console in it. In the top-right corner of the slicer, click **More Options** and select Search.

7. Go back to the Insert ribbon and select Image again. Choose CloseIcon.png and select open. Place this image in the top-right corner of the rectangle and resize it so it appears as shown in Figure 23-8.

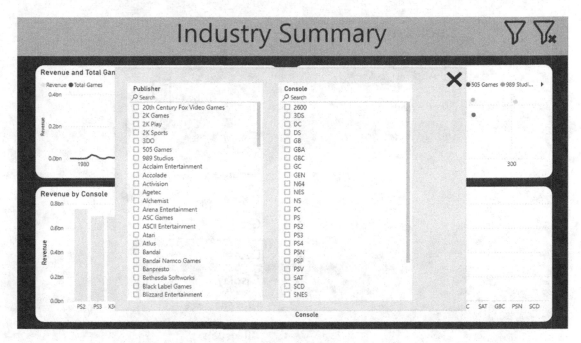

Figure 23-8. *Layout of this pop-up design pattern*

8. In the Bookmarks pane, select Add to create a new bookmark.
    Rename this bookmark Launch Slicer Pop-up. On this new
    bookmark, select the More options ellipsis and uncheck Data as
    shown in Figure 23-9. Unchecking Data means that the visual
    layout will be saved to the bookmark, but any data changes are not
    saved.

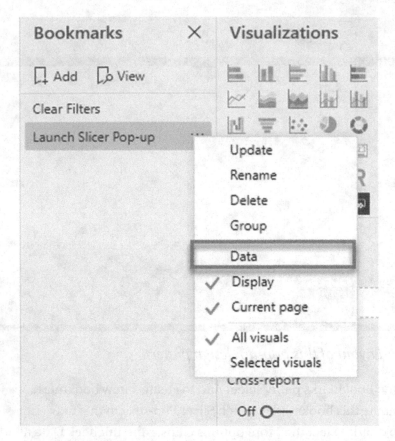

Figure 23-9. *Unchecking Data from the Launch Slicer Pop-up bookmark*

9. Select the FilterIcon.png previously imported. Under the Format
    image pane, expand and turn on the Action section. Set the **Type**
    to Bookmark and set Launch Slicer Pop-up as the bookmark that
    should be launched when this image is selected.

10. In the Selection pane, hide the top four items on the list by
    clicking the icon to the right of Image, Slicer, Slicer, and Shape.

11. In the Bookmarks pane, select Add to create a new bookmark.
    Double-click the new bookmark and rename it Clear Filters.

12. Select the Image, ClearFilterIcon.png. Now, under the Format
    image pane, expand and turn on the Action section. Set the **Type**
    to Bookmark and set Clear Filters as the bookmark that should be
    launched when this image is selected.

13. Add a third bookmark by clicking Add in the Bookmarks pane. Double-click this bookmark and rename it Hide Slicer Pop-up. Uncheck Data under the More options menu.

14. This bookmark needs to be bound to the CloseIcon.png, which is not visible now. To make it visible again, select the Launch Slicer Pop-up bookmark.

    Select the CloseIcon.png image, and under the Format image pane, expand and turn on the Action section. Set the **Type** to Bookmark and set Hide Slicer Pop-up as the bookmark that should be launched when this image is selected.

15. Try interacting with this report to experience the enhancements you have made. Remember you have to control-click your buttons to get the action to work while in the Power BI Desktop.

CHAPTER 24

Sharing Power BI Solutions

The most time-consuming part of your Power BI design is over. You have spent much of your time in the Power BI Desktop fine-tuning your report, and you are now ready to share it with others. This means you are changing "hats" from being a Power BI analyst or developer to being a Power BI administrator. With that role change, the things that you are concerned about have also changed. No longer are you worried about a report's layout. Instead, you are now concerned with things like "How do I ensure everyone can view this solution?" and "How do I ensure the data in this model stays up to date?" The second of those questions will be addressed in the next chapter, but the point is there is a state of mind shift once you start considering the distribution of any solution.

Understanding the Power BI Service

Power BI's default deployment is within Microsoft's cloud ecosystem and is referred to as the Power BI service. The Power BI service not only provides a location to publish your Power BI collateral but also allows you to distribute, secure, and refresh solutions that you have designed. These key features are most important for you to remember for now, but as you will learn through this chapter and the next, there are many elements dedicated to each of these processes.

Using any of these capabilities will likely require a Power BI Pro license. The intent of this chapter, however, is to focus on answering the "what," "how," and "why" type of questions. An in-depth discussion about licensing will not be addressed intentionally as it can vary drastically based on your organization's plan for deploying Power BI.

© Mitchell Pearson, Brian Knight, Devin Knight, Manuel Quintana 2020
M. Pearson et al., *Pro Microsoft Power Platform*, https://doi.org/10.1007/978-1-4842-6008-1_24

> **Tip**   Learn more about how Power BI is priced here: `https://powerbi.microsoft.com/en-us/pricing/`.

It should be noted that while the Power BI service is the default deployment of Power BI, it is not the only method. For organizations not currently using the cloud, they may find an alternative called the Power BI Report Server. Since the Power BI Report Server is not a cloud service, it is not updated as frequently which means you could be missing out on some of the latest features. This is why non-cloud users must use a special install of the Power BI Desktop called the Power BI Desktop (Optimized for Power BI Report Server). This alternative install will prevent users from attempting to deploy a feature that does not exist on their version of Power BI.

What Are Workspaces?

Before you can publish a solution to the Power BI service, you first must have a workspace. Think of workspaces like a folder where any of your Power BI collateral can be published to and shared with others. This is a relatively simplistic understanding of workspaces because they allow for far more. For example, a workspace gives you an opportunity to have a collaborative work environment where multiple team members contribute to a solution.

Any users who log in to the Power BI service will notice that by default they have a workspace assigned to them called My Workspace. This workspace is personal to you and should be seen as a personal testing ground for your reports before you share them with others. Since its purpose is meant more for testing, many of the key features in the service, like Power BI Apps, are disabled in your My Workspace.

Thus, if you want to share your solution with others, you will need to create a new workspace. To do so, log in to PowerBI.com using a Power BI Pro license, then expand the Workspaces node on the left menu, and select Create a workspace as shown in Figure 24-1.

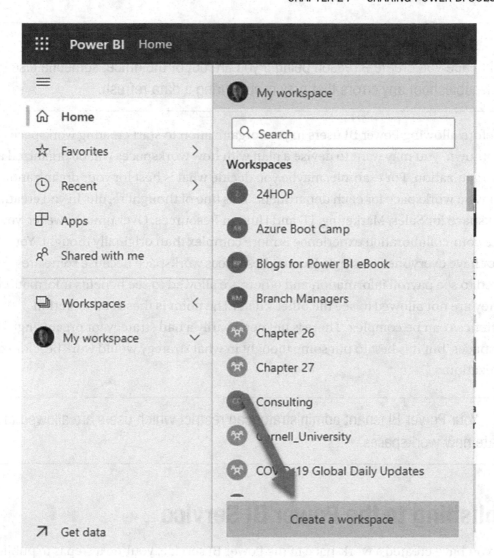

Figure 24-1. *Creating a new workspace*

You will give the new workspace a name and then assign users to it. Generally, the users that you assign to a workspace are not for viewing your solution but for collaborating and building additions to your solution. When you want users to only view and not collaborate, you will utilize a Power BI App.

> **Tip**   It is generally a good idea to have at least two users as an admin of any workspace you create – reason being if you are out of the office, someone else can still troubleshoot any errors that may occur during a data refresh.

Before allowing Power BI users in your organization to start creating workspaces on their own, you may want to devise a plan with how workspaces will be organized at your organization. For example, maybe you decide what is best for your organization is to have a workspace for each department. This line of thought results in you creating a workspace for Sales, Marketing, IT, and Human Resources. Over time, however, you realize your collaboration experience is more complex than originally thought. You cannot have everyone in a single Human Resources workspace because some are allowed to see payroll information and others are allowed to see benefits information, but they are not allowed to see the other's data. The point is these collaboration experiences can be complex. There is not necessarily a bad strategy for organizing workspaces, but it is best to put some thought in what strategy would work best for your organization.

> **Tip**   Your Power BI tenant administrator can restrict which users are allowed to create new workspaces.

Publishing to the Power BI Service

After you have created a workspace in the Power BI service, your next step is to publish your solution to it. This is done within the Power BI Desktop. With your solution open in the Power BI Desktop, simply click Publish under the Home ribbon as shown in Figure 24-2.

Figure 24-2. *Publishing to the Power BI service*

This will first prompt you to save a local copy of your .pbix file (if you have not already), and then you will choose which workspace you would like to publish to. When you publish to a workspace, the dataset and report will be included.

The report is the most obvious of the two items. It includes any report pages and data visualizations you have defined. The dataset is really everything else, which includes but is not limited to connections to the data sources, any data cleansing operations done within the Power Query Editor, relationships defined in the model, and DAX calculations defined.

Creating Dashboards

Something that is often confusing to Power BI beginners is dashboards. Some of this confusion is simply because of how Power BI defines a dashboard vs. what most users assume a dashboard is. Power BI dashboards can only be created from within the Power BI service. This means anything you build in the Power BI Desktop is considered to only be a report. The visuals on your report can be added to a dashboard once the report has been published to the Power BI service. So what exactly is a dashboard? A dashboard is made up of visuals that you select or "pin" from reports that have been deployed to the same workspace. Figure 24-3 shows a report visual being pinned to a dashboard. Once a visual is pinned to a dashboard, it is then referred to as a dashboard tile.

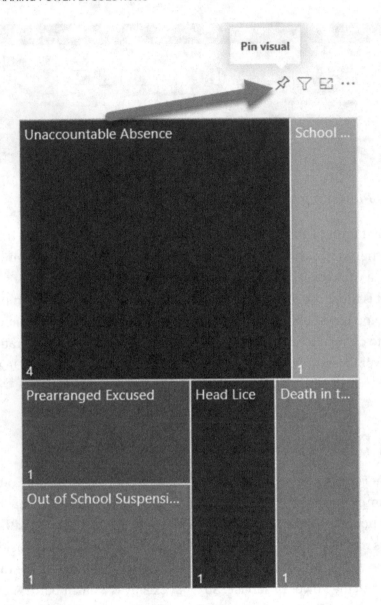

Figure 24-3. Pinning a report visual to a dashboard

You may also have visuals from completely separate reports feed into a single dashboard as long as they are in the same workspace. Let's think of a use case where this might be helpful. Maybe you work with a group of finance analysts. You have been assigned the task of building a Power BI solution for your general ledger data. Meanwhile, one of your colleagues has been assigned the task of building a solution on the accounts receivable data. Your CFO likes to look at the details of each solution but would prefer to have a single financial dashboard that takes from the GL data and the AR data presented side by side. Using Power BI dashboards gives you the ability to combine visuals from these separate solutions into a single view. If the CFO were to click any of the dashboard tiles, they would be taken to the underlying report from which the visual came.

Notice the click behavior is different with dashboard tiles compared to report visuals. When you click a report visual, it could do a drill down, cross-filter, or cross-highlight. When you click a dashboard tile, none of those behaviors are available. For some Power BI specialists, this can cause some debate as to whether they even really need a dashboard at all. If your users like the interaction that selecting report visuals provide and you have no need to combine multiple solutions together as described with our pretend CFO, then a Power BI report may be all you need. In those cases, you can skip the dashboard creation and just provide your users with the published report. Now, let us get into how you would grant your users access.

Sharing with Power BI Apps

When sharing solutions in Power BI, you will find there are multiple levels of access that can be given. The decision you make here may be based on what type of user you are interacting with. If you want to share with others that will be developing and collaborating with you, then you would likely grant them access to your workspace. If you intend to share with those that are only viewing your solution without collaboration, then you will likely leverage Power BI Apps. This chapter will focus on sharing to that large audience of end users who want to view your solution.

Power BI Apps give you the ability to package up any content that you have within a workspace so that it can be shared. You can even pick which items you wish to include or exclude from the app. For instance, maybe you have five reports in your workspace, but you are only ready to share three of them through your app. In that case, you simply turn off the Included in App setting shown in Figure 24-4. By default, all items in your workspace are automatically included to be published in the app.

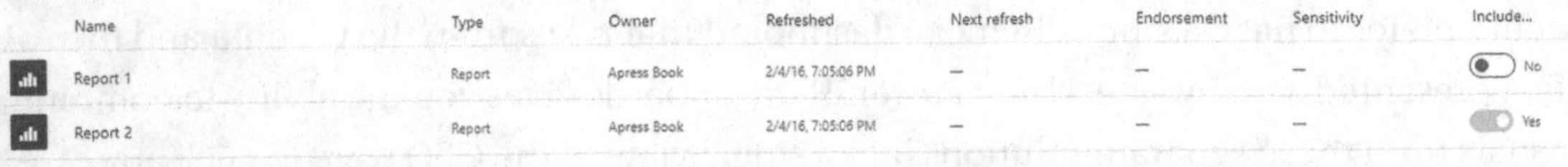

Name	Type	Owner	Refreshed	Next refresh	Endorsement	Sensitivity	Include...
Report 1	Report	Apress Book	2/4/16, 7:05:06 PM	—	—	—	⬤ No
Report 2	Report	Apress Book	2/4/16, 7:05:06 PM	—	—	—	⬤ Yes

Figure 24-4. *Excluding items from your Power BI App*

Once you are happy with the included components, you would select Create app. When publishing the app, you can specify a set of theme colors, navigation, and most importantly who will have access to the app. You can either add individual users to the app or ideally use your Azure Active Directory integration to select groups of users you would like to have access to the app.

Test this out for yourself. The "Try It Out" section of this chapter will walk you through creating a workspace, publishing to that workspace, building a dashboard, and then sharing an app.

Try It Out

In this "Try It Out" section, you learn how to dispense a Power BI solution to the masses. Taking the solution that was developed in the previous chapter, you will publish it to the Power BI service. From there, you will build a simple dashboard using items from the report that was previously built. Using Power BI Apps allows you to package up your solution and easily distribute it to groups or individuals

Lesson Requirements

You feel confident in your design skills based on what you have learned about the Power BI Desktop. The next step is to share your solution and get feedback from a larger audience. Your boss has asked you to set up a method by which your design can be viewed by a new group of users.

Hints

- Create a workspace and deploy the completed solution from the previous chapter.

- Build a dashboard by pinning two visuals from the report.

- Create a Power BI App to share with others.

- You will need at least a Power BI Pro account to do many of the demonstrations in this section.

Step by Step

Create a Workspace

1. In your web browser, navigate to the Power BI service by going to PowerBI.com. Once there, sign in with your Power BI Pro account.

2. From the navigation on the left side of the screen, expand Workspaces and then select **Create a workspace**.

3. Name the new workspace Chapter 24 and then click **Save**.

Publish to the Workspace

1. In the Power BI Desktop, open the example you created from the previous chapter or the file Video Game Analysis.pbix from the book support files.

Tip If you open the completed example, make sure you change the data source settings to point to the location on your local workstation for Video Games.xlsx.

---

2. Under the Home ribbon, click **Publish**.

3. Choose the workspace that you just created called Chapter 24 and click **Select**. Once Power BI has completed publishing, you should see a confirmation that looks like Figure 24-5.

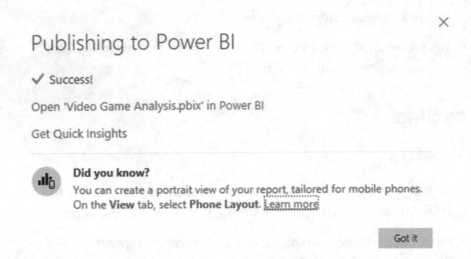

Figure 24-5. *What the Power BI Desktop displays after deployment is complete*

4. Click **Open 'Video Game Analysis.pbix' in Power BI** to launch this example in your default web browser.

Pinning to a Dashboard

1. Once your web browser launches, you will see the same report appear in your web browser that was in the Power BI Desktop.

2. Place your mouse above the Line chart and click **Pin visual** when it appears as shown in Figure 24-6. This will prompt you to select or create a dashboard to place this visual.

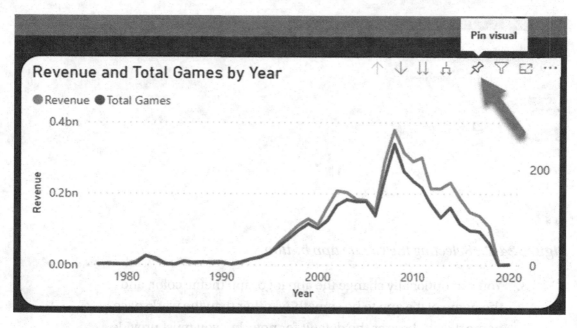

Figure 24-6. *The Pin visual icon*

3. Since a dashboard has yet to be created, you will need to create a new one. Name the dashboard "Chapter 24 Dashboard" and then click **Pin**.

4. Place your mouse above the Scatter chart and click **Pin visual**. This time you will click **Pin** to the existing dashboard you created in the previous step.

5. Expand the workspace on the left navigation and select the dashboard to view the two visuals pinned to it. With the dashboard now complete, you will now learn how to share your solution with a Power BI App.

Sharing with Power BI Apps

1. Select the Chapter 24 workspace on the left navigation pane.

2. With the workspace selected, click **Create app**, as shown in Figure 24-7.

Figure 24-7. *Selecting the Create app button*

3. You can optionally change the app logo, app theme color, and the name of the app to be something other than the workspace name. Leave these as the default for now, but you must provide a description for this app before moving further. Provide any description you see fit and then click **Navigation**.

4. In the navigation builder, you can provide sidebar navigation for the users that receive access to this app. You can add custom links to other websites or just make it easier to navigate to other Power BI assets. For this example, you will not need to customize the navigation. Click **Permissions**.

5. Under the Permission section, you can decide who you would like to assign access to the app that you created. Normally, you would put in a list of users or groups here, but for the purposes of this demo, leave it blank and click **Publish app** to continue. You may be prompted a second time. If so, click **Publish** again.

6. Once the app is finished publishing, you will be prompted to copy a link to the app or go to the app. Click the button labeled **Go to app**.

7. After the app launches, use the navigation on the left to explore what the app provides. This is the experience your end users will have.

8. Users can find the app again by either favoriting the app, clicking a link you provide, or searching for the app under the **Apps** section of your Power BI navigation as shown in Figure 24-8.

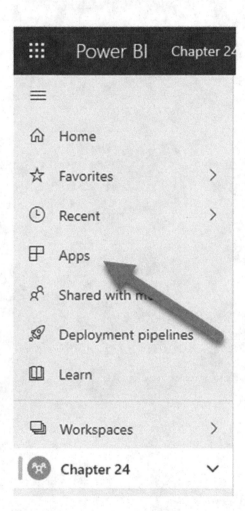

Figure 24-8. *Navigating to the Apps section of Power BI*

CHAPTER 25

Administering Power BI

In addition to sharing, the Power BI service contains several other operations that can assist in administering Power BI solutions. For instance, to ensure your data stays up to date, you may need to set up a data refresh plan. Setting up a data refresh schedule is done within the Power BI service on the solutions dataset. You may also add row-level security to your dataset. Assigning the users to a role is also an administrative task done in the Power BI service. In this chapter, you will learn about using the Power BI service to complete several of these essential administrative tasks.

Adding Security to Your Solution

In the previous chapter, you learned how you can share your Power BI solutions with others. Sharing is a form of object-level security. This means a report is an object and a user either has access to it or they do not. In this section, you will learn another deeper level of security informally referred to as data-level security. With data-level security, more formally known as row-level security inside Power BI, you can specify specific rows that each user should be allowed to see. For example, your company has four sales regions and you would prefer the southeast salesperson not be allowed to see the data associated with the northwest salesperson. Power BI gives you the ability to manage a scenario like this and only allow specific users to see the data that applies to them.

Setting up row-level security in Power BI is a two-step process. The first step begins in the Power BI Desktop where a role is created. The role is the definition of which rows can be seen by users. Under the Modeling ribbon, select Manage roles and then click Create to begin defining a security role. Figure 25-1 shows an example of a role being defined.

© Mitchell Pearson, Brian Knight, Devin Knight, Manuel Quintana 2020
M. Pearson et al., *Pro Microsoft Power Platform*, https://doi.org/10.1007/978-1-4842-6008-1_25

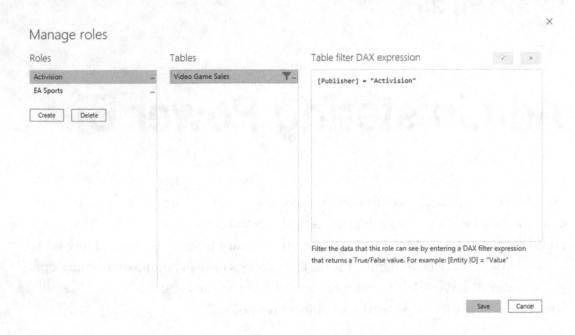

Figure 25-1. *Creation of a role in the Power BI Desktop*

The second step in enabling row-level security is done within the Power BI service. After selecting Security under the dataset settings in the workspace, you will find all roles that have been previously created. From there, you can assign users or groups from your Azure Active Directory to any created role. You can even test the role to validate that it behaves the way you would anticipate it should. If a user is assigned to more than one role, then they would have access to the cumulative of all roles assigned to them.

Step one is performed in the Power BI Desktop where you will define the role, and step two is where you assign users to the role within the Power BI service.

Tip   There are many complex security scenarios that you may find yourself needing to understand. This book only covers the basics, but you can watch this video to learn about more complex design patterns: `www.youtube.com/watch?v=uyxesN_nGnQ`.

Setting Up Automated Data Refreshes

Depending on the type of data source you have and even perhaps how you have configured the source, you will likely need to set up a process to refresh your datasets. Automating your data refresh gives you a hands-off approach to ensuring your users are always looking at the most up-to-date data possible.

As mentioned previously, how you have configured your data source settings can determine whether a refresh is even necessary. Remember connectivity mode types of DirectQuery and Live Connection do not require data refresh plans because they connect directly to their data sources. Thus, if you are like most individuals new to Power BI, you have likely chosen the default connectivity mode of import when setting up your data source. This means your data is physically imported into Power BI, which also means you must have a plan to ensure that your model's imported data continues to show up-to-date data.

The next thing to consider is whether you need a data gateway. This is really a question of where your data resides. If your data is on-premises (not in the cloud), then you must install a data gateway. The data gateway is used to form a secure connection between your on-premises data source and the cloud, which in this case is Power BI. You can use the same data gateway configured in either Power Apps or Power Automate for the purposes of Power BI as well.

Note   The data gateway installation can be found under the download section of the Power BI service, or you can visit `https://powerbi.microsoft.com/en-us/gateway/`. Recommendations for the type of machine to install it on can be found here: `https://docs.microsoft.com/en-us/power-bi/guidance/gateway-onprem-sizing`.

After installing the data gateway, you must then configure the data sources that will use the gateway from within the Power BI service. While in the Power BI service, you must go to the Settings icon and select Manage gateways (Figure 25-2). Here, you will define each data source that will leverage the data gateway you have created.

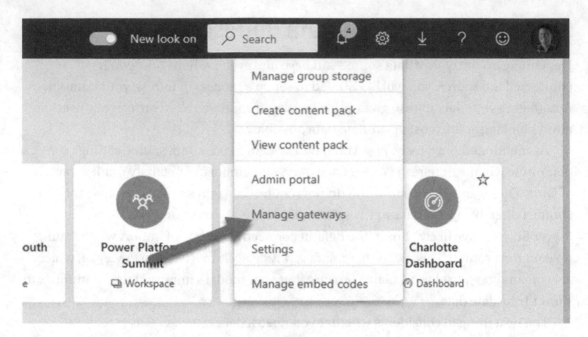

Figure 25-2. *Where to go when managing your gateways*

After the gateway configuration is complete, you are ready to schedule the data refresh. To schedule a data refresh, locate the dataset you desire to refresh and click Scheduled refresh as shown in Figure 25-3. These actions will launch the settings of the dataset you have chosen.

	Name		Type	Owner	Refresl
⊘	Chapter 24 Dashboard		Dashboard	Chapter 24	—
ılı	Video Game Analysis	Schedule refresh	Report	Chapter 24	4/10/20
▤	Video Game Analysis	↻ ⊡ ⋮	Dataset	Chapter 24	4/10/20

All   Content   Datasets + dataflows

Figure 25-3. *Selecting the Scheduled refresh option*

In the dataset settings configuration, you will select which of your available gateways you would like to use for the dataset and then configure the Scheduled refresh settings. Figure 25-4 shows a dataset configured to refresh eight times daily. Power BI Pro accounts have a limit of 8 refreshes a day, while Power BI Premium accounts can refresh up to 48 times a day using this user interface and an unlimited number of times when using the Power BI API.

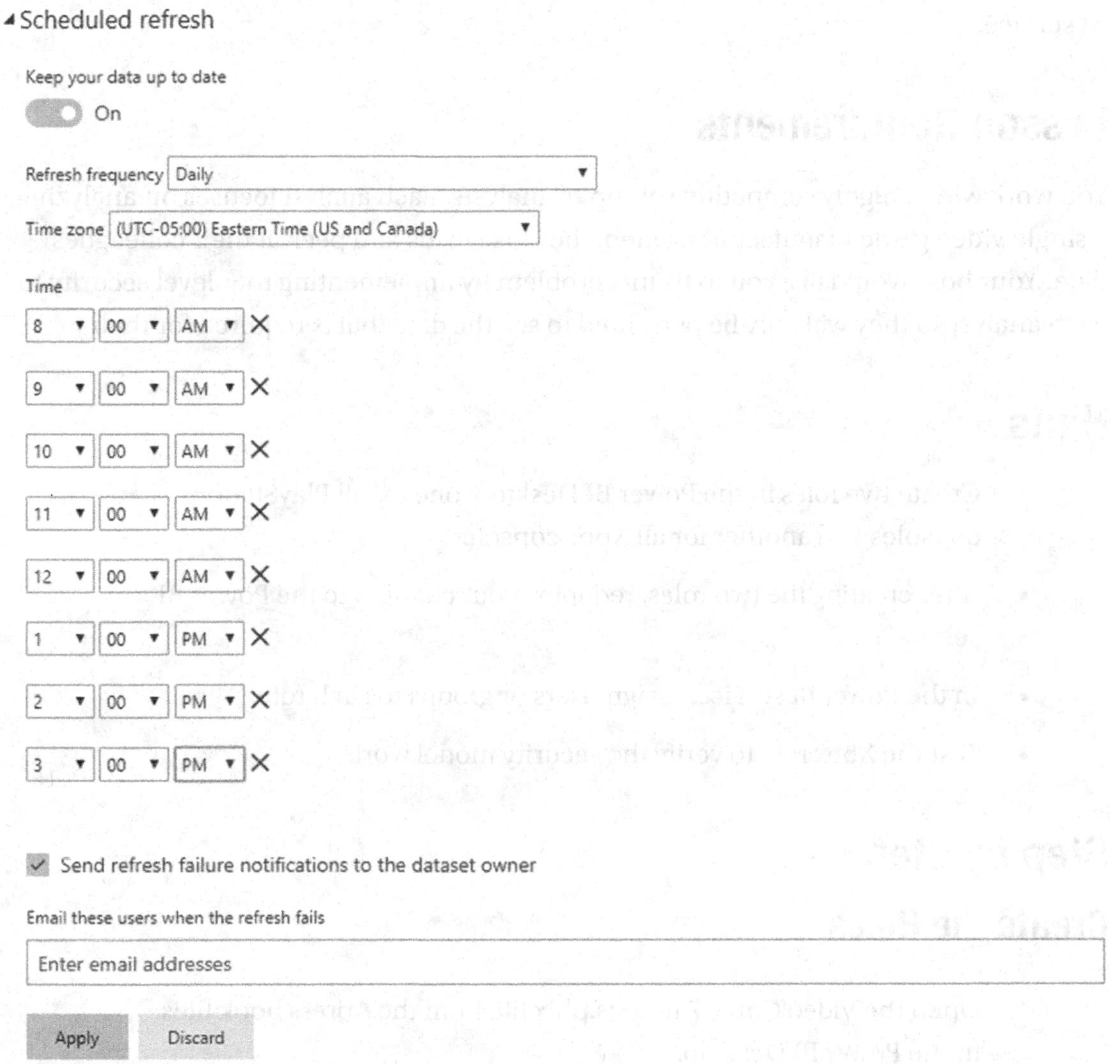

◢ Scheduled refresh

Keep your data up to date

⬤ On

Refresh frequency Daily   ▼

Time zone (UTC-05:00) Eastern Time (US and Canada)   ▼

Time

8 ▼ 00 ▼ AM ▼ ✕

9 ▼ 00 ▼ AM ▼ ✕

10 ▼ 00 ▼ AM ▼ ✕

11 ▼ 00 ▼ AM ▼ ✕

12 ▼ 00 ▼ AM ▼ ✕

1 ▼ 00 ▼ PM ▼ ✕

2 ▼ 00 ▼ PM ▼ ✕

3 ▼ 00 ▼ PM ▼ ✕

☑ Send refresh failure notifications to the dataset owner

Email these users when the refresh fails

| Enter email addresses |

| Apply | Discard |

Figure 25-4.   Configuring refresh times for a dataset

The "Try It Out" section will focus on the row-level security discussed earlier in the chapter.

Try It Out

In this "Try It Out" section, you will learn to apply row-level security to the data model you created in Chapter 23 and later deployed to the Power BI service in Chapter 24. Implementing this level of security will allow you to share one model with multiple users while only permitting each to view data that is relevant to them. This requires that you first create a role in the Power BI Desktop and then assign users to that role in the Power BI service.

Lesson Requirements

You work with a highly competitive group of analysts. Each analyst focuses on analyzing a single video game manufacturer. Often, they lose focus and peek at their colleagues' data. Your boss would like you to fix this problem by implementing row-level security to each analyst so they will only be permitted to see the data that is required for their job.

Hints

- Create two roles in the Power BI Desktop: one for all PlayStation consoles and another for all Xbox consoles.

- After creating the two roles, redeploy your changes to the Power BI service.

- In the Power BI service, assign users or groups to each role.

- Test the Xbox role to verify the security model works.

Step by Step

Create the Roles

1. Open the Video Game Analysis.pbix file from the Apress book files in the Power BI Desktop.

2. On the Modeling ribbon, select **Manage roles**.

3. Click **Create** and name the role PlayStation.

4. Click the ellipses next to Video Game Sales and select **Add Filter**
   ➤ [Console].

5. Replace the word Value between the double quotes with PSN. Add
   multiple Console filters as you did in step 4 to add all the
   PlayStation consoles. The final DAX expression should look like
   this:

   **[Console] = "PSN" || [Console] = "PSV" || [Console] = "PSP"
   || [Console] = "PS" || [Console] = "PS2" || [Console] = "PS3"||
   [Console] = "PS4"**

   Notice the && symbols were replaced with double pipes (||). In the
   DAX language, this means you have replaced an AND filter with
   an OR filter. This is required because the records will never meet
   the requirement of an AND since no game has been a part of every
   console.

6. Repeat steps 3–5 but now for Xbox. The final solution should
   appear as shown in Figure 25-5. Once complete, click *Save*.

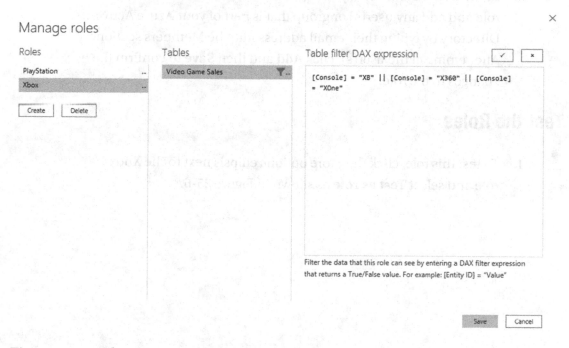

Figure 25-5. *The two completed roles*

7. Switch back to the Home ribbon and select **Publish** to redeploy these changes back to the Power BI service.

8. Go ahead and reuse the workspace called Chapter 24 that was created in the previous chapter. If you followed along with the previous chapter, you will be prompted to replace the existing dataset. Confirm this by selecting **Replace**.

9. Once the publishing process completes, click Open 'Video Game Analysis.pbix' in Power BI. This will launch your web browser and take you to the report within the Power BI service.

Assign Users to the Roles

1. Select the workspace name from the left navigation and then choose Datasets.

2. On the Video Game Analysis dataset, click the More options ellipsis and select **Security**.

3. In the Row-Level Security configuration section, select the Xbox role and add any user(s) or group that is part of your Azure Active Directory by typing their email address into the Members section. After typing in the user(s), click **Add** and then **Save** to confirm the changes to the role.

Test the Roles

1. To test this role, click the More options ellipsis next to the Xbox role and select **Test as role** as shown in Figure 25-6.

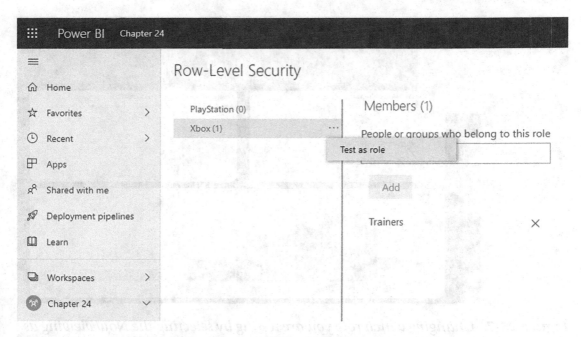

Figure 25-6. *Launching the Test as role option*

2. This will launch the report again, but now you will only see what the Xbox role can see. If you would like to change to the PlayStation role or even type in the specific user you tested with, then you can do so by clicking the **Now viewing as** selector, as shown in Figure 25-7.

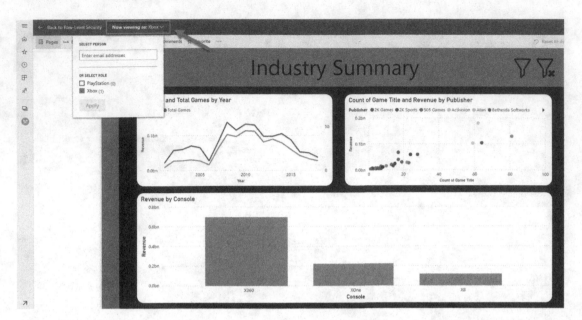

Figure 25-7. *Changing which role you are testing by selecting the Now viewing as selector*

Well done on implementing row-level security to your data model. In the part four of this book, you will learn about how the major Power Platform tools (Power Apps, Power Automate, and Power BI) all integrate together.

PART IV

Integrating the Power Platform Tools Together

CHAPTER 26

Power Platform Integration in Power Apps

Through the course of this book, you have learned how each of the individual tools within Microsoft's Power Platform work individually. In this final section, you will learn more about how these tools are optimized to work together to solve business problems. A true citizen developer will need to be skilled in all Power Platform tools to build a well-rounded solution that can not only provide a data collection system but also provide reporting and analytics to better understand your incoming data.

In this chapter, you will learn how Power Automate and Power BI can be integrated inside the Power Apps solutions you develop. You will start by learning about how Power Apps can execute flows to initiate additional external processes. Then, in the "Try It Out" section, you will see how Power BI dashboard tiles can be embedded into your canvas app design.

Power Automate Integration with Power Apps

By now, you have learned that Power Automate can be used to program the automation of one or more operations which are triggered by a schedule, an event, or manual execution with a button. What you haven't learned is how this capability can be harnessed to improve Power Apps. For example, within Power Apps, you could have an Edit Form control that a user fills out, but when they click the Submit button on the screen, it actually executes a Power Automate flow. That flow could take the user-entered data and place it in an invoice template using the Word Online connector. The final result could even convert the Word document to a PDF.

Both the flow and the app can be developed independently of each other and then brought together to orchestrate this more complex operation. So while it is great for you

© Mitchell Pearson, Brian Knight, Devin Knight, Manuel Quintana 2020
M. Pearson et al., *Pro Microsoft Power Platform*, https://doi.org/10.1007/978-1-4842-6008-1_26

to be an expert in the entire Power Platform, this gives you the ability to split a project's work to those that consider themselves to be an expert in one product over another.

The integration of these two tools is fairly simple. When you create a new flow in Power Automate, start with the Power Apps trigger as shown in Figure 26-1. Doing this will make this flow available to any app that is in the same environment. Any actions that are added after this trigger will run once Power Apps initiates the flow. Each flow action has the ability to call upon Power Apps to pass it values that impact the flow run.

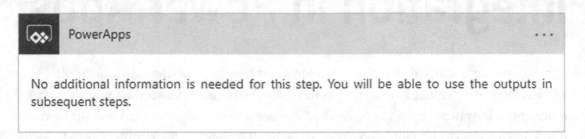

Figure 26-1. *The Power Apps trigger inside Power Automate*

Once the flow is configured, you call on it to execute from inside any app using the Action ➤ Power Automate menu; see Figure 26-2. Typically, you will configure this on a button so that when the button is selected, the flow is executed.

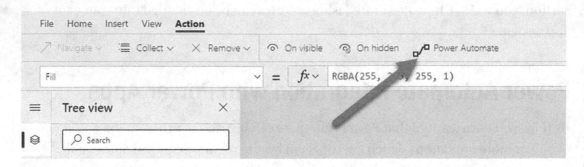

Figure 26-2. *The menu inside Power Apps used for selecting a flow*

In the final chapter of this book, you will see an end-to-end example of the Power Platform working together. As part of that, you will walk through a step-by-step configuration of executing flows inside Power Apps.

Power BI Integration with Power Apps

You may find the need while developing an app to display data using various visuals. Power Apps includes a Column, Line, and Pie chart visual built-in for you to use. However, you are not limited to these three visuals. You can optionally choose to integrate Power BI into your app with the Power BI tile control.

Using this control, you can display any visual that appears in a Power BI dashboard tile. Simply add the Power BI tile control to your app, then configure it by selecting the workspace, dashboard, and tile you wish to display. Any user of the app must also have permission to the Power BI dashboard for this control to work properly.

Test this out for yourself. The "Try It Out" section of this chapter focuses on building and adding the Power BI tile control to an app.

Try It Out

In this "Try It Out" section, you will combine the capabilities of Power Apps and Power BI using the Power BI tile control to embed Power BI visuals into your apps. Doing this will help your app stand out more than just using the standard charts that are provided within Power Apps.

Lesson Requirements

You are working on an app for your local high school to better track absences. Power Apps makes for a quick and simple paperless method for tracking each absence, but you would like to integrate Power BI to present the data in a more unique fashion. For this lesson, you will need to build an app for entering new absences with a Power BI visual to display the results.

Hints

The following are hints and reminders to keep in mind as you work through the step-by-step process in the next subsection:

- From the book support files, take the School Absence.xlsx file and move it to a OneDrive for Business location.

- Build a Power BI report directly in the Power BI service using the School Absence file.

- Use the Power BI tile control to embed a Power BI dashboard tile into Power Apps.

Step by Step

The step-by-step process can be broken into two. First, you create the dashboard. Then, you embed the dashboard into Power Apps.

Creating the Power BI Dashboard

The following are the steps for creating the dashboard:

1. Take the School Absence.xlsx file from the book support files and upload it to any location on your personal OneDrive for Business.

2. Next, log in at `https://app.powerbi.com/` and create a new workspace called Chapter 26.

3. Immediately after the new workspace is created, you are provided several options for bringing in data. Select **Get** next to the Create new content from the Files option as shown in Figure 26-3.

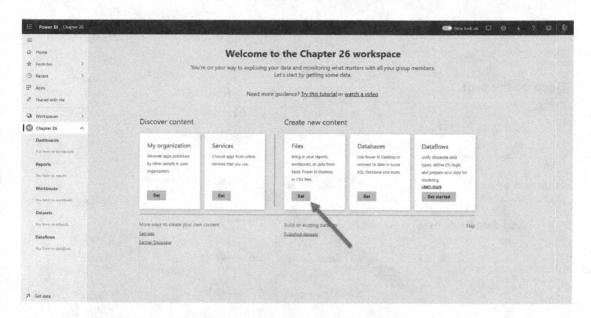

Figure 26-3. *Choosing a file source in the Power BI service*

4. Next, choose the **OneDrive – Business** option and then navigate
    to the location where you uploaded the School Absence.xlsx file in
    step 1. Select this file and then click **Connect**.

5. When presented the option to Connect or Import the data from
    your Excel workbook, choose **Import**. This will automatically
    create a new dataset and dashboard in your workspace.

Tip   If your data is stored in OneDrive for Business or SharePoint Online, Power
BI will automatically check for updates every hour. If a change has occurred, then
Power BI will refresh your dataset.

---

6. Navigate to the School Absence dataset to begin building the
    report visual that will be embedded into Power Apps.

7. With this dataset open, select the **Treemap** visual and
    add the AbsenceCount field to the **Values** section and the
    AbsenceCodeDESC field to the Group.

8. Go to the Format options menu and turn on Data labels for the
    Treemap as shown in Figure 26-4.

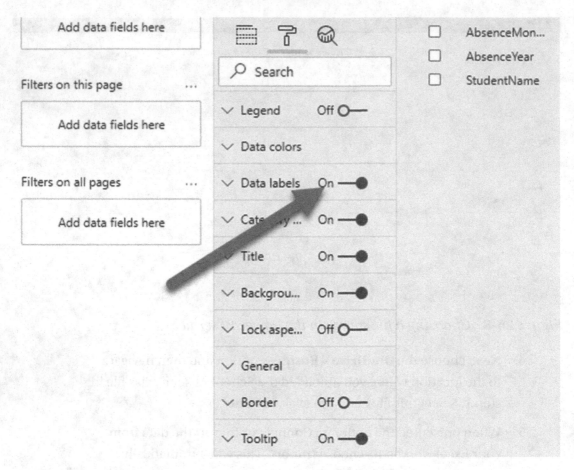

Figure 26-4. Modifying the Format properties to turn on Data labels

9. Now pin this visual to the dashboard by selecting the **Pin visual** icon found at the top-right corner of the visual when you hover above it.

10. When you do this, you will likely first be prompted to save your report. Name the report School Absence and then click **Save**.

11. Next, you will be prompted to "Pin to dashboard." Choose to pin this visual to the existing dashboard and then click **Pin**.

Embedding Power BI in Power Apps

And in this section are the steps to embed the dashboard into Power Apps:

1. Navigate to `https://make.powerapps.com/` to begin building the app to track absences.

2. After signing in, select **Other data sources** under the Start from data section as shown in Figure 26-5.

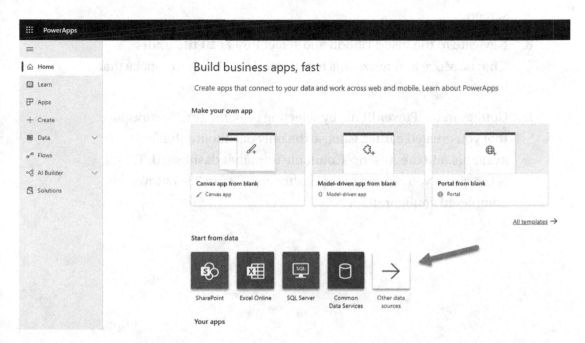

Figure 26-5. *Choosing Other data sources which is needed to connect to the OneDrive for Business file*

3. Select **New Connection** and select **OneDrive for Business**, then click **Create**. This will then prompt you to sign in to your OneDrive for Business account if you haven't done this previously.

4. Navigate to and select the School Absence.xlsx file in the location that you uploaded the file to in step 1. Once the file is selected, choose the only table available and then click **Connect**. This will begin the process of automatically building your app. Once it's complete, click **Skip** on the "Welcome to Power Apps Studio" dialog box.

5. Change the header on BrowseScreen1 to be "Absentees."

6. Select BrowseGallery1 from the Tree View, then click **Edit** on the Fields property. Here you will change Title1 to be StudentName, Subtitle1 to be AbsenceDate, and Body1 to be AbsenceCodeDESC.

7. Next, select BrowseGallery1 from the Tree View again and resize it to make space for the Power BI tile control. Grab the bottom anchor points and resize the gallery to only take up about half the screen.

8. Navigate to the Insert ribbon and select **Power BI tile** under **Charts**. Move and resize this new control to take up the space that was left by the resizing of the gallery.

9. Configure the Power BI tile by selecting the Chapter 26 workspace that you created earlier. Choose the only dashboard that is available and the AbsenceCount tile from that dashboard. This is the visual you pinned to the dashboard. Figure 26-6 shows this completed configuration.

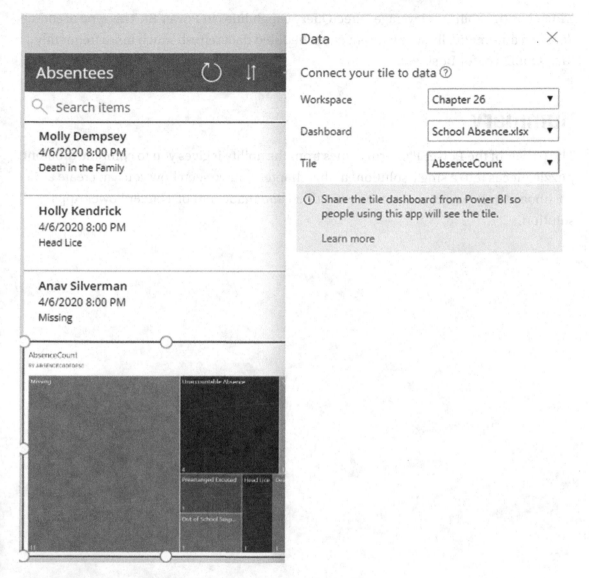

Figure 26-6. *Configuring the Power BI tile control*

Now go to the file menu to give this app the name of Student Absence Tracker and then click **Save**.

You have now successfully integrated Power BI dashboard tiles inside Power Apps. In this case, we have used OneDrive for Business as the data source which means the data will automatically be refreshed on any Power BI visuals every hour. An even better data source would be something like Azure SQL Database or the Common Data Service which has the ability to leverage DirectQuery capabilities in Power BI. This type of source data can automatically sync without any scheduled data refresh much more frequently than OneDrive for Business.

Summary

The power of the Power Platform comes from the ability it gives you to combine different puzzle pieces into a single solution. In this chapter, you've seen how you can create a dashboard in Power BI that can be embedded and made part of a larger Power Apps solution.

CHAPTER 27

Power Platform Integration in Power Automate

While this part of the book is devoted to Power Platform product integration, you likely already have learned that Power Automate is a tool devoted to integration among hundreds of products. Within the Power Platform, it is sometimes referred to as the glue that brings all things together. In this chapter, you will learn about the integration points that exist between Power Automate and the other Power Platform products.

Power Apps Integration with Power Automate

In the previous chapter, you learned about how flows can be executed from within Power Apps. This however is not the only integration point that exists between Power Automate and Power Apps. With this integration, you are provided similar capabilities to what you can do with PowerShell cmdlets for Power Apps, but rather than using a command-line interface, this can all be done within Power Automate connectors. The connectors that will be the focus of this section are Power Apps for App Makers, Power Apps for Admins, and Power Platform for Admins. Let's discuss these connectors a little further.

Tip Microsoft has provided an exported Power App called the Connector Browser that helps you learn more about what is possible with Power Apps for App Makers, Power Apps for Admins, and Power Platform for Admins connectors. You can download this sample app here: `https://powerapps.microsoft.com/en-us/blog/new-connectors-for-powerapps-and-flow-resources/`.

© Mitchell Pearson, Brian Knight, Devin Knight, Manuel Quintana 2020
M. Pearson et al., *Pro Microsoft Power Platform*, https://doi.org/10.1007/978-1-4842-6008-1_27

Power Apps for App Makers

The Power Apps for App Makers connector is focused on the tasks that are often important for app designers. This includes but is not limited to publishing an app, removing an app, changing the name of an app, and changing permissions on an app. A practical example of using this connector could be when a new employee is added to your company, they are automatically added to the permissions of a Power Apps app using the Edit App Role Assignment action.

Another example of using this connector could be that you don't want to publish the latest changes to your app in the middle of the day when it is being used. Instead, you could choose to use Power Automate to schedule the deployment of your latest version of an app by using the Publish App action as shown in Figure 27-1.

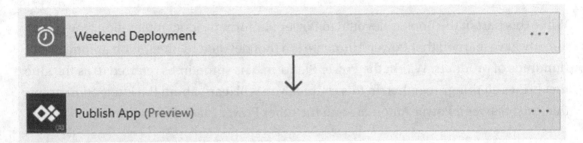

Figure 27-1. *Using the Power Apps for App Makers connector to publish an app*

Methods like the examples given earlier can make the adoption of Power Apps much smoother for both app users and app makers.

Power Apps for Admins

The Power Apps for Admins connector is largely similar to the Power Apps for App Makers connector but has limits to the type of operations that are available to things that an administrator would need to control. For example, this connector can also change the permissions of an app, but it cannot publish or rename the app. Since renaming and publishing an app are generally tasks for an app maker, those tasks can be found only in the Power Apps for App Makers connector.

Power Platform for Admins

The next connector, Power Platform for Admins, has a fairly short list of operations that it can perform. These operations are exclusive to configuring an environment's permissions or completely removing the existence of a selected environment.

Power BI Integration with Power Automate

One of the biggest challenges in Power BI is keeping the data in your reports up to date. Often business processes are designed in a way that users would expect to see results updated immediately in their Power BI reports, but due to your dataset configuration, users are left waiting until the next scheduled data refresh. You have already learned in this book about the options within Power BI for managing data refreshes, but Power Automate introduces new methods of synchronizing data.

Refreshing Power BI Datasets

Built into Power Automate is a Power BI action that allows you to initiate the data refresh of an existing Power BI dataset. No matter what your flow trigger is, this Refresh a dataset step, as shown in Figure 27-2, can be added to update data.

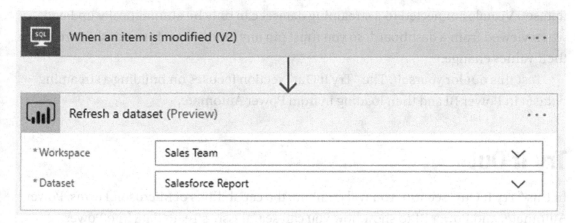

Figure 27-2. A Refresh a dataset action in Power Automate

There are any number of use cases for this but imagine you wanted to promptly update your Power BI dataset once a record gets modified in your SQL Server table. Using Power Automate, you can configure a trigger to monitor that table for changes, and when a change occurs, initiate a Power BI dataset refresh immediately. It is simple to configure but extremely powerful as an integration point between the two products.

Any dataset that you select to refresh with this action must follow the licensing rules defined in Power BI. For example, if you select to refresh a dataset that is not in a Power BI Premium workspace, then you can only initiate a refresh up to eight times a day. However, if the dataset is in a Premium workspace, then you do not have a limit to the number of refreshes that can occur in a day.

Streaming Datasets in Power BI

Another method for working with Power BI datasets in Power Automate is with streaming datasets. The concept of streaming datasets means that you can have a real-time dashboard that leverages the REST API available in Power BI to push data into the available endpoint and see up-to-date data in seconds.

The configuration within Power Automate is simple. Create a trigger from your desired data source and send it into the Power BI action called "Add rows to a dataset." The more complex elements of this type of solution exist on the Power BI side. You must first create a streaming dataset and then build report visuals on top of the streaming dataset. Visuals connected to a streaming dataset can only be automatically updated when viewed from a dashboard, so you must pin any report visuals to a dashboard to see their values change.

Test this out for yourself. The "Try It Out" section focuses on building a streaming dataset in Power BI and then loading in from Power Automate.

Try It Out

In this "Try It Out" section, you will combine the capabilities of Microsoft Forms, Power Automate, and Power BI to show how you can seamlessly stream data into Power BI. Power Automate will be used for both the purposes of collecting survey results from Forms and for transmitting the results into a Power BI streaming dataset. Exclusively using these business-ready applications, you will see the power provided in these tools that are designed for citizen developers.

Lesson Requirements

You are organizing a conference of like-minded individuals to learn more about your favorite, your favorite technology, Power Platform. During one of the breaks between presentations, you came up with the idea to have an ice cream social to encourage more networking between attendees. To make sure you order the right amount of ice cream and toppings, you have decided to create and send a survey to attendees in advance of the conference. Since you are such a Power Platform enthusiast, you have decided to take the results of the survey and present them in a Power BI report.

You will need to design and build the following:

- A new survey called Dessert Survey created in Microsoft Forms that can be used to collect responses

- Power BI streaming dataset to store the results of the survey in Power BI

- Power BI report and dashboard to display the values found in the streaming dataset

- Power Automate that watches for new survey responses and, when they are found, transmits them to the Power BI streaming dataset

Read on for some hints before you tackle the step process.

Hints

Here are just a couple of hints to keep in mind as you build out the example:

- To see the dataset results stream into Power BI, you must pin the visuals to a dashboard.

- You will need to create the Power BI streaming dataset before attempting to complete the flow for this example.

Step by Step

You'll begin by creating a data source. Then you'll create a dataset that feeds into a dashboard. Finally, you'll use Power Automate to load from the data source into the dataset.

Creating a Data Source in Microsoft Forms

Here are the steps to follow in creating the data source:

1. Open a web browser and navigate to the website `https://forms.office.com`. Sign in with the O365 account and select **Create a new form**.

2. Replace the name "Untitled form" with the new name of "Dessert Survey."

3. Begin to add new questions to the form by clicking **Add new** and then **Choice** for the question type.

4. Make the question on "Which ice cream flavor would you prefer?" and provide the options of Vanilla, Chocolate, and Strawberry as shown in Figure 27-3.

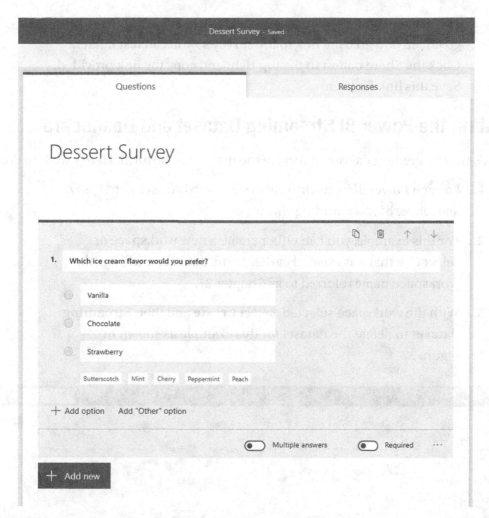

Figure 27-3. Creating your first question in Microsoft Forms

5. Click **Add new** again to add a second question. Choose **Choice**
    for the question type and then add the question "What toppings
    would you like?" Provide the following choices to the questions:
    Sprinkles, Chocolate syrup, Bananas, Gummy Bears.

6. Click **Add new** again to add a third question. Choose **Text** for the
    question type and then add the question "Where are you from?
    (Provide answer in City, State format. For example: Orlando, FL)."

7. The survey should automatically save as you are working on, but go ahead and grab the link to the survey so you can test it later. Click the Share button in the top right and copy the link provided. Save this link for later.

Creating the Power BI Streaming Dataset and Dashboard

Now it's time to create a dataset to receive the data from the form. Here's what to do:

1. Launch Power BI by navigating in your web browser to `https://app.powerbi.com/` and signing in.

2. For this example, you can either create a new workspace or select one that was created earlier in the book. You will see the workspace name referred to as Chapter 27.

3. With the workspace selected, select **Create** and then **Streaming dataset** to define the dataset for this example as shown in Figure 27-4.

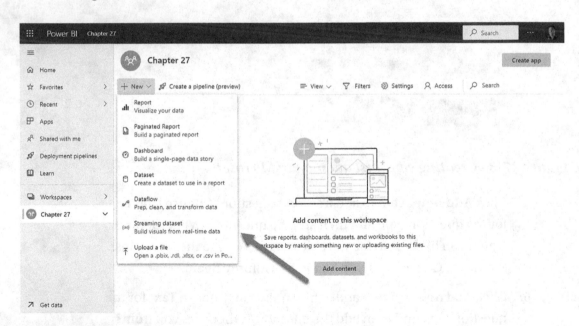

Figure 27-4. *Creating a Power BI streaming dataset*

4. Choose API for the type of streaming dataset and then click **Next**.

5. Name the dataset "Survey Results" and then add the following values: Flavor, Toppings, and Location. Each of these values should have a data type of Text.

Change the property of **Historic data analysis** to On before finally clicking **Create**. This will allow you to track a history of survey responses over time. Figure 27-5 shows this step being completed.

Once the streaming dataset is created, click **Done**.

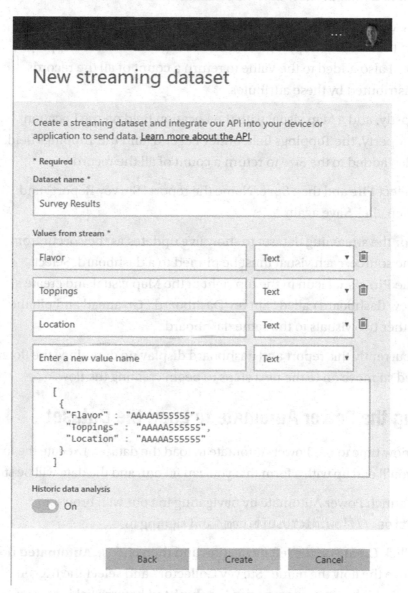

Figure 27-5. *Entering in the required values for this dataset*

6. Navigate to the new dataset in your workspace and click **Create Report**.

7. First, add a Table visual to the report that includes all three fields to verify each value is returning as expected once the streaming begins.

    You will notice currently no rows are returned because we have yet to define the flow that will load this dataset.

8. Next, create a new Stacked Column chart with the Flavor field on the Axis, the Toppings field on the Legend, and the Toppings field also added to the Value to return a count of all the records distributed by these attributes.

9. Lastly, add a Map visual with the Location field on the Location property, the Toppings field under Legend, and the Toppings field also added to the Size to return a count of all the records.

    Select **File** and then **Save**. Name the report "Survey Report" and then click **Save** again.

10. For the streaming dataset to show live updates as they occur from the source, each visual must be pinned to a dashboard. Select the **Pin visual** icon in the top right of the Map visual and create a new dashboard called "Survey Dashboard." Go ahead and pin the other two visuals to the same dashboard.

Again, currently this report and dashboard display no data since the flow has not been created so move on to the next steps to begin creating the flow.

Designing the Power Automate to Load the Dataset

Finally, it's now time to use Power Automate to load the dataset. Execute the following steps, and you'll end up with a form that you can fill out, and the data will be stored for you.

1. Launch Power Automate by navigating in your web browser to `https://flow.microsoft.com/` and signing in.

2. Click **Create** on the left navigation and then choose **Automated flow**. Give the flow the name "Survey Collector" and select the trigger called **When a new response is submitted** before clicking **Create**.

This will start the creation of the flow for this example. You may be prompted to sign in to your Microsoft Forms account.

3. Now select the Form Id that corresponds with the form you created. The Form Id should be Dessert Survey.

4. Next, you will need to configure the flow to iterate over each survey response that is received. To do this, click **New step** and then search for and select the Microsoft Forms action called **Get response details**.

5. Select the Form Id of Dessert Survey again, and for the Response ID, choose **List of response notifications Response ID** from the Dynamic content fields that are available.

    When you do this, Power Atuomate will automatically wrap this action in an Apply to each loop so it can iterate over each response.

6. Inside the newly created Apply to each loop, click **Add an action** and then search for and select the Power BI action called **Add rows to a dataset**.

    If you are prompted to sign in to your Power BI account, go ahead and do so.

7. In the new Power BI action configuration, select the **Workspace** where you created the streaming dataset. For the purposes of this demonstration, it was called Chapter 27.

    Select Survey Results as the **Dataset**, and the **Table** will be RealTimeData.

8. Once you select the table property, you will see the fields from the streaming dataset you created will now appear.

    Map Flavor to the Dynamic content field named **Which ice cream flavor would you prefer?**

    Map Toppings to the Dynamic content field named **Which toppings would you like?**

    Map Location to the Dynamic content field named **Where are you from? (Provide answer in City, State for...**

9. With these changes completed, click **Save** to complete this flow.
    Your completed flow should look like Figure 27-6.

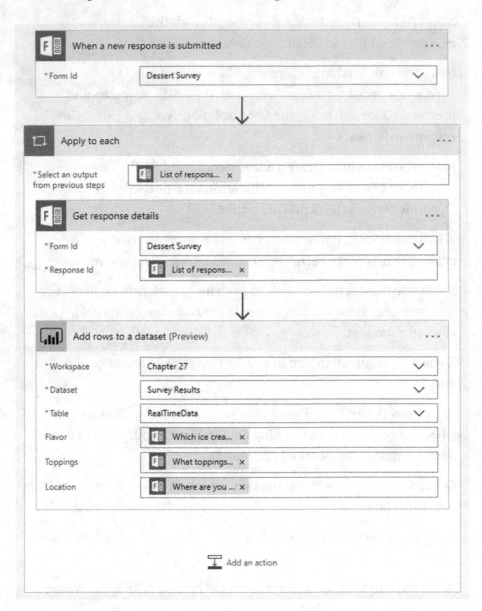

Figure 27-6. *The completed flow for this example*

10.   The final step is to test the whole process by using the link for the survey that was created. Fill out the form several times providing different variations of answers to the questions and watch your Power BI dashboard to see how the values stream in without any scheduled data refresh required.

Summary

Power Automate's role within the Power Platform can be thought of as the glue that brings together the other elements. This chapter showed how you can use Power Automate to stream data from Microsoft Forms directly into a Power BI dataset and then to see that dataset refreshed in real time.

CHAPTER 28

Power Platform Integration in Power BI

While Power BI is by far the most widely used of the Power Platform tools, it is also the tool with the fewest built-in integration features compared to the other tools. Both Power Apps and Power Automate do have integration points within Power BI, but the ability to execute flows is not a smooth process. In this chapter, you will learn how you can integrate the apps you design with Power Apps inside your Power BI reports and how you will take on the more difficult task of executing Power Automate flows into your data cleansing process within the Power Query Editor.

Power Apps Integration with Power BI

Power Apps and Power BI are often thought of as opposite ends of the data life cycle. Power Apps is used for data collection through features like Forms, while Power BI is used for presenting and analyzing your data. If you could combine these two elements of the data life cycle, then you would have a rather powerful combination of features that is not available in many business-ready tools on the market. In this section, you will learn about the Power Apps Visual and how it allows you to combine both data collection and data visualization in a single interface for your users.

Power Apps Visual

The Power Apps Visual was originally one of the many custom visuals that was kept separate from the built-in Power BI data visualizations. However, in September of 2019, the Power Apps Visual was elevated to become one of the default visuals that is available to every Power BI user by default when you open the Power BI Desktop. Leveraging this

© Mitchell Pearson, Brian Knight, Devin Knight, Manuel Quintana 2020
M. Pearson et al., *Pro Microsoft Power Platform*, https://doi.org/10.1007/978-1-4842-6008-1_28

feature allows you to embed any canvas app into your Power BI report design. Using this visual is one of the most powerful integrations between products in the Power Platform because it gives you the capability to enable the concept of writeback for your Power BI users.

The Power of Writeback

Have you ever been looking at a Power BI report and noticed incorrect data that you wish you could fix the source data from inside the report itself? Normally, this is unheard of within Power BI since it is designed to display data from your data source but not change data in your data source. However, with the Power Apps custom visual, you can do just that and writeback new values or update existing values back to the reports data source.

There are many scenarios where this could be useful. For example, imagine you are looking at a report displaying budget vs. actual data, and you realize while looking at the Power BI report that you underbudgeted an expense for March. Using the Power Apps Visual, you could embed an app that is connected to the same data source as the report, make a modification to the budget, and see the results appear immediately in your report without ever leaving Power BI.

This is incredibly powerful and can get even better when you set your Power BI data source to DirectQuery. The benefit you gain with this is you never have to refresh your data. When an update occurs, you can see the results immediately in the report because DirectQuery sources point directly to the data source instead of importing the data into Power BI.

To see an example of this writeback with the Power Apps Visual inside Power BI, skip to the "Try It Out" section of the next chapter. In that chapter, you will see an end-to-end demonstration of using all the Power Platform tools together.

Power Automate Integration with Power BI

The integration between Power Automate and Power BI is likely the least user-friendly of all the integration points within the Power Platform. With most other integration features, you will find a convenient button to add a Power Apps app to Power BI or call upon a Power Automate flow inside Power Apps, for example. However, when it comes to bringing together Power Automate inside Power BI, it is a more manual process using the Power Automate REST API.

Since there is not a user-friendly method of calling a flow within Power BI, you must instead initiate your flow using a REST API call. This can be done using a Request trigger inside of Power Automate. The Request trigger provides an HTTP POST URL that can be executed from any app, including custom apps you develop or in this case Power BI.

The "Try It Out" section will now cover more about how to configure a Power Automate flow that uses a Request trigger and can be used in Power BI.

Try It Out

In this "Try It Out" section, you will learn how Power Automate flows can be integrated into your data cleansing process inside Power BI. Using the Power Query Editor, you will write a small section of M code that will be used to call upon a flow that will give you new capabilities inside Power Query that would not normally be possible.

Lesson Requirements

You work for a multilingual organization that often has the need to translate customer-entered data into English before presenting it in a report. To manage this, you will need to build a process that can manage automatic text translation. That process will then need to be integrated into your data cleansing process so any new rows will continue to get translated.

You will need to design and build the following:

- A Power Automate flow that uses Microsoft Translate to convert Spanish phrases to English using a trigger that can be initiated using a REST API call.

- A Power BI Desktop file that calls upon the Power Automate flow you created using M code in the Advanced Editor.

Hints

The following are some items to keep in mind as you work through the step-by-step example:

- Use the "When an HTTP request is received" to begin the flow.

- The data source for this demonstration can be found in the book support files and is called Spanish Phrases.xlsx.

- Create a parameter using M to pass in the list of values you need to convert.

Step by Step

There are two parts to the step-by-step sequence. First is to create the flow using Power Automate. Next is to invoke that flow from within Power BI.

Creating the Flow

1. Open a web browser and navigate to the website `https://powerautomate.com/` and sign in with the account.

2. Once signed in, select **Create** from the navigation on the right side of the screen. You will then choose the **Instant flow** option.

3. Name the flow "Power BI Translator" and select the trigger called **When an HTTP request is received** and then press **Create** in the Build an instant flow wizard. This will build the initial flow.

4. Click **New step** to add a new action after the trigger and then search for and select **Translate text** from the Microsoft Translator connector. You may be prompted to establish a connection to Microsoft Translator.

5. Within this new action, select the Text property and choose **Body** from the dynamic content values. Also, change the Target Language to **English**.

6. Add another step by clicking **New step** and then search for and select Response from the Request Connector.

7. In the new action, select the Body property and choose **Translated Text** from the dynamic content values.

    Once this is complete, click *Save*. The flow you designed should match Figure 28-1.

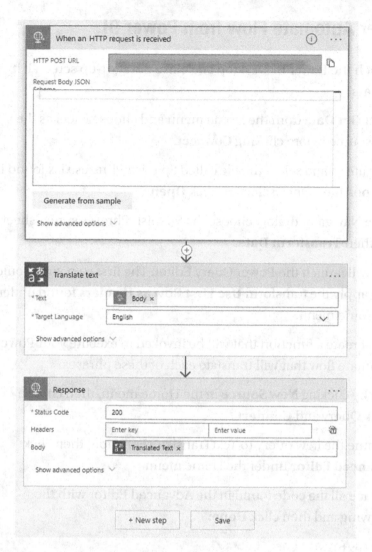

Figure 28-1. *The completed Power Automate flow*

8. Go back and expand the trigger "When an HTTP request is received" and then copy the URL found next to the HTTP POST URL property. This URL will not appear until after you save the flow.

    You may want to paste this URL in a Notepad document because you will need to find it later in this lab.

Call a Power Automate Flow from Power BI

1. Launch the Power BI Desktop and close the start-up screen if it appears.

2. Select **Get Data** from the Home menu and choose Excel as the data source before clicking **Connect**.

3. Navigate to and select the file called Spanish Phrases.xlsx found in the book files. Once selected, click **Open**.

4. In the Navigator dialog, choose the Spanish Phrases spreadsheet and then **Transform Data**.

5. This will launch the Power Query Editor. The first step you should do is apply the transform **Use First Row as Headers** found under the Home menu.

6. Next, create a function that will be invoked to execute your Power Automate flow that will translate each of these phrases.

    Start by clicking **New Source** in the Home menu, then choose Blank Query and **Connect**.

7. Rename the new query to TextTranslatorFunction, then click **Advanced Editor** under the Home menu.

8. Replace all the code found in the Advanced Editor with the following and then click **Done**:

```
(getText)=>
let
    Source = (Web.Contents("Insert the URL you
    copied from Power Automate here", [Content=Text.
    ToBinary(getText)])),
    TextFromBinary = Text.FromBinary(Source)
in
    TextFromBinary
```

In this section of code, a parameter is created called getText. This parameter is then used to pass in each Spanish phrase into the flow you created. Notice the section where you should pass in the URL you copied from the trigger in the previously created flow.

9. Select the Spanish Phrases query, then select **Invoke Custom Function** from the Add Column menu.

10. Change the New column name property to "English Phrase" and select TextTranslatorFunction for the Function query property before clicking OK. Figure 28-2 shows the completed configuration of this step.

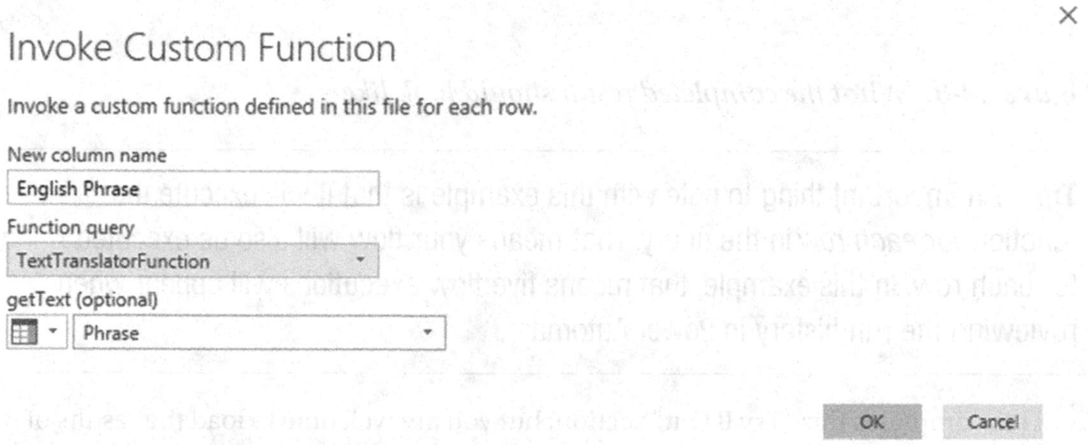

Invoke Custom Function   ×

Invoke a custom function defined in this file for each row.

New column name

English Phrase

Function query

TextTranslatorFunction   ▾

getText (optional)

▦ ▾ Phrase   ▾

OK   Cancel

Figure 28-2. *Configuring the Invoke Custom Function option*

11. You will likely see a warning bar appear at the top of the editor that says, "Please specify how to connect." Click **Edit Credentials** to complete this step.

12. When prompted, keep the default setting of Anonymous authentication and then click **Connect**.

13. Another warning bar will appear, this time stating "Information is required about data privacy." Click **Continue** to complete this step.

14. For this example, it is OK to check the box that states you will be ignoring privacy level checks of this file and then click **Save**.

15. Figure 28-3 shows that this will now execute the function for each row in the Spanish Phrases, creating a new column called English Phrase, which has each value translated to English.

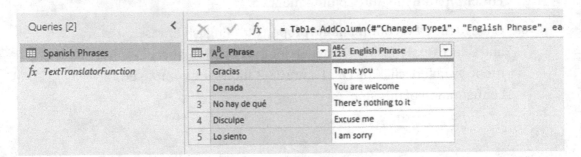

Figure 28-3. What the completed result should look like

Tip   An important thing to note with this example is that it will execute the function *for each row* in the query. That means your flow will also be executed for each row. In this example, that means five flow executions will appear when reviewing the run history in Power Automate.

This completes this "Try It Out" section, but you are welcome to load the results of this query into a Power BI data model and visualize the results if you would like.

Summary

The ability to execute Flows from within Power BI is not as smooth and easy as one might like. It is possible to do so though, and this chapter has shown how you can take an app created in Power Apps, then invoke that app from inside Power BI. The chapter's example showed how to use the M language from inside Power BI to invoke a flow.

CHAPTER 29

Designing a Fully Integrated Power Platform Solution

In this final chapter, you will take many of the skills that you have learned throughout this book to do one final end-to-end solution using the entire Power Platform together. It is important to understand how these tools really do complement each other, and that is exactly what this chapter is designed to show you through a complete end-to-end demonstration. Since this chapter does not introduce any new topics, you will now jump straight into your final "Try It Out" section.

Try It Out

In this final "Try It Out" section, you will put to test all of the skills you have learned throughout this book and apply them together in building an end-to-end solution that uses Power Apps for data collection, Power Automate for automating an approval process, and Power BI for reporting and analytics. Additionally, you will see how the Common Data Service can be used from start to finish as an ideal data source.

Lesson Requirements

You are tasked with building a beginning-to-end Power Platform solution to support the needs of the company Vet on the Go, Inc. Office administrators will use the app that you develop to add new appointments for the veterinarians that make house calls for customers unable to take their pets to their office. Using the app, veterinarians should

© Mitchell Pearson, Brian Knight, Devin Knight, Manuel Quintana 2020
M. Pearson et al., *Pro Microsoft Power Platform*, https://doi.org/10.1007/978-1-4842-6008-1_29

have the ability to approve or reject appointments that have been assigned to them. Lastly, executives at Vet on the Go, Inc. must have the ability to report on the house calls to see which veterinarian is bringing in the most revenue over time.

Hints

The following are some things to keep in mind as you work your way through the final example in the book:

- This demonstration will assume you have already signed up for the Power Apps Community Plan discussed in Chapter 1.

- The fields and data necessary for the Vet Appointments entity can be found in the file named VetOnTheGo-DataSource.xlsx available in the book support file.

- The app that is designed should have the ability to execute a flow and retrieve a value from the approval response.

Step by Step

There are four major activities involved in building this chapter's example. To address the business problem, you will need to build the following:

- A new Common Data Service entity named Vet Appointments with the fields and data necessary to build

- A Power Apps app that uses the Vet Appointments entity as a data source for entering in new appointments

- A Power Automate flow that gives each veterinarian the ability to accept or reject appointments that are assigned to them.

- Finally, a Power BI report showing the amount of appointments and revenue brought in from each veterinarian.

The step-by-step sections to follow walk you through designing each of these parts to the solution.

Creating and Loading a CDS Entity

Complete the following to create a Common Data Service entity for veterinary appointments:

1. Open a web browser and navigate to the website `https://make.powerapps.com`. Sign in with the account you set up with the Power Apps Community Plan.

2. Once signed in, ensure that the environment is set to your personal environment that leverages the Power Apps Community Plan.

3. On the left navigation, expand **Data** and select **Entities**.

Tip   If this is your first time working with the Common Data Service, then you may be prompted to create a database. If so, select the Create a database button to get started. This may take 5–10 minutes to create the database.

---

4. Choose **New entity**, as shown in Figure 29-1, to create the data source that will be used throughout this "Try It Out" section.

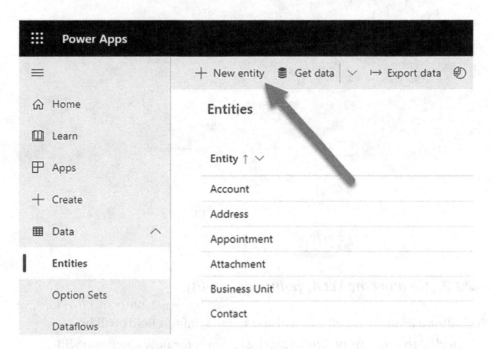

Figure 29-1. Launching the CDS entity dialog

5. In the New entity pane that now appears, provide the Display name
    Vet Appointment and ***AppointmentID*** for the Display name of the
    Primary Field. Notice in Figure 29-2 that the name of the entity and
    Primary Field is prefixed with a value that you cannot change. This prefix
    is automatically generated to ensure that your custom entity is unique
    across your entire environment. You will likely have a different prefix
    than what is displayed below. Select ***Create*** once this step is complete.

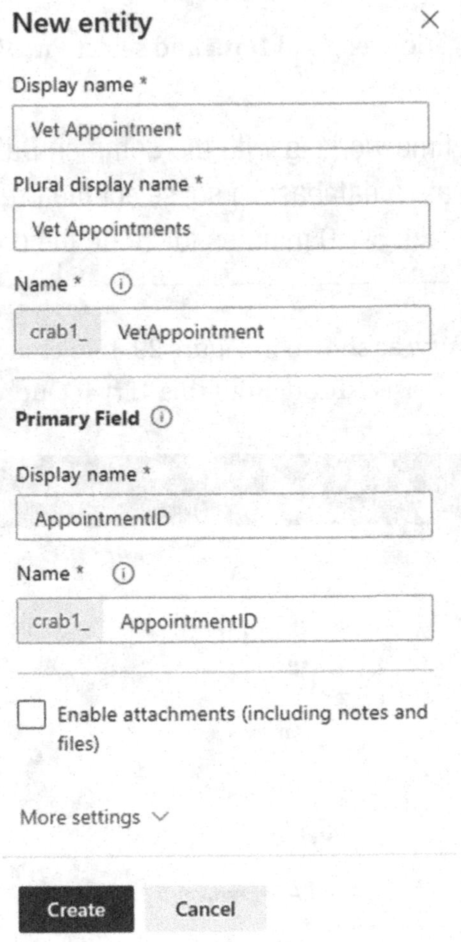

Figure 29-2. *Creating the Vet Appointments entity*

6. After a few moments, you will see several default fields will be
    added to your entity. These can be ignored for now since you will
    soon begin to add your own custom fields to this new entity.

7. The first change to make is on the Primary Field. This field should be changed so that it autogenerates a new numeric value for each row entered. This is commonly referred to as an identity column in data warehouse design.

   Select the AppointmentID field, then make the changes as shown in Figure 29-3. This image shows how to modify the Data type property and set it to *Autonumber*. Click *Done* after this is complete.

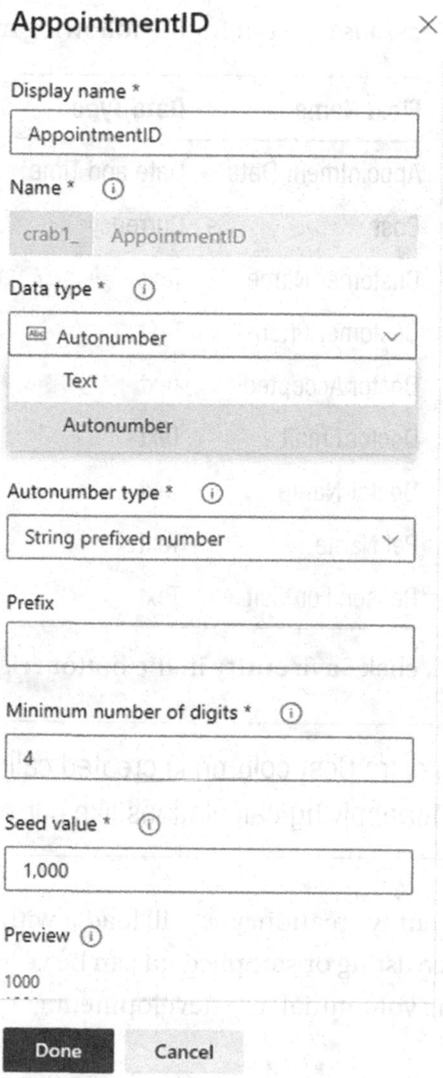

AppointmentID   ✕

Display name *

AppointmentID

Name *   ⓘ

crab1_   AppointmentID

Data type *   ⓘ

🔤 Autonumber   ⌄

    Text

    Autonumber

Autonumber type *   ⓘ

String prefixed number   ⌄

Prefix

Minimum number of digits *   ⓘ

4

Seed value *   ⓘ

1,000

Preview ⓘ

1000

[Done]   Cancel

Figure 29-3. *Modifying the Primary Field Data type*

> **Tip**   As with any tool, it is a good idea to save your changes frequently to protect
> yourself from loss of work. In CDS, you will find a **Save entity** button on the
> bottom-right corner of the screen.

8. Next, add another new field by clicking the **Add field** button on
    the top menu. This new field should be called Animal Type and be
    a Text data type. Click **Done** once this field is set correctly.

9. Now repeat the previous step but for the following new fields:

Field Name	Data Type
Appointment Date	Date and Time
Cost	Currency
Customer Name	Text
Customer Phone	Text
Doctor Accepted	Text
Doctor Email	Text
Doctor Name	Text
Pet Name	Text
Reason For Visit	Text

Once these are created, click **Save entity** in the bottom right.

> **Tip**   You may notice an extra Cost column is created called Cost (Base). These two
> columns could be used for applying calculations like currency conversions.

10. To finish off the entity creation, you will load it with some sample
     data. Having preexisting or sample data can be very helpful when
     it comes to doing your initial app development.

There are multiple ways to load data into an entity, but one simple method for this example is to click the **Edit data in Excel** option on the top bar. This will download a new Excel file to your machine with a connection tied directly into this CDS entity. Save and open this file to continue.

11.   Once this Excel file opens, you may need to click Enable Editing at the top of the Excel ribbon. Copy the data from the file provided with the book called VetOnTheGo-DataSource.xlsx and paste the results in the corresponding columns in the Excel file that was downloaded from CDS. Once the data is set in the correct columns, click the **Publish** button in the Microsoft Power Apps Office Add-in window, as shown in Figure 29-4. You may be required to sign in to Power Apps first.

If prompted, click **Yes** to confirm that you are OK with the changes that will overwrite what is currently in this entity.

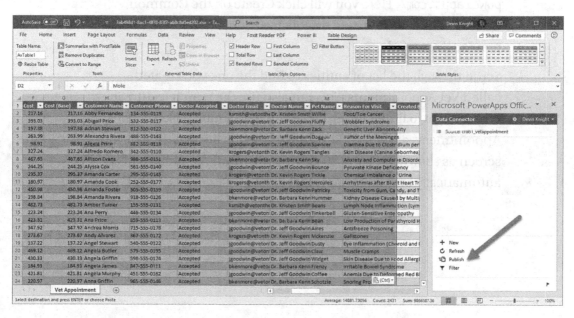

Figure 29-4. *Loading the sample data into your CDS entity using Excel*

12. Congratulations! Our first step is now complete, and your Common Data Services entity has now been created and loaded. This will be what you use for the following sections as a data source. You can now close any instances of Excel that were opened during these first steps.

Building the Power App

Next comes the task of building the app that will use the entity you just created as a data source for adding new appointments.

1. Back in your web browser, return to `https://make.powerapps.com` to begin building the app for this example.

2. From the Home screen, select Common Data Service under the **Start from data** option.

3. This will redirect your browser screen to `https://create.powerapps.com/`. Here you will click Create on the Common Data Service data source to establish a connection to the entity previously created.

4. Scroll through the list of entities to find the one you created called Vet Appointments. You can also use the search feature in the top right to find it faster. Once you have found it, select Vet Appointments and then click **Connect** in the bottom right of your screen as shown in Figure 29-5. This will begin the process of automatically building your initial app.

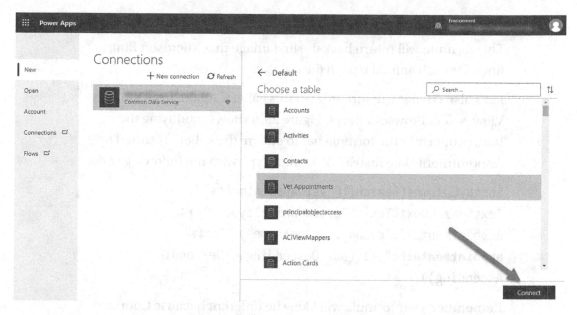

***Figure 29-5.** Choosing the entity Vet Appointments that we created earlier to be the data source for the Power App*

5.   Once the app is created, click **Skip** on the "Welcome to Power Apps Studio" screen.

6.   Since you have already learned about customizing apps in previous chapters, you will only make small modifications to this one. Select **BrowseGallery1** from the Tree View on the left side of your screen. With this selected, change the Layout property on the Properties menu on the right to **Image, title, subtitle and body**.

7.   Next, with BrowseGallery1 still selected, click Edit next to the Fields property also located in the Properties menu. Make the following changes:

   •   Change Body to **Reason For Visit**

   •   Change Subtitle to **Customer Name**

   •   Change Title to **Pet Name**

8.   Go back to the Tree View on the left side of the screen and select the **Image** control found within BrowseGallery1. Modify the Image property in the formula bar to use the following code:

"`http://tse1.mm.bing.net/th?q=`" & 'Animal type'

This formula will return back the first image that Microsoft Bing finds for each animal type in the dataset.

9. Let's also change the sort order of this gallery. Again, from the Tree View, select BrowseGallery1. Figure 29-6 shows modifying the Item property in the formula bar to ensure the gallery is sorted by Appointment Date instead of Animal Type with the following code:

```
SortByColumns(Search([@'Vet Appointments'],
TextSearchBox1.Text, "cr4a4_animaltype","cr4a4_
appointmentid","cr4a4_customername"), "cr4a4_
appointmentdate", If(SortDescending1, Descending,
Ascending))
```

Remember, your formula will likely be different because Common Data Service entities have autogenerated prefix names. In my case, each field is prefixed with "cr4a4_", but yours will be different.

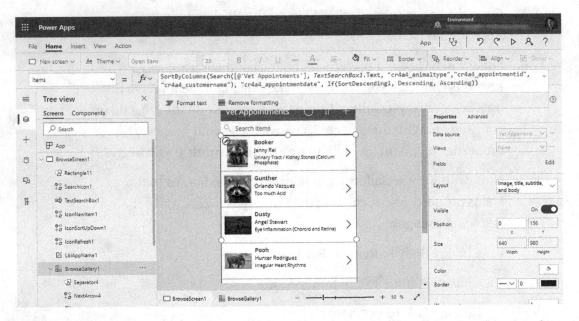

Figure 29-6. *The current state of the app after the modifications completed so far*

10. Next, navigate to the detail screen to make some small modifications. Select DetailScreen1 in the Tree View and then select DetailForm1 from inside of that screen.

11. Click the **Edit fields** link in the Properties menu to add some of the missing fields.

12. Click **Add field** and select the following fields to add them to the detail form:

    - Customer Name

    - Animal Type

    - Pet Name

    - Appointment Date

    - Cost

    - Reason for Visit

    - Customer Phone

    - Doctor Name

    - Doctor Email

    - Doctor Accepted

    Click **Add** after each of these have been selected.

13. Delete the Created On and AppointmentID columns from the form fields by hovering above the field name in the Fields list and then clicking the ellipsis that appears to the right to find **Remove**.

14. Next, you will modify the edit screen so all the necessary fields can be entered in by the office administrators when new appointments need to be added. Use the Tree View to expand EditScreen1 so you can find and select **EditForm1**.

15. Select the Edit field link from the Properties menu on the right side of the screen. Choose **Add field** and select the following fields in the listed order:

    - Customer Name

- Animal Type

- Pet Name

- Appointment Date

- Cost

- Reason for Visit

- Customer Phone

- Doctor Name

- Doctor Email

- Doctor Accepted

Once all of these are selected, click **Add**.

16. Delete the Created On column from the form fields by hovering above the field name in the Fields list and then clicking the ellipsis that appears to the right to find **Remove**.

17. Next, change the **Control Type** on the AppointmentID field to Edit text. Finally, move the AppointmentID column to the bottom of the form by clicking and dragging it in the Fields list to the bottom of the fields listed. You might find it helpful to collapse all the fields first by clicking the ellipses to the right of the Add field button.

18. Next, you will begin setting up our app to integrate with Power Automate so doctors can approve or reject appointments that are sent their way. Before you begin building the flow, there are a few tweaks you will need to make to the app first.

    Select EditForm1 from the Tree View and go to the Advanced tab on the right side of the screen. In the OnSuccess property, remove Back() and leave it blank.

    This property controls what happens after a successful entry into the form. By default, it will return the user back to the previous screen they were viewing, but in this example, we want to change the default behavior.

19.   Go to the Insert menu at the top of Power Apps Studio and select Rectangle from the Icons menu.

20.   With the new rectangle selected, choose the Fill property from the Property selector and change the code in the formula bar to the following:

RGBA(0, 0, 0, .7)

21.   Resize the rectangle so it takes up the entire screen and then add a second rectangle on top of this one.

22.   With the new rectangle selected, choose the Fill property from the Property selector and change the code in the formula bar to the following:

RGBA(255, 255, 255, 1)

23.   Resize the second rectangle to take up about a quarter of the screen and then move it to the middle as you see in Figure 29-7.

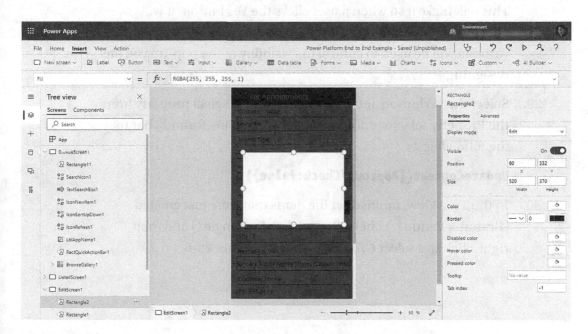

Figure 29-7. *The beginning of a pop-up design that will be used for sending approvals*

24. Go to the Insert menu at the top of Power Apps Studio and select Label from the Text menu. Move this new label on top of the white rectangle.

25. With the label selected, change the text to "Ready to send approval to the doctor?"

26. Bring in two buttons from the Insert menu and place them within the white rectangle below the text label.

27. Resize the buttons so they fit next to each other and change the text on these buttons, so the one on the left says "Yes" and the other one says "No."

28. Select the Yes button and then choose the OnSelect property from the Property selector and change the code in the formula bar to the following:

UpdateContext({ApprovalCheck:false})

This will make it so when a user clicks the Yes button, it will change the value of a new variable called ApprovalCheck. This variable will be used to control the visibility of the pop-up you are designing.

29. Select the No button and then choose the OnSelect property from the Property selector and change the code in the formula bar to the following:

UpdateContext({ApprovalCheck:false})

30. In the Tree View, multiselect the items that were just created (Button2, Button1, Label1, Rectangle2, Rectangle1) and then right-click and select *Group* as shown in Figure 29-8.

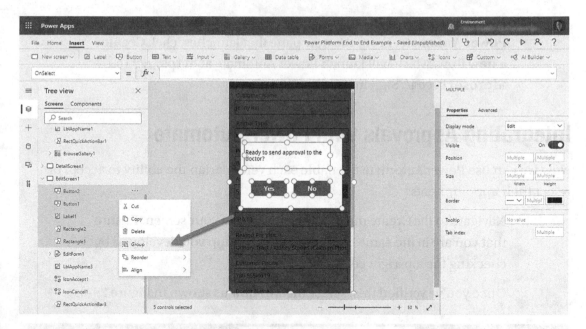

Figure 29-8. *Placing the controls into a group*

31. With the newly created group selected, choose the Visible
    property from the Property selector and change the code in the
    formula bar to the following:

    ApprovalCheck

32. You will notice the group will disappear for the moment. Next,
    select IconAccept1 from the Tree View. Then choose the OnSelect
    property from the Property selector and change the code in the
    formula bar to the following:

    SubmitForm(EditForm1); UpdateContext({ApprovalCheck:true})

    This makes it so that when new rows are inserted into our entity,
    our pop-up is displayed. Our next steps will be to create the Power
    Automate flow that will initiate the approval process.

33. Before moving to Power Automate, save the app design by clicking
    the File menu, then Save. Name the app "Power Platform End to
    End Example" and then click **Save**. Click the back arrow in the top
    left to return back to the app design screen.

34. Navigate to the Action tab at the top of your screen, then select **Power Automate**. From the new pane that launches, click **Create a new flow**, which will launch Power Automate at `https://flow.microsoft.com/`. Sign in if you are not already.

Integrating Approvals with Power Automate

Now we can use Power Automate to enable each veterinarian the ability to accept or reject their appointments:

1. Navigate to the Create menu on the left side of your screen. Ensure that you are in the same environment as the app you developed by checking the top-right corner of your screen.

   Once you've verified this, select **Instant flow** as shown in Figure 29-9.

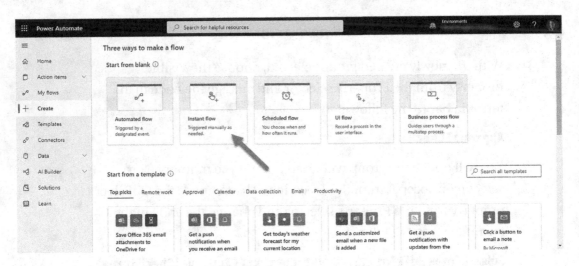

Figure 29-9. *Launching the Instant flow menu*

2. This will launch the Build an instant flow dialog box. Click **Skip** here because you will provide a name and trigger later.

3. This will launch the designer for Power Automate where you will start by searching for Power Apps in the "Search connectors and triggers" search box.

There is only one type of trigger available for Power Apps that can be selected here. Choose it so that this flow will be initiated from some action in the Power App you designed earlier.

4. Click **New step** and then use the "Search connectors and triggers" search box to find approvals. Choose the approval called **Start and wait for an approval**.

5. Set the Approval type property to **Approve/Reject – First to respond**. After this is set, several new options will appear. Change the configuration of the following properties, as shown in Figure 29-10:

   - Set the Title property to **Do you accept this appointment?**

   - Set the Assigned to property to a dynamic input from Power Apps by clicking Ask in Power Apps under the Dynamic content dialog box.

   - Set the Details property to *Please select approve if you accept this appointment*.

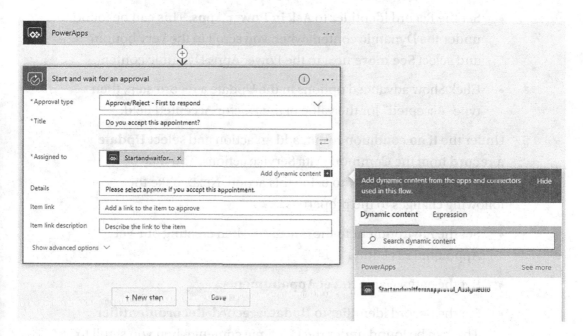

Figure 29-10. *The approval step being configured*

6. Click **New step** again, but this time add a **Condition** control. This will control what happens when an approval is approved or rejected.

7. Set the Condition to use the Dynamic content field called **Responses Approver response**. As soon as you make this selection, a new item will be added to your flow called Apply to each. This is automatically added for you so the flow can iterate over multiple approval responses should it need to.

   Click the Condition step to expand the settings and complete this step by setting it equal to "Approve."

8. Under the **If yes** condition result, add an action and select **Update a record** from the Common Data Service actions. You may be prompted to sign in prior to using this action. Next, make the following changes to the properties:

   • Set the Environment to the one used when creating our Vet Appointments entity.

   • Set the entity Name to **Vet Appointments**.

   • Set the Record identifier to **Ask in Power Apps**. This can be found under the Dynamic content when you scroll to the very bottom and select **See more** next to the Power Apps Dynamic content.

   • Click Show advanced options in the Update a record step, then type "Accepted" for the value of the Doctor Accepted field.

9. Under the **If no** condition result, add an action and select **Update a record** from the Common Data Service actions. You may be prompted to sign in prior to using this action. Next, make the following changes to the properties:

   • Set the Environment to the one used when creating our Vet Appointments entity.

   • Set the entity Name to **Vet Appointments**.

   • Set the Record identifier to **Updatearecord_Recordidentifier**. This can be found under the Dynamic content when you scroll to the very bottom.

- Click Show advanced options, then type "Rejected" for the value of the Doctor Accepted field.

10. Rename the flow from Untitled to "Power Platform End to End Example" in the top left as shown in Figure 29-11. Then click **Save**.

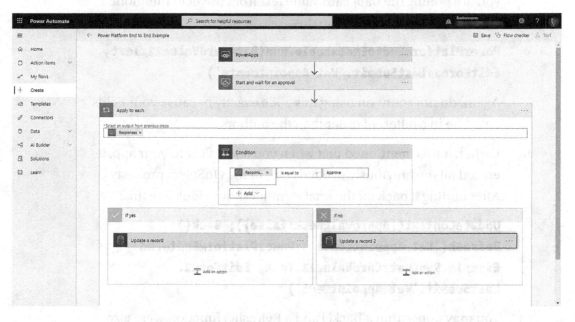

Figure 29-11. *What a completed version of this flow should look like*

11. Now, return back to editing the Power App you developed earlier so that the flow can be integrated into it.

    Once the app is open, go to EditScreen1 in the Tree View and select the Yes button inside of Group1 that was created earlier. You may need to change the visibility of the group temporarily to determine which button is Yes.

12. Go to the Action tab and select Power Automate. You should now see the flow you created a few moments ago appear here. If you don't for some reason, it is likely that you accidently created the flow in a different environment, or perhaps you did not save the flow.

    You must select the flow to make it available in this app. However, when you select it, any formulas you had written in the OnSelect property will be overwritten.

13. Modify the OnSelect property to pass in the data card value text from the Doctor Email field. You will also pull back the unique identifier for the entity that will be needed for running the update.

    This formula may be a little different for you, so please verify you are pulling the data card value text from the field mentioned earlier. My formula looks like this:

    ```
    PowerPlatformEndtoEndExample.Run(DataCardValue22.Text,
    EditForm1.LastSubmit.'Vet Appointments')
    ```

    Again, do not count on using this code exactly because your fields could be in a different order than the authors.

14. Earlier, it was mentioned that when you add a flow to your app, it erased all the previously needed code in the OnSelect property. After adding it back in, the final formula should look like this:

    ```
    UpdateContext({ApprovalCheck:false}); Back();
    Refresh('Vet Appointments');PowerPlatformEndtoEnd
    Example.Run(DataCardValue22.Text, EditForm1.
    LastSubmit.'Vet Appointment')
    ```

    You may notice that a Back() and a Refresh() function were also added to this for usability.

15. The app is now ready to test. Go to BrowseScreen1 in the Tree View and then click the Preview button in the top right of the screen.

16. Add a new record, as if you were the office administrator, by clicking the plus button in the top-right corner of the app. Fill in whatever information you would like in the form except for the Doctor Email. For this field, ensure that you use your email address that you use to sign in to Power Apps with.

    You should also skip filling in the Doctor Accepted field because this will be provided an input from our flow.

    Put in a number higher than 2000 for the AppointmentID. Once complete, click the check mark button at the top right.

Tip   If you want to be really creative, put a formula on the AppointmentID text input default property to make sure it brings back whatever the next highest value. Something like this would do the trick.

```
Max('Vet Appointments', AppointmentID)+1
```

This will launch the pop-up you created to start the Power Automate flow that will notify the doctor of a new appointment. They will then be able to accept or reject the appointment. Click Yes.

17. Save and publish the changes to this app. Go to the File menu and select the **Save** button. Once the save is completed, go ahead and click **Publish** to push out the changes.

Reporting and Analytics with Power BI

Now to the last phase of this project. Let's generate a report showing the number of appointments each veterinarian is handling along with the amount of revenue that each is bringing in to the practice. Follow these steps:

1. Launch the Power BI Desktop and select Get Data to define the data source.

    Choose Common Data Service for the connector type and then click **Connect** as shown in Figure 29-12.

Figure 29-12. *Choosing CDS as the data connector*

2. Provide the Server URL for the Vet Appointments entity. If
    you're uncertain on what your URL is, you can find it by clicking
    Advanced Settings under the gear icon while on `https://make.`
    `powerapps.com/`.

    The URL should follow this pattern: `https://`
    `yourenvironmentid.crm.dynamics.com/`

    Once this is provided, click **OK**.

If this is the first time connecting to this environment, you may
be prompted to provide your credentials. After you do this, click
Connect.

3. Next, the Navigator pane will appear. Expand the Entities folder
    and search for the word "vet" to find the entity you created at the
    beginning of this demo.

4. Select the VetAppointment (custom entities will be prefixed with a
    unique identifier) entity, then click **Load**.

5. Select the Line chart from the Visualization pane and add the
    following fields to it:

    - Add appointmentid to Values.

    - Add appointmentdate to the Axis but remove Year and Quarter
      from the hierarchy it creates.

    - Add doctorname to the Legend.

6. Click somewhere in the background of the report, then select the
    Matrix from the Visualization pane. Add the following fields to this
    visual:

    - Add cost to Values.

    - Add doctorname and customername to Rows.

    - Add appointmentdate to Columns but remove Year and Quarter
      from the hierarchy it creates.

Figure 29-13 shows what this quick report should look like.

Count of cr4a4_appointmentid by Month and cr4a4_doctorname

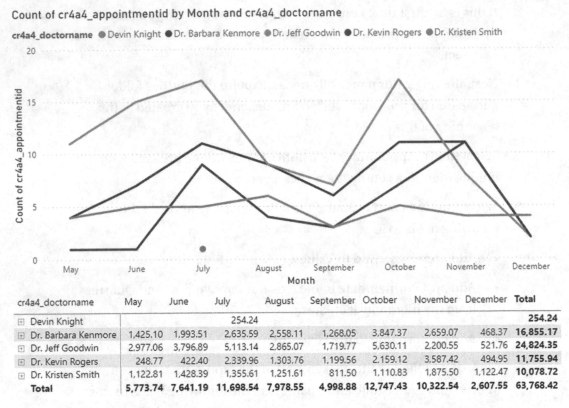

Figure 29-13. *The completed Power BI report*

cr4a4_doctorname	May	June	July	August	September	October	November	December	Total
⊞ Devin Knight			254.24						254.24
⊞ Dr. Barbara Kenmore	1,425.10	1,993.51	2,635.59	2,558.11	1,268.05	3,847.37	2,659.07	468.37	16,855.17
⊞ Dr. Jeff Goodwin	2,977.06	3,796.89	5,113.14	2,865.07	1,719.77	5,630.11	2,200.55	521.76	24,824.35
⊞ Dr. Kevin Rogers	248.77	422.40	2,339.96	1,303.76	1,199.56	2,159.12	3,587.42	494.95	11,755.94
⊞ Dr. Kristen Smith	1,122.81	1,428.39	1,355.61	1,251.61	811.50	1,110.83	1,875.50	1,122.47	10,078.72
Total	**5,773.74**	**7,641.19**	**11,698.54**	**7,978.55**	**4,998.88**	**12,747.43**	**10,322.54**	**2,607.55**	**63,768.42**

7.   Save the report and name it "Power Platform End to End
       Example."

Summary

You should now have a working end-to-end example. Building the example had you
drawing on many of the skills that you have learned from reading this book. You can
see now how the different tools in the Power Platform complement each other and
can be connected together in ways that enable citizen developers to create powerful
applications.

Index

A

Actions
    connectors permissions, 82
    power automate, 85
Admins connector, 343, 344
Administration
    data gateway (*see* Data gateway)
    exporting flows, 162, 163
    roles, Power BI
        creation, 326, 327
        test, 328, 330
        users assign, 328
    sharing flows, 160–162
Advanced condition builder, 131
Application, building
    connections, 17, 19
    controls
        adding and editing data, 19
        display data, 19
    designer environment, 12, 13
    previewing, 14
    saving and version control, 13, 14
    start with data option, 11
Application lifecycle management (ALM)
    processes, 58
App Makers connector, 344
Approval action, 143
    availability of Markdown, 145
    start and wait, 144
Approval flows

actions, 143
advanced options
    disable notifications, 146
    reassigning, 147
    requestor, 146
clipboard, 157
copy action to clipboard, 157
industry agnostic, 143
markdown language supported, 145
pending approval request, 158
responding, 147, 148
start and wait, 144
update item, 156
ArcGIS map, 267
Area chart, 262
Automated data refreshes, 323–325
Automated workflow, 74, 75
Automation, 75, 76
Azure Logic Apps, 74, 97

B

Bar chart, 259
Blog storage, 200
Bubble map, 266

C

Calculated columns, 245, 246, 248
Calculated measure, 246, 247, 249
Calculated table, 248

389

© Mitchell Pearson, Brian Knight, Devin Knight, Manuel Quintana 2020
M. Pearson et al., *Pro Microsoft Power Platform*, https://doi.org/10.1007/978-1-4842-6008-1

Printed in the United States
by Bookmasters

Printed in the United States
By Bookmasters